The Rhetoric of Heroic Expec

M000211645

NUMBER TWENTY-FOUR
Presidential Rhetoric and Political Communication
Vanessa B. Beasley, General Editor

The Rhetoric of Heroic Expectations

ESTABLISHING THE OBAMA PRESIDENCY

Edited by Justin S. Vaughn & Jennifer R. Mercieca

TEXAS A&M UNIVERSITY PRESS | COLLEGE STATION

Manufactured in the United States of America

This paper meets the requirements of ANSI/NISO Z39.48–1992 (Permanence of Paper).

Binding materials have been chosen for durability.

LIBRARY OF CONGRESS CATALOGING-IN-PUBLICATION DATA

The rhetoric of heroic expectations : establishing the Obama presidency / edited by
Justin S. Vaughn and Jennifer R. Mercieca. — 1st ed.
    p. cm. — (Presidential rhetoric and political communication ; no. 24)
Includes bibliographical references and index.
ISBN 978-1-62349-042-3 (cloth : alk. paper) —
ISBN 978-1-62349-043-0 (pbk. : alk. paper) —
ISBN 978-1-62349-121-5 (e-book)
1. Obama, Barack. 2. United States—Politics and government—2009–
3. Presidents—United States—Election—2008. 4. Rhetoric—Political aspects—
United States. I. Vaughn, Justin S., 1978– II. Mercieca, Jennifer R.
III. Series: Presidential rhetoric and political communication ; no. 24.
E907.R47 2014
973.932092—dc23
2013022042

We dedicate this book

to the memory

of our dear friend,

mentor, and colleague,

James Arnt Aune

1953–2013

Contents

Preface

For many, election night November 4, 2008, seemed as though it might be the moment when Martin Luther King's long "arc of the moral universe" finally did bend "toward justice."[1] The seemingly impossible came true as the United States of America stood on the cusp of electing and then inaugurating its first African American president, Barack Obama. Many readers, of course, will remember those days and will have been equally cognizant of the importance and possibility in those events as they were transpiring. Contemporary politics, however, rarely lets us linger in such moments, but instead always rushes ahead with new stories about transitions and appointments and policy initiatives and the like. Nevertheless, we contend that it is not only worth remembering those early moments of what became the Obama presidency but also analyzing them, particularly with an eye to the way that the moment was rhetorically constructed and how this construction shaped the early fortunes of this historic administration.

The essays in this volume represent the work of an interdisciplinary group of scholars who participated in Texas A&M University's March, 2010, "Rhetoric, Politics, and the Obama Phenomenon" conference. When we began planning a conference on Barack Obama's meteoric rise from little-known Illinois state senator to president of the United States, we thought that we would focus on what seemed like the "Obama Phenomenon"—the throngs of crowds, the celebrity-like popularity, the strategic use of new media, and the talent for powerful oratory. What we could not have predicted was that one year into Obama's first term the Obama phenomenon would have turned into Obama's phenomenal burden as overlapping sets of responsibilities, hurdles, and constraints shaped the ways he approached and performed his new position. The essays in this volume reflect an interest both in the phenomenon that won him the presidency and the historic and contemporary burdens of that presidency.

Since Obama's victory, scholars have published numerous commentaries on the significance of the Obama campaign and election. Some of these pieces can be found in special issues of journals or edited volumes like this one,[2] others in monographs and articles that analyze the 2008 campaign and election,[3] particularly the role race played in it,[4] or volumes that assess the new president's performance in various dimensions of his administration.[5] Other scholars, in various ways, engage the transformative nature of Obama's rise to power, providing insight into how it came to be and offering wise explanations for why Obama's successes required careful and precise navigation of several political, cultural, and historical hurdles. For example, Horace G. Campbell explains how Obama motivated and mobilized a movement of networks and organizations that marked the possibility of progressive change in contemporary American politics,[6] a notion embraced by Ian Reifowitz, who makes the case that Obama's vision of American identity as inclusive and based upon shared bonds provides the new president with an opening to redefine and transform the American polity.[7] Other scholars take a more cautious view as they urge awareness of deeply entrenched factors of American life that challenge and limit Obama's ability to lead and succeed. For example, Thomas J. Sugrue shows how, despite the apparent evidence of Obama's election, post–civil rights era racial divisions continue to challenge not only the nation but also Obama's administration.[8] Sugrue notes that much of the corresponding battle has already been fought within Obama, as the future president painstakingly searched for and embraced his identity as an American and as an African American.[9] Stephen J. Wayne has also focused on the internal dimensions of Obama's leadership, showing how Obama's character, beliefs, and style function as their own set of resources and constraints in shaping his response to political challenges and opportunities.[10] At the same time, Jeffrey C. Alexander locates the promise of Obama's candidacy and future as president in distinctly external ways, presenting a narrative of Obama's rise to power as one that emphasized performance and image.[11] Alexander argues that on that momentous and memorable election night in November, 2008, Americans "elected a civil hero," one who was charged with restoring "the utopian spirit of the nation's revolutionary origins and the promise of its founding fathers to create a more perfect democracy."[12] Indeed, in a moment Obama went from accomplishing one heroic task—becoming the first African American to win election to the White House—to being charged with another, even more Herculean one: returning the ship of state to its original course toward its glorious destiny. Alexander contends that the Americans who voted for Obama voted for themselves—for the very best idea of America, a nation of diversity and equality and hope.

Election-night celebrations must eventually end, however. So, too, inaugural balls. And when the unimaginably hard work of reaching goals and satisfying heroic expectations begins, new questions of how and whether these things can be done arise. It is this conversation that this volume endeavors to join. By focusing on the early days of the Obama presidency and the campaign season that led up to it, the essays in this volume address three questions: First, how can we understand the rhetoric of presidential expectations and the associated burdens of office? Second, how did President Obama negotiate the institutional, contextual, and personal burdens of his presidency in his first year in office? And finally, how is Obama judged, based upon our expectations and upon his specific presidential burdens? We focus our analysis upon three kinds of burdens: institutional burdens (specific to the office of the presidency itself); contextual burdens (burdens specific to the historic moment within which the president assumes office); and, personal burdens (burdens specific to the man or woman who becomes president). It may be too soon to give a definitive answer about whether President Obama met the world's expectations, but the question of how those expectations were constructed and how the Obama administration negotiated those expectations in its first year is worth considering in depth because of what answering it can teach us about the US presidency in general and about Barack Obama's presidency in particular.

Path of the Volume

Chapter 1 begins this volume with an introductory essay that roots Obama's rhetoric and the establishment of his presidency within the context of Americans' heroic expectations for their presidents. After identifying the structural and constitutive dimensions of these expectations—as well as the gap that exists between expectations and actual presidential powers to meet them—the authors elaborate upon the three types of burdens faced by every president: institutional, contextual, and personal. Showing how Obama's predecessors generally experienced each burden and how Obama specifically was challenged by burdens in the early days of his presidency, this chapter provides an organizational frame that is sustained throughout the volume. Following this introduction, the chapters proceed in an order that parallels the three types of burdens identified above and analyzed in chapter 1.

The next four chapters link to the institutional burdens faced by all presidents, including Barack Obama. Jay Childers's focus in chapter 2 concerns the role of the president in a democratic republic rife with conflict and competition. Childers grounds his analysis in one of Obama's more controversial public outings of his new administration: the 2009 commencement address at Notre Dame University. Childers argues that the new president's conception of political engagement—a cornerstone of Barack Obama's political philosophy since his days working south Chicago streets as a community organizer—may be understood best as a model of agonistic democracy.

In chapter 3, Eric Dieter builds on Kenneth Burke's frame of consubstantiality as he depicts Obama's campaign for high office as a balancing effort between his substance and that of his audience with what Burke calls "acting-together." Noting that no matter how talented a presidential candidate may be at harnessing identification through ethos, audiences do not merely submit to rhetorical force, but rather make the sovereign choice to "act together" with the leader in question. Dieter deftly links the academic theory with the Obama campaign's "Yes, We Can" slogan, rooting it conceptually in consubstantiality and assessing the prospects and inherent pitfalls of such strategic communication.

In chapter 4, Brandon Rottinghaus responds to a sharpening divide in the empirical literature concerning whether presidents are able to lead the public. Seeking a middle position between scholars like George C. Edwards III, who argue that presidential appeals fall "on deaf ears," and several other scholars who find evidence of successful opinion leadership for select presidents, often in particular moments or on certain policy issues, Rottinghaus develops a conditional theory of presidential public opinion leadership and uses the early Obama administration's public leadership efforts as a test case.

In chapter 5, Matthew Eshbaugh-Soha narrows his focus to a particular dimension of the public presidency, asking explicitly about the media's role in structuring Obama's public leadership performance. Arguing persuasively about the filtering power of the contemporary news media, Eshbaugh-Soha demonstrates the power of the news media to impede the president's efforts to reform health care, leading him to advise Obama and his successors to first lead news coverage before seeking to change the minds of the masses.

The next three chapters of the volume relate to key dimensions of the contextual burden faced by Barack Obama as he campaigned for, won, and ascended to the office of the presidency, most notably foreign policy challenges abroad in the midst of continuing global fallout from the nation's war on terror and economic crises at home following the massive collapses in the banking, housing, and employment sectors. In chapter 6,

David Zarefsky situates Obama's foreign policy rhetoric at the end of a declining trajectory of exceptionalist expectations. Borrowing language from Kenneth Burke, Zarefsky notes that leadership failures on the part of Obama's predecessor, George W. Bush, combined with shifting global economic and political dynamics "cracked the frame" of American exceptionalism, taking the phenomenon to the "end of the line."

Jason Edwards continues the examination of exceptionalism and Obama in chapter 7 by exploring a particular vein of the president's rhetoric: democratic exceptionalism. Edwards argues that the rhetoric of democratic exceptionalism acknowledges America's continuing global leadership, yet tempers traditional exceptionalism with a greater enthusiasm for partnership and interdependence rather than for hegemonic dominance and coercion. In so doing, Edwards puts a conceptual label to the changes Zarefsky delineated in the previous chapter.

James Aune returns the contextual frame to the domestic sphere, shifting focus away from international affairs and toward the economic crisis that befell the nation in the final weeks of the 2008 campaign. Examining Obama's response to the crisis in the early months of his administration, Aune argues that the new president's response was indicative of his typical rhetorical approach, one that combines soaring appeals with a host of policy details but that fails to link the two dimensions with digestible narratives for the viewing audience. Aune further contextualizes this analysis by locating not just Obama but all modern presidents and their efforts to exhibit economic leadership within the heritage of the divine right of kings.

The next four essays take in turn different dimensions of the personal burdens Barack Obama faced as he vied for and eventually became the nation's forty-fourth president, including questions about his religious beliefs and affiliations and especially challenges he had to face because of his racial identity. Following a campaign in which Obama was dogged by allegations that his Chicago pastor, Reverend Jeremiah Wright, held anti-American sentiments, President Obama faced widespread allegations that he was secretly Muslim. In short, the relative religiosity of this president has contributed to his presidential burden. In chapter 9, Catherine L. Langford uses Obama's 2006 speech at a high-profile evangelical conference about the role of religion in a democratic government as source material to explore the religious characteristics of the then-senator's political speech. Langford argues that Obama drew upon the "secular messianic style" of oratory, a prudential strategy fusing secular humanism and traditional religious discourse.

Dave Tell argues in chapter 10 that Obama's rhetoric indicates how his chosen religious tradition—and particularly the centrality of its Exodus narrative–explains the president's entrance into political life. Tell demonstrates that the Exodus narrative plays an important role in Obama's rhetoric, which allows him to reevaluate Sacvan Bercovitch's seminal research to show how Exodus works within the Jeremiadic tradition to invest political agency in his auditors.

In the next two essays, the focus is broadened to include not just Obama's rhetoric and actions but also the way Americans see the nation's first African American president and his family, particularly against the raced and gendered cultural and historic expectations that preceded his election. In chapter 11, Cara Finnegan provides empirical substance to Forrest McDonald's apt observation that "the president lives in a museum of the history of the presidency," utilizing a recent and unique data source to explore how Obama uses fine art to situate himself within the historical dimensions of the White House.[13] Drawing from photographs of President Obama featuring White House art from the White House Flickr photostream, Finnegan shows how pictures of the president with paintings and busts of mythic presidents authorize the president's leadership and associate him, despite obvious visual disjunctions, with the long and storied history of the presidency.

Bonnie Dow's essay in chapter 12 presents a provocative analysis of how the Obama phenomenon has forced confrontations with more than traditional concepts of the American presidency. Dow builds from Karlyn Kohrs Campbell's argument that "the First Ladyship is a vital part of the presidency," by examining how Michelle Obama's mediated public image displays a tension between sameness and difference in understandings of American citizenship.[14] Dow argues that Michelle Obama's embodiment and embrace of idealized heteronormative familialism provides, to some degree, a status quo–friendly balance to the otherwise disjunctive elements of her arrival and entrenchment on the national stage.

Finally, the volume concludes with an epilogue that advances the narrative a few years as it attempts to explain the toll the burdens discussed throughout the volume took on Obama's presidency over the course of his first term and shaped how he would make the case for a second one in the fall 2012 election against Republican former governor of Massachusetts Mitt Romney. Taken together, the essays in this volume trace an elegant path from the way the institutional burdens all presidents face shape the construction of their presidencies to the ways contemporary context and

Barack Obama's own unique burdens matter. Each essay grapples with the tension between general presidential phenomena and the unique vagaries of the Obama example. By approaching the question of Obama's presidency from an interdisciplinary perspective, this book contributes to ongoing conversations in political science and communication on the presidency, the rhetorical presidency, presidential leadership, and presidential rhetoric. Furthermore, by examining Obama's rhetoric with an emphasis upon how it helped to establish his presidency, the essays in this volume allow readers to interrogate the current state of American presidential rhetoric.

Notes

1. The quotation comes from Martin Luther King's 1965 Selma Speech, but as National Public Radio (NPR) notes, King borrowed the phrase from the nineteenth-century Abolitionist Theodore Parker: http://www.npr.org/templates/story/story .php?storyId=129609461.

2. Notable among these are two issues guest-edited by Jeffrey Cohen in *Presidential Studies Quarterly* in 2010 (vol. 40, Issues 2–3) and volumes such as Janet M. Box-Steffensmeier and Steven E. Schier's collection *The American Elections of 2008* (Lanham, MD: Rowman & Littlefield, 2009); Robert E. Denton Jr.'s *The 2008 Presidential Campaign: A Communication Perspective* (Lanham, MD: Rowman & Littlefield, 2009); and Larry J. Sabato's *The Year of Obama: How Barack Obama Won the White House* (New York: Longman, 2010).

3. James W. Ceaser et al., *Epic Journey: The 2008 Elections and American Politics* (Lanham, MD: Rowman & Littlefield, 2011); Kate Kenski et al., *The Obama Victory: How Media, Money, and Message Shaped the 2008 Election* (Oxford: Oxford University Press, 2010); Heather E. Harris et al., *The Obama Effect: Multidisciplinary Renderings of the 2008 Campaign,* (Albany, NY: SUNY Press, 2010); Nicholas Yanes and Derrais Carter, eds., *The Iconic Obama, 2007–2009: Essays on Media Representations of the Candidate and New President* (Jefferson, NC: McFarland, 2012).

4. Michael Tesler and David O. Sears, *Obama's Race: The 2008 Election and Dreams of a Post-Racial America* (Chicago: University of Chicago Press, 2010); T. Denean Sharpley-Whiting, ed., *The Speech: Race and Barack Obama's "A More Perfect Union"* (New York: Bloomsbury, 2009); Ama Mazama and Molefi K. Asante, *Barack Obama: Political Frontiers and Racial Agency* (Washington, DC: CQ Press, 2011); Clarence E. Walker and Gregory D. Smithers, *The Preacher and the Politician: Jeremiah Wright, Barack Obama, and Race in America* (Charlottesville, VA: University of Virginia Press, 2009); Susanna Dilliplane, "Race, Rhetoric, and Running for President: Unpacking the Significance of Barack Obama's 'A More Perfect Union' Speech," *Rhetoric & Public Affairs* 15 (2012): 127–52; David A. Frank, "The Prophetic Voice and the Face of the Other in Barack Obama's 'A More Perfect Union' Address, March 18, 2008," *Rhetoric & Public Affairs* 12 (2009): 167–94; and Robert C.

Rowland and John M. Jones, "One Dream: Barack Obama, Race, and the American Dream," *Rhetoric & Public Affairs* 14 (2011): 125–54.

5. See, for example, the June 2011 special issue of *Presidential Studies Quarterly* (vol. 41, Issue 2) dedicated to the early Obama presidency, as well as Bert A. Rockman et al.'s *The Obama Presidency: Appraisals and Prospects* (Washington, DC: CQ Press, 2012); Andrew Dowdle et al.'s *The Obama Presidency: Change and Continuity* (New York: Routledge, 2011); Robert P. Watson et al.'s *The Obama Presidency: A Preliminary Assessment* (New York: SUNY, 2012); Lawrence R. Jacobs and Desmond King's *Obama at the Crossroads: Politics, Markets, and the Battle for America's Future* (Oxford: Oxford University Press, 2012); and Steven Schier's *Transforming America: Barack Obama in the White House* (Lanham, MD: Rowman and Littlefield, 2011).

6. Horace G. Campbell, *Barack Obama and Twenty-First Century Politics: A Revolutionary Moment in the USA* (New York: Palgrave MacMillan, 2010).

7. Ian Reifowitz, *Obama's America: A Transformative Vision of Our National Identity* (Dulles, VA: Potomac Books, 2012).

8. Thomas Sugrue, *Not Even Past: Barack Obama and the Burden of Race* (Princeton, NJ: Princeton University Press, 2010).

9. For more information, Obama's own memoir, *Dreams from My Father: A Story of Race and Inheritance* (New York: Times Books, 1995) provides a first-person account of this process of discovery. See also James T. Kloppenberg, *Reading Obama: Dreams, Hope, and the American Political Tradition* (Princeton, NJ: Princeton University Press, 2011); and Edward McClelland, *Young Mr. Obama: Chicago and the Making of a Black President* (New York: Bloomsbury Press, 2010).

10. Stephen J. Wayne, *Personality and Politics: Obama For and Against Himself* (Washington, DC: CQ Press, 2012).

11. Jeffrey C. Alexander, *The Performance of Politics: Obama's Victory and the Democratic Struggle for Power* (Oxford: Oxford University Press, 2010).

12. Ibid., 268.

13. Forrest McDonald, *The American Presidency: An Intellectual History* (Lawrence, KS: University of Kansas Press, 1994), 466.

14. Karlyn Kohrs Campbell, "The Rhetorical Presidency: A Two-Person Career," in *Beyond the Rhetorical Presidency,* Martin J. Medhurst, ed. (College Station: Texas A&M University Press, 1996), 179–99, 180.

Acknowledgments

The genesis of this volume occurred via text message during a conference we coordinated in Bryan, Texas, in March, 2010. Representatives from a range of disciplines—communication, political science, history, English, gender studies, business administration, Africana studies, and more—had gathered to discuss "Rhetoric, Politics, and the Obama Phenomenon," and over the three days of conversation and conviviality we had begun to notice a few themes emerging across the different plenary and panel presentations.

We owe tremendous gratitude to a number of individuals and institutions for their assistance both in supporting our efforts to organize the "Obamenon" conference and for working with us over the many months since as we sought to investigate those themes and build this book. We wish to thank and acknowledge Texas A&M University's College of Liberal Arts, the Melbern Glasscock Center for the Humanities, and the Department of Communication Colloquium Series, as well as Cleveland State University's College of Liberal Arts and Social Science and the Department of Political Science, for their financial support of our conference; these institutions provided generous resources that enabled us to host an event that was both stimulating and enjoyable. We are also grateful for the support of the City of Bryan. We also want to note the individuals who helped steer these resources in our direction, including Donnalee Dox, Rodger Govea, Gregory Sadlek, Virginia Varaljay, Leroy Dorsey, and Jim Rosenheim. We would also like to thank Kathryn Kelly and Zoë Carney for their capable organizational assistance and John Greiner (aka John G) for creating the inspired image for the conference, art that now graces the cover of this volume.

Many individuals attended, participated in, and presented innovative work at this conference, helping to create the intellectual context from which this volume emerged. All of them deserve our hearty thanks: Karrin Anderson, James Andrews, Julia Azari, David Bailey, Jennifer Jones Barbour, Vanessa Beasley, Kimberly Brown, Patrick Burkart, Tasha Dubriwny, Carl Cannon, Ken Collier, Marcia Dawkins, Leroy Dorsey, George Edwards, Janice Edwards, David Frank, Adam Gaffey, Stephen Goldzwig, Ron Greene, Ulrike Gretzel, Joshua Gunn, Diane Heith, Jeremiah Hickey, Edward Hinck, James Jasinski, Connie Johnson, Nancy Kassop, Mark McPhail,

Marty Medhurst, John Murphy, Stirling Newberry, Phillip Perdue, Kristan Poirot, Ian Reifowitz, Kurt Ritter, David Richardson, Michael Shaw, Paul Stob, Patricia Sullivan, Christopher Swift, Kerri Thompson, José Villalobos, Stephen Wayne, Kirt Wilson, Dan Wood, and Susan Zaeske.

Several individuals have also earned our appreciation for their help, patience, and support as this set of essays became a book. First and foremost are the brilliant authors who agreed to share their contributions with us. We are honored to have been able to work with them. Second, Mary Lenn Dixon and the staff at Texas A&M University Press have been outstanding to work with; their demand for the finest intellectual product and commitment to excellence hopefully show in this volume. Finally, we are forever indebted to Vanessa Beasley, who has been a champion of this project since those spring days in Bryan. In the months since, she has been the very model of professionalism in the academy, someone who has been able to challenge us while also supporting our vision. There is no hyperbole involved when we say that this book would not exist without her intellectual leadership and guidance.

Over the course of the many months between first conceptualizing the Obama Phenomenon conference and submitting the final version of this manuscript, both of our lives have seen significant change, including most importantly the people who have come into them and those who have departed. During this time, we both married the loves of our lives, Elena Tomorowitz (Justin) and Dwayne Raymond (Jennifer), cementing partnerships that make us both hopeful and excited for the years to come. An immeasurable loss was also suffered when Jim Aune passed away in January 2013. An exceptional scholar, Jim was also a treasured colleague and friend. We are humbled to include what may be his final essay in this volume, and we dedicate this book to his memory.

The Rhetoric of Heroic Expectations

CHAPTER 1

Barack Obama and the Rhetoric of Heroic Expectations

JENNIFER R. MERCIECA
JUSTIN S. VAUGHN

"As we stand at this crossroads of history, the eyes of all people in all nations are once again upon us," President Barack Obama observed in his February 24, 2009, *Address Before a Joint Session of Congress*. He believed that the world was "watching to see what we do with this moment, waiting for us to lead. Those of us gathered here tonight have been called to govern in extraordinary times. It is a tremendous burden, but it is also a great privilege, one that has been entrusted to few generations of Americans. For in our hands lies the ability to shape our world for good or for ill."[1] That President Obama overtly recognized the "crossroads of history," the "moment," the "extraordinary times," indeed, the "tremendous burden" of his presidency, only one month into office is a comment both on the awesome responsibility of the presidency in general and upon Barack Obama's presidency specifically. Does the "moment" within which a president assumes office really affect their presidency, as Obama suggested? We believe that the answer is unequivocally yes; the moment within which a president takes office can matter and it can matter a great deal.

In President Obama's case, after nearly two years of promising "hope" and "change" on the campaign trail many Americans listening to his address that night, only a month after his inauguration, might well have believed that Obama's presidency really could reshape the world for good. Other Americans listening that night might have worried that the Obama presidency would reshape the world for ill. Still others might have wondered if the "extraordinary times"—the startling economic collapse of 2008 while America fought two wars abroad, coupled with increased political partisanship at home, America's diminished international reputation, a media environment that thrived upon division, and his historic role as the nation's first African American president—would hinder Obama's ability to lead and reshape the world at all. As Obama noted, leading in extraordinary times is both a "tremendous burden" and a "great privilege," for such moments of profound change demand heroic leadership in the face of insurmountable obstacles.

Along with President Obama in his February 24, 2009, *Address,* this volume asks: With the eyes of all the world watching, would Barack Obama be able to meet the high expectations of his office; would he be able to lead? In this chapter, we engage with two under-theorized notions of the presidency. So doing enables us to rethink how we judge presidential leadership: first, the expectations gap; and second the burden of the presidency. We argue that there is a rhetoric of presidential expectations, which has grown more heroic since the Progressive Era, and that these heroic expectations set up three kinds of presidential burdens: institutional burdens (the "glorious burdens" specific to the office of the presidency itself); contextual burdens (burdens specific to the historic moment within which the president assumes office); and, personal burdens (burdens specific to the man or woman who becomes president). We judge all presidents based upon both our heroic expectations and how they handle their various burdens, both shared and unique. Although many presidents have acknowledged the overwhelming expectations of the office, scholarly work on how those expectations are rhetorically constructed and how a president's burden affects his or her ability to lead remains largely undone. This is a regrettable lacuna because the president's burden forms an important element of the rhetorical context within which he or she operates, and thus ought to be understood.

The Rhetoric of Presidential Expectations

That Americans have what we can think of as "heroic expectations" for the president cannot be denied. We expect that the president will act at a minimum as the chief administrator, chief diplomat, chief legislator, chief magistrate, commander in chief, chief executive, ceremonial head of state, manager of the economy, party leader, and national leader—much more than the US Constitution prescribes. Yet Dennis M. Simon argues that "there is no corpus of work that constitutes the normal science on public expectations."[2] He argues further that we could usefully distinguish between "image-based expectations" that "refer to both the desirable personal traits of presidents and how presidents should conduct themselves in office" and "performance-based expectations" that "focus upon what presidents should accomplish in office." Ray Price, an aide to Richard Nixon during his 1968 campaign for the presidency, demonstrates these "image-based expectations" in his warning to the eventual thirty-seventh president:

> People identify with a President in a way they do no other public figure. Potential presidents are measured against an ideal that's a combination of leading man, God, father, hero, pope, king, with maybe just a touch of the avenging Furies thrown in. They want him to be larger than life, a living legend, and yet quintessentially human; someone to be held up to their children as a model; someone to be cherished by themselves as a revered member of the family, in somewhat the same way in which peasant families pray to the icon in the corner. Reverence goes where power is.[3]

Additionally, empirical documentation supports Simon's claims about "performance-based expectations." For example, George Edwards and Stephen Wayne show that prior to his inauguration, significant percentages of Americans expected Barack Obama to satisfy a wide range of lofty tasks, including working effectively with Congress (89 percent), managing the executive branch wisely (84 percent), and fulfilling the proper role of the United States in world affairs (80 percent).[4] These numbers were comparable to (and in some cases up from) the high expectations preceding George W. Bush's inauguration in January, 2001, when 81 percent of Americans hoped that Bush would set a good moral example for the nation; 78 percent hoped that he would use military force wisely; 74 percent expected him to work well with Congress; and 72 percent anticipated proper fulfillment of the United States in world affairs.[5] These numbers compare with expectations of other recent presidents. In *The Public Presidency*, for example, George Edwards reported public opinion data that demonstrated sizeable majorities expected both Jimmy Carter and Ronald Reagan to accomplish policy tasks such as reducing unemployment and inflation, increasing government efficiency while reducing its cost, and dealing effectively with foreign policy while strengthening the national defense.[6] In short, Americans have significant, often even unrealistic, expectations that the President of the United States has the power to control every facet of government. How did Americans come to expect so much from their presidents?

Scholarly consensus indicates these outsized expectations are a function of our cultural tradition of glorifying presidential memories, the distance between the presidency and most Americans that prevents them from actually knowing and understanding the office and those who hold it, and the way the presidency is presented in mediated forms to the public. Along these lines, Joseph Pika and John Maltese argued, "[W]e have glorified the memories of past presidents. The 'great presidents,' particularly those who took decisive action and bold initiatives, and even some of the 'not so great' are treated as folk heroes and enshrined in a national mythology."[7] The effects of this enshrinement are exacerbated by the fact that most Americans will never have direct knowledge of the presidency; therefore, as Trevor Parry-Giles and Shawn Parry-Giles observe, "[F]or most citizens the presidency is only and always a representation, an image of a reality that can never be known."[8] That the representation is glorified and heroic means that "for most Americans, the presidency is larger than life, transcending normal human limitations."[9]

These representations and the expectations that they inculcate affect both the presidency in general and specific presidents in particular, thanks in part to media portrayals of presidential leadership and politics. Indeed, as Dennis M. Simon writes, they "are part of the historical inheritance that awaits every new president. They are, in a sense, imposed on every incumbent, regardless of party or ideology." Whether or not the president has heroic ambitions, "These expectations shape how presidents are covered by the press as well as how they are perceived and evaluated by elites and the mass public."[10] Scholars have previously argued that we develop our expectations about the presidency through media portrayals, school textbooks, and political campaigns.[11] We agree that all of these sources contribute to building presidential expectations, but we believe that scholars have not yet recognized the constitutive role that historical rankings of presidents play in setting presidential expectations and that the standards established by polls of presidential greatness, in turn, influenced how media, textbooks, and campaigns portray the presidency. We believe that these polls of presidential greatness help to define how we think about presidential leadership and, as we explain below, these polls constituted the "great president" as a heroic leader rather than as a competent chief executive.[12]

"The "great Presidents," argued Arthur M. Schlesinger Sr., in *Life Magazine,* "were strong Presidents. Each of them magnified the executive branch at the expense of the other branches of the government."[13] Since Schlesinger Sr. began polling historians about presidential greatness in 1948, historians have consistently rated George Washington, Abraham Lincoln, and Franklin Delano Roosevelt (FDR) "great." Experts have less consistently rated Thomas Jefferson, Andrew Jackson, James K. Polk, Theodore Roosevelt, Woodrow Wilson, and Harry S. Truman as "great" or "near great" and identified the bottom "failure" presidents as Ulysses S. Grant, Warren G. Harding, James Buchanan, Herbert Hoover, and (eventually) Richard Nixon. Yet despite these consistencies, the polls are controversial, with presidential fortunes rising and falling based upon new assessments of the past, current values, and pollsters' ideological leanings.[14]

"How the hell can you tell?" asked President John F. Kennedy, when Schlesinger Sr. sent him the poll in 1962. "Only the president himself can know what his real pressures and real alternatives are. If you don't know that, how can you judge performance?"[15] Schlesinger agreed that Kennedy had a point—to a degree—but that did not stop him, or his son Arthur M. Schlesinger Jr., from continuing to inquire after presidential greatness. Stephen Skowronek believes that Progressive Era historians like the Schlesingers were "advocates of presidential power" who "left an indelible mark on the operations of American government."[16] Progressive Era historians "wanted a more powerful presidency" and "they saw in [Franklin] Roosevelt's political skill and reform vigor a model for political leadership in modern America, and they distilled from his example the personal attributes likely to prove most valuable to incumbents in negotiating the governing challenges of the future."[17] We could think of the "great" presidents as those who abided by the letter of the constitution, balanced the budget, did not interfere with setting national policies, or any other number of metrics. Yet we do not. Since the Progressive Era, we think of great presidents, as Schlesinger noted in 1948, "as strong presidents."

Schlesinger Sr. explained the 1962 poll results by arguing that historians judged presidents based upon a series of questions, all indicating a president's power and his success in changing history: "Did the President head the nation in sunny or stormy times? Did he exhibit a creative approach to the problems of statecraft? Was he the master or servant of events? Did he use the prestige and potentialities of the position to advance the public welfare? Did he effectively staff his key government posts? Did he properly safeguard the country's interest in relation to the rest of the world? How significantly did he affect the future destinies of the nation?"[18] Although Schlesinger Jr.'s 1973 work, *The Imperial Presidency*, decried the consolidation of power in the Nixon administration, Gene Healy and others have noted that "Schlesinger Jr.'s polls, like his father's, heavily favored imperial presidents."[19] In 1948, 1962, and 1996, Americans were treated to the Schlesinger interpretation that great presidents were strong presidents who changed history. As Stephen Skowronek and others have shown, the consistency of the ratings across polls since 1948 demonstrates that the Schlesinger interpretation influenced the modern public's understanding of how a president should be judged, if not the precise judgments for particular presidents.[20] Indeed, recent scholarship by Curt Nichols, which itself is predicated upon Skowronek's notion of "political time,"[21] has empirically evaluated and underscored this sentiment, showing that experts systematically "reward presidents who succeed in taking advantage of the opportunity to reorder—while also punishing those presidents helping to bring about enervated conditions as well as those failing to overcome them."[22]

Even though empirical evidence seems to support the conclusion that polls of presidential greatness have tilted toward the "strong presidents," one might wonder how much of an influence these polls might really have in constituting the public's expectations of the presidency. After all, how many Americans read these polls, and how much weight do citizens and politicians give to the musings of historians? These are certainly difficult questions to answer with any certainty, but we argue that by providing a consistent standard by which to judge presidential "greatness," these polls helped to constitute if not the presidency, then at least expectations about the presidency. Polls of presidential greatness both reflected preexisting notions of who and what should count as excellence in office, as well as created benchmarks for others to judge future presidential excellence. It may seem tautological to argue that polls of presidential greatness constitute how we think of presidential greatness, but that is precisely what we mean. Polls of presidential greatness are a kind of rhetorical discourse that helps Americans to understand, position, frame, and delimit the presidency; the polls, in effect, have a constitutive function in our understanding of the American presidency.[23] One way to understand these polls, then, is that through them Americans learned that the only great presidents were those "strong presidents" who consolidated power in the executive branch—or who acted as what scholars today call an "imperial president."[24]

Heroic Expectations, Heroic Burdens

Not only did Progressive Era historians like Arthur M. Schlesinger Sr. and his followers constitute the "great president" as the "strong president," but their efforts to increase the power of the executive branch reconstituted the president in the public imagination as the nation's hero rather than as the nation's chief executive. Progressive Era historians may not have intended to cultivate heroic expectations for the president, but it is hard to read Schlesinger Sr.'s approving description of the "great presidents" without also learning to applaud those heroic presidents who had the fortitude to expand the powers of the presidency, change history, and protect freedom and democracy: "Every one of these men left the executive branch stronger and more influential than when he found it. As a matter of course they magnified the powers expressly granted them by the Constitution and assumed others not expressly denied by it."[25] Even if today we might question whether any one person has the agency to change the course of history, we seem to expect that the president would have the heroic ability to do just that. As Schlesinger Jr. explained in 1963, the heroic leader has the "Promethean responsibility to affirm human freedom against the supposed inevitabilities of history." He goes on to note, "A purposeful and vital democracy must rest on a belief in the potency of choice—on the conviction that individual decisions do affect the course of events."[26] Promethean responsibilities ought not to fall on just anyone, for only a select few heroic humans can wield the power of the gods.[27]

The longest standing account of the influence of heroic expectations on our understanding of the presidency is that of Thomas Cronin, who has found that school textbooks written since FDR and the influence of Progressive Era historians have portrayed presidents as omniscient, omnipotent, benevolent, and moral, which in turn has enabled presidents to argue for more power.[28] Scholars of presidential rhetoric like John Murphy and Trevor and Shawn Parry-Giles have argued that media portrayals of the president have become increasingly heroic in character. "Over the past decade an unusual number of movies and television episodes have portrayed the presidency," observed Murphy, and in these portrayals, like the school textbooks studied by Cronin, "the president is a good guy."[29] Likewise, Jeffery C. Alexander has recently described presidential campaigning as the construction of hero narratives. "Struggles for big-time political power are narrated in terms of crisis and salvation," explained

Alexander: "According to those who would be president, Americans face a unique moment in our history. There are unprecedented dangers and opportunities; a world-historical crisis domestically and internationally threatens to derail the nation's triumphant, mythical history. America has fallen on tough times." Therefore, all political campaigns are persuasive attempts in which candidates attempt to convince the American public that they are the right hero for the moment.[30] Taken together, these studies demonstrate that the post-Schlesinger view of presidential greatness asks us to view the "great president" as a hero who protects human freedom and democracy by changing the course of history; these are not small expectations to be sure. Below we explain how acknowledging the rhetoric of heroic expectations can help us to make sense of three kinds of presidential burdens: institutional burdens, contextual burdens, and personal burdens. The notion that the presidency is a "glorious burden" is both widely accepted (the Smithsonian American History Museum's exhibit on the institution is titled "The American Presidency: A Glorious Burden," for example) and completely uninterrogated; indeed, the phrase stems from Stefan Lorant's epic 1968 *The Glorious Burden: The American Presidency,* in which Lorant neither defines the term nor traces its provenance.[31] We attempt to do some of this work here.

INSTITUTIONAL BURDENS

"There are no easy matters that will ever come to you as president," Dwight D. Eisenhower counseled President-elect John F. Kennedy on January 19, 1961, as Kennedy prepared to assume office. "If they are easy, they will be settled at a lower level. So that the matters that come to you as president are always the difficult matters, and matters that carry with them large implications." Two years into office, President Kennedy believed that these difficult decisions were a large part of what he described then as the "burdens of the office of the presidency."[32] Kennedy was not alone in referring to the presidency as a "burden." Although it was true that eighteenth-century presidents like George Washington described the office as an "arduous but pleasing task" and nineteenth-century presidents like Andrew Jackson described the office as "arduous duties," by the twentieth century it was common for presidents to characterize the responsibilities of the office by using the word *burden.*[33] For example, at the dawn of the twentieth century, William McKinley believed that "[a]nyone who has borne the anxieties and burdens of the Presidential office, especially in time of National trial, cannot contemplate assuming it a second time without profoundly realizing the severe exactions and the solemn obligations which it imposes, and this feeling is accentuated by the momentous problems which now press for settlement."[34] As McKinley explained, anxieties, burdens, exactions, obligations, and problems would weigh on the minds of all of those who held the office.

Whether described as an "arduous but pleasing task" or as a "burden," as Eisenhower told Kennedy, the office has always required its occupant to make tough decisions under difficult circumstances. The job is indeed arduous, but is there more at stake than word choice in the difference between thinking of the presidency-as-task and the presidency-as-burden? Indeed, our heroic expectations for the presidency bear little relationship either to the constitutional limits on the president or to any president's ability to fulfill those expectations—or what Richard E. Neustadt explained in "the last of the great Progressive tracts" as the "expectations gap."[35] These heroic expectations contribute to the president's burden because they ask the president to seek to control every facet of the political community—to make laws, conduct wars, control the economy, create a lasting worldwide peace, and so on—regardless of whether he or she has the constitutional power to do so. Thus, the nation's heroic expectations for the presidency directly translate into what we can think of as the "institutional burdens" of the office.

Although scholars have not previously described the "institutional burdens" of the presidency, we believe that the concept helps to explain contradictory scholarship on presidential leadership. For example, although Richard E. Neustadt famously argued that presidential power lies in a chief executive's power to persuade rather than in any positive legal tool, George Edwards has (also famously) demonstrated that the president's ability to influence Congress is marginal at best.[36] Edwards argues that the president's failure to move Congress is a reflection of a persistent inability to move public opinion,[37] which is a cornerstone requirement of Samuel Kernell's seminal "going public" thesis and Neustadt's own model of leadership.[38] If a president's chief power is the power to persuade, but there is no proof that presidential speechmaking actually persuades anyone, then either we have misperceived what a president's "chief power" is, or we have overly exaggerated presidential power. Either way, the occupant of the office is burdened by the expectation that he or she will successfully set the public's agenda and move public opinion. Dennis M. Simon describes this conundrum as the "trap of the textbook presidency," whereas B. Dan Wood explains that "[a]lthough it *seems* evident that presidents should be influential agenda setters at both the systemic and institutional levels, hard scientific evidence showing that presidents *are* influential agenda setters is limited."[39] Consider, for example, any president's ability to influence the economy—one of the most salient issues for rendering judgments of presidential greatness. Forrest McDonald explains that although presidents are "supplied with a council of economic advisors to tell him how" to manage the economy, presidents are "given none of the tools to implement policy, if indeed policy is capable of altering economic reality in desired directions. The president cannot raise or lower taxes, cannot hire or fire people, cannot reward productivity or punish inefficiency, and has but an indirect voice in setting interest rates and expanding or contracting the money supply. Moreover, the emergence of a global economy has made the American economy subject to gust and squalls from the world over, quite beyond anyone's control."[40] What is true for the president's ability to control the economy is true for most of the issues that we use to judge the effectiveness of presidential leadership. Quite simply, the heightened expectations placed upon all presidents since the Progressive Era have translated into the increased institutional burdens of the office of the presidency.

Astute observers of the Obama presidency have recognized the consequences that such expectations have had on the president's ability to lead in a manner consistent with the vision of the presidency he offered during the 2008 campaign. As Todd Purdum notes in *Vanity Fair*:

> The modern presidency—Barack Obama's presidency—has become a job of such gargantuan size, speed, and complexity as to be all but unrecognizable to most of the previous chief executives. The sheer growth of the federal government, the paralysis of Congress, the systemic corruption brought on by lobbying, the trivialization of the "news" by the media, the willful disregard for facts and truth—these forces have made today's Washington a depressing and dysfunctional place. They have shaped and at times hobbled the presidency itself.[41]

A seemingly impossible task, to be sure, but one also made all the more complicated and cumbersome by the promises and assurances

Obama offered to voters during his campaign. In step with his predecessor presidential aspirants—and matched by his opponent Senator John McCain—Obama offered an almost limitless range of ways in which his presidency would solve policy problems facing the nation and remedy the dysfunctional dimensions of national politics that dismayed so many in the electorate. Such promises crossed a range of ambitious, yet substantive policy initiatives, including: universal health care, immigration reform, shuttering Guantanamo Bay's enemy combatant prison, repealing the George W. Bush tax cuts, increasing government transparency, limiting the role played by professional lobbyists, and creating a cap-and-trade program to battle the burgeoning global warming crisis. The president's early record of accomplishments on these issues was mixed, and he quickly learned that even on the most noteworthy successes, a myriad of structural barriers limited his ability to accomplish all of his aims. Congress watered down his health care bill and tabled consideration of immigration and climate change legislation, while the president was quickly forced to either compromise or back away entirely from promises concerning Guantanamo Bay and the Bush tax cuts.

Making matters even more muddled, many of Obama's campaign promises were ambiguous and arguably unachievable by any measure. Casting his candidacy as one dedicated to hope and change, his supporters expected to see change, not just in policy but in how Washington worked, and to see it immediately. Obama nurtured this expectation, promising to turn the page on dysfunctional partisanship and restore Americans' fair shot at their dreams, lofty yet vague goals that he would be poorly positioned to achieve.[42] That is, he was poorly positioned, as would be any president, to control the partisan behavior of not only his side but also that of the opposition. Presidents certainly serve as the heads of their parties, but they can hardly count on unlimited and consistent support from their fellow partisans, particularly in Congress,[43] and they can be increasingly certain of the opposition's disinclination toward cooperation. Further, while Republicans were relatively timid in their support for their 2008 presidential nominee, John McCain, they were united and full-throated in their disdain for candidate and then new President Obama—so much so that Republican congressional leaders identified the defeat of Obama in 2012 as their single greatest priority. Similarly, on the two important votes in Congress in the opening days and weeks of the new administration, Obama received only three Republican votes in the Senate and no Republican votes in the House of Representatives on the economic stimulus bill, while receiving only one Republican vote in the Senate and none in the House on the health care reform bill. This overwhelming opposition, on votes and in tone, prompted a chastened Obama to acknowledge, less than a year after his inauguration, that the promise for a new American politics had gone unfulfilled. In a 2010 speech at Vermont Avenue Baptist Church in Washington, D.C., in honor of Martin Luther King Jr., Obama noted:

> There were those who argued that because I had spoke of a need for unity in this country that our nation was somehow entering into a period of post-partisanship. That didn't work out so well. There was a hope shared by many that life would be better from the moment that I swore that oath. Of course, as we meet here today, one year later, we know the promise of that moment has not yet been fully fulfilled.[44]

The promise of a new era of politics, one where ugly partisanship was diminished and the lives of every day Americans enriched, remained unfulfilled largely because of the structural and constitutional obstacles standing between the president's goals and political reality. Perceptively, however, Obama went on to note other important reasons why his campaign promises remained unfulfilled, reasons we turn to in the next section of this essay. According to Obama, the historical context, particularly the banking crisis and related economic troubles, was the primary reason why the promise of the moment in Grant Park on election night 2008 remained unfulfilled on Martin Luther King Jr. Day 2010.

CONTEXTUAL BURDENS

Although every president faces institutional expectations upon assuming office, some presidents assume the office during what George Forgie has called a "heroic age," or what we can understand as a time of national crisis.[45] Presiding over the nation in a heroic age raises the expectations for presidential greatness both because the stakes are so high and because judgments of success or failure are based upon the immediate consequences of actions taken to resolve the crisis.[46] Presidents face heightened contextual burdens during national crises, to be sure, but Stephen Skowronek's "political time" thesis can help us to think more carefully about how all presidents face contextual burdens. "A broad view of American political development reveals recurrent sequences of political change," Skowronek argued; "leadership problems are reconfigured in typical ways along these sequences, and each configuration yields a corresponding pattern in presidential performance." The potential for presidential leadership is therefore "episodic rather than evolutionary": only certain presidents (the ones who head a "regime change" or set the nation on an entirely new course) have the opportunity to become heroic leaders.[47] As a result, all presidents do not have an equal opportunity for presidential greatness, which means that the context within which a president assumes office has to be understood by both situating it within its context in history and within its context in the presidency. "What if the political demands on incumbents change in significant ways even within the same historical period?" asks Skowronek. "What if the leadership capacities of the office vary widely from one administration to the next? Much of what we take to be evidence of character and strategic acumen might actually be an expression of changing relations between the presidency and the political system."[48] Indeed, Curt Nichols's recent analysis of presidential ratings and political time supports Skowronek's thesis about the importance of context: "historical context—especially that associated with the challenges and opportunities identified in the latest extension of political time theory—does matter in structuring ratings."[49]

Furthermore, political campaigns may actually heighten the sense of heroic times and increase the incoming president's contextual burden. If Jeffery C. Alexander is correct in saying that presidential candidates largely frame their campaigns through the strategic deployment of hero narratives, then in their attempt to persuade Americans that they are the appropriate hero for the moment, candidates both ratchet up fears of crisis and expectations that they will be the hero who saves America from impending doom. Political campaigns are centered on "narrating time, about building a new temporality that is radically discontinuous, and about weighting the imminent break with immense significance," explained Alexander. Every candidate's opponent is portrayed as "so dangerous that electing that person will plunge the nation into apocalypse. Rather than transcending the troubled present, history will be set in reverse. If the antihero is elected, the progressive arc of our collectivity will be broken, and we will no longer be able to move into future time and change for the better."⁵⁰ The goal of any presidential campaign is therefore to convince Americans that their candidate is "the right kind of hero: once a political figure's hero character is formed, it is history that decides whether it will fit with that particular time."⁵¹ With the nation convinced that the candidate is the right hero to save America, incoming presidents will be judged accordingly, as heroes who *ought* to save America.

The 2008 presidential election had been framed as a comment on heroic leadership as early as May 2006, when Sean Wilentz attempted to explain to the readers of *Rolling Stone* why 81 percent of the 415 historians surveyed by the *History News Network* in 2004 had ranked the presidency of George W. Bush a "failure." Wilentz observed that President Bush was faring equally poorly in public opinion polls, which in mid-2006 showed that only about 35 percent of the American population approved of Bush's job performance—a figure matched only by Richard Nixon right before "his resignation in 1974." In his explanation of Bush's meager presidential reputation, Wilentz listed a long train of Bush's supposed abuses and usurpations, which he argued equaled nothing less than a reverse of "presidential greatness." Wilentz explained that the great presidents—Washington, Lincoln, and FDR—"were the men who guided the nation through what historians consider its greatest crises: the founding era after the ratification of the Constitution, the Civil War, and the Great Depression and Second World War. Presented with arduous, at times seemingly impossible circumstances, they rallied the nation, governed brilliantly and left the republic more secure than when they entered office." Bush's performance ranked him alongside those "calamitous presidents"—Buchanan, Andrew Johnson, and Hoover—who "divided the nation, governed erratically and left the nation worse off." Wilentz believed that the attacks of September 11, 2001, provided Bush with "an extraordinary opportunity to achieve greatness," but believing himself to be a "messianic liberator and profound freedom fighter, on a par with FDR and Lincoln," Bush acted "in ways that have left the country less united and more divided, less conciliatory and more acrimonious."⁵²

We can observe that Sean Wilentz's explanation of how historians judged presidential greatness in 2006 is the same as that used by the Schlesingers in 1948, 1962, and 1996: the "great" presidents were Washington, Lincoln, and FDR because, facing great crises, they were able to act as heroic leaders who controlled history, united the nation, and used the power of the presidency to leave the nation better off than they had found it. Second, in Wilentz's negative assessment of Bush's presidency we can observe the continued contradictions of heroic expectations: Wilentz compared Lincoln's use (or abuse) of presidential power during the Civil War to Bush's and argued both that Bush was secretive/duplicitous about his expansion of presidential powers *and* that Bush overtly argued that the president had such powers during war time. In either case, according to Wilentz, Lincoln—governing brilliantly—was justified in expanding the reach of the presidency, but Bush—governing erratically—was not. Bush's calamitous failure meant that the next president would have an even greater burden than Bush because that president would have to deal with an even more troubled nation, an even larger crisis—the same situation in which Lincoln and FDR found themselves following the presidencies of Buchanan and Hoover. And finally, in judging Bush's presidency a failure, we learn that both historians and citizens rejected Bush's use of imperial presidential power, which meant that whoever won the 2008 election would face increased scrutiny over its use. If Wilentz's analysis was correct, then the forty-fourth president indeed would have one of the largest burdens in American history.

As Obama launched his bid for the Democratic Party nomination in late 2006 and early 2007, he therefore had some sense that the calamitous failure of the Bush presidency had created a great need for heroic leadership, but few could have predicted how grave the nation's crises would become by the November 2008 election.[53] Between February 2007 and November 2008, the nation witnessed an astounding collapse of the economy: Rising gas prices in the spring and summer of 2008 (up to $4.49 a gallon) contributed to rising commute and food prices.[54] American wages, which had been stagnant since 1999, actually regressed.[55] More and more Americans were unemployed or underemployed, with unemployment rates increasing in each month of 2008 until they reached 6.5 percent by October, the highest levels since 1994.[56] Housing prices had been falling in some markets since 2006, but by April 2008, news outlets reported that home prices across the United States had dropped 15.3 percent since the year before, the largest drop since The Standard & Poor's/Case-Shiller home price index began keeping track of prices in 2000.[57] By June, the Mortgage Bankers Association released data that showed that one in every one hundred US homes was in foreclosure (double the rate from the previous year), which led to short sales and the loss of property tax revenues for state and local governments.[58] In the Summer and early Fall of 2008, big

Wall Street firms like Bear Stearns, Lehman Brothers, Merrill Lynch, and AIG collapsed due to their "toxic investments" in subprime mortgages.[59] In early September 2008, the government placed mortgage giants Fannie Mae and Freddie Mac into "conservatorship" in order to prevent a complete collapse of the financial system.[60] And on September 29, 2008, the stock market tumbled 778 points, the largest ever single-day loss.[61] The economic crisis overshadowed, but did not eclipse, the nation's many other crises: the unpopular, unsuccessful, and costly wars in Iraq and Afghanistan; the nation's poor health care system; the nation's crumbling infrastructure; the nation's dependence on foreign oil; the world's changing climate; the poor quality of the nation's public schools; the nation's declining international reputation; the growing disparities between the rich and the poor; the growing vehemence in partisanship; the problems of immigration, and on and on. In short, just like the election of 1860 or 1932, the times themselves called for a heroic leader. Obama's 2008 presidential campaign attempted to constitute him as that leader. As one would expect, his opponents—Hillary Clinton, John McCain, and Sarah Palin—repeatedly questioned whether he was ready to lead.

Clearly, the central question of the 2008 presidential campaign was who was best prepared to lead the nation out of its many crises. Yet although the times called for heroic presidential leadership, we must remember that the nation also was wary of the imperial presidency. Thus, every presidential hopeful in 2008 had both to argue for his or her leadership credentials and do so in such a way as to appear to be a brilliant leader like Washington, Lincoln, and FDR rather than a calamitous leader like Buchanan, Hoover, or Bush. Obama negotiated this rhetorical situation by positioning himself as a Washington outsider who could bring necessary change, as the only candidate who had the good judgment to oppose the war in Iraq, and by promising to lead by sharing the burden of heroic times with all American citizens. In so doing, Obama created an even greater burden of heroic expectations for himself—his very campaign and victory seemed to promise that he was indeed Washington, Lincoln, or FDR.

Barack Obama raised more money, and from more donors, than anyone in the history of American politics ($750 million total, $500 million online, from more than two hundred thousand individuals).[62] By election night in November 2008, his campaign had an e-mail list of over ten million supporters—the largest database of its kind.[63] When Obama made a public appearance, he regularly drew crowds in excess of forty thousand.[64] His image sold more T-shirts, more posters, more coffee cups, more newsmagazine covers, more swag than most celebrities.[65] Obama had won the presidency by over nine million votes—the largest margin for a nonincumbent and the sixth largest ever.[66] After Barack Obama's election, comparisons between his presidency and those of the perennial greats became ubiquitous: President-elect Obama appeared as Abraham Lincoln on the cover of the November 15, 2008, *Newsweek;* as FDR on the November 24, 2008, cover of *Time;* as George Washington the cover of the January 26, 2009, *New Yorker,* and on and on.[67] We can read these comparisons, along with the entirety of the Obama phenomenon, as proof of our expectations for him to rise to the challenge of the heroic age. When he took office on January 20, 2009, his approval rating was 65 percent.[68] In the presidential greatness poll conducted by Siena College in 2010, Obama already ranked fifteenth, in the "almost great" category.[69]

PERSONAL BURDENS

Whereas institutional burdens come with the office and contextual burdens situate the duties of office within its historical moment, personal burdens are attached to the person who assumes the office. Each president has personal burdens: whether the president comes into office because the Supreme Court halted a state level recount or following the resignation of a sitting president under duress; or whether a president has hidden the fact that his struggle with the debilitating effects of polio means that he is often forced to use a wheelchair; or whether a president assumes office as half of the nation that he has sworn to protect believes that he intends to illegally abolish slavery; or whether a vice-president who was elected as a compromise to southern slaveholders suddenly finds himself accidentally elevated to the presidency by the effects of long winded speech-making, every president's personal circumstances form a part of the burden of the office. We can think of any president's personal burden as a part of what Dennis M. Simon described as "image-based expectations" and what Donald R. Kinder, Mark D. Peters, Robert P. Abelson, and Susan T. Fiske describe as "presidential prototypes." Indeed, Kinder and colleagues' analysis of the public's expectations about the president found that citizens have specific expectations about *who* a president ought to be and *how* presidents ought to act: "[A]n ideal president is honest, knowledgeable, and open-minded, but neither power-hungry nor unstable. An ideal president provides strong leadership, appoints good advisors, solves economic problems, avoids unnecessary wars, and never uses power for personal gain."[70] Citizens judge their presidents based upon these expectations of presidential character, which then form a portion of any president's personal burden. Each president faces unique personal burdens as well as the common prototypical personal burdens associated with the office.

For Barack Obama, his great personal burden in becoming and being president centered less on his character than it did on his race. For most observers, an African American president was something unconceived of (and, possibly, inconceivable) until Obama's rise as a serious candidate for the Democratic nomination in 2007, itself made possible by Obama's star turn at the 2004 Democratic National Convention. Other African American candidacies, namely those of Jesse Jackson and Shirley Chisholm, though path breaking, never rose to the level of plausibility. Obama himself, of course, had spent a great deal of time imagining himself as a black president, though it was a notion that only emerged after nearly a lifetime of contemplating his own blackness and its role in shaping his sense of self. Obama was well aware of the burden his race played in his life, both privately and publicly. Indeed, in his celebrated memoir, *Dreams from My Father*, Obama reflected at length on the role of race in his life, making a careful yet earnest assessment of his place in the world. In a particularly illuminating passage, where he writes about the way his mother taught him to think about the role race played in his life and in modern American public life, he noted that to be black was "to be the beneficiary of a great inheritance, a special destiny, glorious burdens that only we were strong enough to bear."[71]

Obama's optimism about the ability for African Americans to bear this burden, at least all the way to the White House, was not universally shared. In a thoughtful, though not entirely prescient, volume published less than a year before Obama's 2008 general election victory over John McCain, Shelby Steele argued that the two-dimensional nature of Obama's appeal would prohibit his ascent to the Oval Office.[72] Calling Obama a "bound man," Steele contended that Obama performed the role of a bargainer with whites, implicitly signaling a willingness to forgive their racism if they will look past his race, while he simultaneously appeared to the black community as a challenger, willing to leverage white guilt into black political advantage. To Steele, this contradiction could not be sustained. Sociologist Thomas Sugrue made a similar argument, rooted in Obama's hybrid vision of race relations, which showed how Obama's style facilitated coalition building and progress for all Americans, including African Americans.[73]

Wilbur Rich has linked Obama's so-called postracial approach with the pressures of heightened expectations, and in so doing notes the way developments in both Obama's campaign and early administration were racialized: from the controversy over candidate Obama's pastor, Jeremiah Wright, and the important speech on race it led Obama to deliver, to events like the arrest of Henry Gates and the firing of USDA employee Shirley Sherrod.[74] These controversies show that regardless of Obama's personal orientation toward race and his uncanny ability to appeal in different ways to different attentive constituencies, unpredictable developments continually force him to respond to race-driven dynamics. Such an observation is consistent with Randall Kennedy's argument, in which he painstakingly demonstrates the inability for Obama to be viewed in any way divorced of racial connotation and context.[75] As moments such as the controversies over Gates and Sherrod demonstrate, the racial euphoria felt in early November 2008—Rich, for example, points to a postelection poll that showed nearly 70 percent of Americans believed that race relations had improved—was temporary. Whereas Obama realized that he was a blank screen upon which people projected their own views, he forgot or perhaps failed to realize that whatever those views might be, nearly all would be colored by racial considerations.[76] As a result, Obama faced not only the expected retrenchment and paranoia of those on the Right who feared that he would govern in a biased manner, one that benefited fellow African Americans at the expense of other groups and communities; he also faced critique, often scathing, from members of the African American community over perceptions that he had not done enough to help their community. While Obama was promising in Grant Park that he would be the president of all people, many of his supporters in the black community (and indeed many of his opponents on the other side of the racial divide) expected him to perform some version of Martin Luther King Jr. in the White House.[77] That he has not been King has earned him little credit from his opponents, but great censure from luminaries such as Cornel West,[78] and calls for more direct presidential engagement with racial divisions by esteemed scholars such as Desmond King and Rogers Smith.[79] Obama's personal burdens thus intersect with his contextual burdens and institutional burdens, because questions over Obama's racial heritage have been a constant part of media coverage of the Obama presidency (the "Birther" controversy continued to reassert itself well into the 2012 election, for example), fueling partisanship and making it more difficult to pass his policy agenda.

Conclusion

"In the United States we like to 'rate' a President," explained Richard E. Neustadt; "We measure him as 'weak' or 'strong' and call what we are measuring his 'leadership.'"[80] We have argued that these kinds of rankings have a constitutive role upon the presidency and form an important element of the president's burden. An understanding of the institutional, contextual, and personal burdens Barack Obama faced in the early days of his administration provide a lens through which to examine his efforts to establish his presidency and to evaluate this landmark presidency in both historical terms and in "political time." Moreover, by focusing on the constitutive discourses surrounding these expectations, these burdens, and this presidency, we can learn more about how these expectations have been constructed and how to assess their fairness and appropriateness, as well as Barack Obama's ability to satisfy them.

When we take into consideration a nation's heroic expectations for presidential greatness, we are enabled to understand more clearly what is at stake in scholarship on the imperial presidency and the rhetorical presidency. First, scholars working on the questions of the imperial presidency would benefit from a recognition that Americans both want an imperial president and do not want an imperial president. We want "great" presidents who can change history, but who do so within the constitutional order. The rhetoric of heroic expectations mandates that the president attempt to act heroically and control history, even if so doing requires working outside of the limits of the constitution. Not only is this contradictory, but these contradictory expectations add to any president's burden because they give ammunition to the opposition party to decry any unwanted policy as an imperial abuse of power. Second, scholars working on the questions of the rhetorical presidency would benefit from a recognition that our heroic expectations require that presidents "go public" or go "over the heads of Congress" and that the rise in the rhetorical presidency during the Progressive Era was concomitant with the rise of heroic expectations. When we judge presidents based upon their ability to act heroically and control history, then we must expect that they would go over the heads of Congress and speak directly to the people, for part of the president's burden is to demonstrate heroic leadership of the public, regardless of the normative and constitutional concerns this might evoke, as Jeffrey Tulis and other scholars have identified and addressed.[81]

Neither are scholars of presidential rhetoric immune to the rhetoric of presidential expectations. Indeed, their judgments of presidential greatness share much in common with the judgments of historians and others. Presidential rhetoric scholars have taken a keen interest in those presidencies that historians and other pollsters have rated "great" or "near great"—especially Lincoln, FDR, Jefferson, Teddy Roosevelt, Woodrow Wilson, and Ronald Reagan—while neglecting those merely "average" or "below-average" presidents like Zachary Taylor, Millard Fillmore, Franklin Pierce, and Rutherford B. Hayes. So little was known about the rhetorical practices of this latter group of presidential not-so-greats that in 2002 Texas A&M University hosted an entire conference devoted to them and collected the essays into the aptly named *Before the Rhetorical Presidency*. The essays demonstrated that all of these "lesser-known chief executives" failed the test of greatness because they failed the "Promethean test" of controlling history. For example, the "Little Magician" Martin Van Buren, "failed to understand—or to rhetorically adapt to—the rapidly changing circumstances of democratic governance"; likewise, "His Accidency," John Tyler, although he deserved credit for helping "to establish the principle of executive independence from both Congress and party," was unable to control history by providing "effective rhetorical leadership"; the "Fainting General," Franklin Pierce, chose to "avoid politics in favor of the language of gentlemanly decorum," which meant that he did not even attempt to control history; and poor "Tennessee Tailor" Andrew "Johnson's 'enactment of the presidency was ill-suited in almost every possible way to the standards of performance requisite to its success.' As both rhetor and statesman, Johnson [was] found wanting."[82] Even while reevaluating these presidential not-so-greats with fresh eyes, the judgments of rhetorical scholars were still based upon the established standards of greatness: Did the president exert his will over the government? Did the president consolidate power in the executive branch? Did the president control history? Did the rhetorical practices of the president satisfy the nation's heroic expectations? Not surprisingly, the presidents traditionally judged to be not so great continued to be judged not so great, likely because these presidents continued to fail rhetorical scholars' heroic expectations.

We have argued that the constitutive discourses of presidential polls, textbooks, and popular culture help to create heroic expectations and that these heroic expectations, in turn, constrain and enable presidential leadership. When we think of the presidency as heroic, then we expect for presidential rhetoric to unify the nation, demonstrate a high degree of agency (the ability to control world history), and seek to consolidate power in the executive branch. Conversely, when we think of the presidency as non-heroic then we expect for presidential rhetoric to divide the nation, acknowledge the interconnectedness of world events without stressing the agency of the president to control history, and seek to equalize power among the three branches. Not only do we judge presidencies as "great," "average," or "failures" based upon heroic expectations, but we also often judge presidential *rhetoric* based upon heroic expectations. Heroic expectations therefore form a part of the burden of the presidency because they set unrealistically high standards for presidential success and mandate that a president use what Robert Hariman has called the "courtly style" within a "republican fiction" that supposedly shuns imperial leaders, no small rhetorical burden for any president to negotiate.[83] Further, we have argued that we both desire "great" presidents who are strong leaders and decry the consolidation of power in the executive branch that such presidential greatness would require. These contradictory expectations for the president form an important element of the rhetorical context within which any president operates and contribute to the president's burden, for how can any president both be a "great" heroic leader who changes history and also work within the confines of constitutional limitations?

Notes

1. Barack Obama, "Address Before a Joint Session of the Congress," February 24, 2009, in *The American Presidency Project* [online], eds. John Woolley and Gerhard Peters, http://www.presidency.ucsb.edu/ws/?pid=85753.

2. Dennis M. Simon, 2009, "Public Expectations of the President," in *The Oxford Handbook of the American Presidency,* eds. George C. Edwards III and William G. Howell (Oxford: Oxford University Press), 135–159, p. 135.

3. Michael Novak, *Choosing Presidents: Symbols of Political Leadership*, 2nd ed. (New Brunswick, NJ: Transaction, 1992), 44; and Joseph A. Pika and John Anthony Maltese, *The Politics of the Presidency,* 6th ed. (Washington, DC: CQ Press, 2004), 25.

4. George C. Edwards III and Stephen J. Wayne, *Presidential Leadership: Politics and Policy Making*, 8th ed. (Boston, MA: Wadsworth, 2010), 109.

5. Ibid, 107.

6. George C. Edwards III, *The Public Presidency: The Pursuit of Popular Support*, New York: Palgrave, 1983), 189.

7. Pika and Maltese, *The Politics of the Presidency,* 23–24.

8. Trevor Parry-Giles and Shawn Parry-Giles, *The Prime-Time Presidency: The West Wing and U.S. Nationalism* (Urbana-Champaign: University of Illinois Press, 2006), 4–5.

9. Buchanan, *The Citizen's Presidency: Standards of Choice and Judgment* (Washington, DC: CQ Press, 1994), 28.

10. Dennis M. Simon, "Public Expectations of the President," in *The Oxford Handbook of the American Presidency,* eds. George C. Edwards III and William G. Howell (New York: Oxford University Press, 2009), 135–59, 135.

11. See, for example: Thomas Cronin, "The Textbook Presidency and Political Science," in *Perspectives on the Presidency,* eds. Stanley Bach and George T. Sulzner (Lexington, MA: DC Heath, 1974), 54–74; J. M. Sanchez, "Old Habits Die Hard: The Textbook Presidency Is Alive and Well," *PS: Political Science and Politics* 29 (1996): 63–66; and Justin S. Vaughn and Lilly S. Goren, "Presenting Presidents: How American Presidents are Portrayed and Why It Matters," *White House Studies* 10 (2010): vii–ix.

12. Of course presidential polls alone did not constitute heroic expectations. The standards and expectations of historians for presidential greatness in combination with the exaggerated accounts of presidential power found in school textbooks, popular culture, and presidential precedent form what previous scholars have Buchanan called "presidential culture" (Buchanan, *The Citizen's Presidency*), "presidentiality" (Parry-Giles and Parry-Giles, *The Prime-Time Presidency*), the "symbolic presidency" (Hinckley, *The Symbolic Presidency*), the "textbook presidency" (Cronin, *The State of the Presidency*), and the "heroic presidency" (Burns, *Leadership*). See Bruce Buchanan, *The Citizen's Presidency* (Washington, DC: Congressional Quarterly, 1987); Trevor Parry-Giles and Shawn Parry-Giles, *The Prime Time Presidency* (Urbana, IL: University of Illinois Press, 2006); Barbara Hinckley, *The Symbolic Presidency* (Routledge: New York, 1990); Thomas E. Cronin, *The State of the Presidency* (Boston: Little, Brown and Co.), 1975; James MacGregor Burns, *Leadership* (New York: Harper & Row, 1978).

13. Arthur M. Schlesinger, "Historians Rate U.S. Presidents," *Life* 25 (November 1, 1948), 65–75; Arthur M. Schlesinger, "Rating the Presidents," *Paths to the Present,* 2nd ed. (Boston: Houghton Mifflin, 1964), 104–14; and Arthur M. Schlesinger Jr. "Rating the Presidents: Washington to Clinton," *Political Science Quarterly* 112 (1997): 179–90.

14. "The context at the time of evaluation also matters in structuring presidential rating scores. This is because ranking polls have not escaped bias working at the cultural level of discrimination. Whether this bias manifests itself as the preferential treatment the founding "patricians" appear to receive or the bonus above-average "progressives" get, it is apparent that historical evaluation is not escaping the milieu in which it is formed." Curt Nichols, "The Presidential Ranking Game: Critical Review and Some New Discoveries," *Presidential Studies Quarterly* 42 (2012): 275–99, 295.

15. Schlesinger Jr., "Rating the Presidents," 180.

16. Stephen Skowronek, *Presidential Leadership and Political Time: Reprise and Reappraisal,* 2nd ed. (Lawrence, KS: University Press of Kansas, 2011), 4.

17. Ibid., 6–7. See also Michael A. Genovese, *Contending Approaches to the American Presidency* (Washington, DC: CQ Press, 2012).

18. Schlesinger, "Rating the Presidents," 104–105. According to Stephen Skowronek, "Assessments of the problem of political agency, or effective political action, in the American presidency have changed a lot over the years, but they have not strayed far from a few basic concerns that the Progressives' vision put at issue: Is the power of the office adequate to the demands placed upon it? How much can we expect a president to get done? How important are the personal qualities of the incumbent to making the system work? For the Progressives themselves, answers to each of these questions could be found in the presidency of Franklin Roosevelt. They saw in Roosevelt's political skill and reform vigor a model for political leadership in modern America, and they distilled from his example the personal attributes likely to prove most valuable to incumbents in negotiating the governing challenges of the future" (Skowronek, "Presidency in American Political Development," 6–7).

19. Gene Healy, *The Cult of the Presidency: America's Dangerous Devotion to Executive Power* (Washington, DC: Cato Institute, 2008), 5. Arthur M. Schlesinger Jr., *The Imperial Presidency* (Boston: Houghton Mifflin, 1973).

20. James Lindgren, Steven G. Calabresi, Leonard A. Leo, and C. David Smith, "Rating the Presidents of the United States, 1789–2000," November 18, 2000, http://www.fed-soc. org/doclib/20070308_pressurvey.PDF

21. Stephen Skowronek, *The Politics Presidents Make* (Boston: Harvard University Press, 1993).

22. Curt Nichols, "The Presidential Ranking Game: Critical Review and Some New Discoveries," *Presidential Studies Quarterly* 42 (2012): 295.

23. Schlesinger, "Historians Rate U.S. Presidents," 73.

24. "Back in 1973 the historian Arthur M. Schlesinger Jr. had affixed an enduring adjective to the Nixon presidency: it was, he said, 'imperial.' This didn't mean that the president literally has become emperor, as some anti-Federalist authors had feared back in the 1780s. But it did suggest both that the occupant of the office exercised more absolute power over more issues than the constitutional framework suggested and, more broadly, that the office itself had expanded in its power relative to other governmental actors." Andrew Rudalevige, *The New Imperial Presidency: Renewing Presidential Power after Watergate* (Ann Arbor: University of Michigan Press, 2006), ix; Lonnie G. Bunch III, Spencer R. Crew, Mark G. Hirsch, and Harry R. Rubenstein, *The American Presidency: A Glorious Burden* (Washington, DC: Smithsonian Institution Press, 2000); and Pika and Maltese, 16–17.

25. Arthur M. Schlesinger, *Paths to the Present,* 111; and William J. Ridings and Stuart B. McIver, *Rating the Presidents: A Ranking of U.S. Leaders, from the Great and Honorable to the Dishonest and Incompetent* (New York, Citadel Press, 2000).

26. Arthur M. Schlesinger Jr., *The Politics of Hope* (Boston: Houghton Mifflin, 1963), 8.

27. "Presidential greatness assumes that considerable talent and expertise, not possessed by everyone, are required for effective service. In addition, the concept of greatness recognizes that whoever fills the role of president comes to personify the government and thus serves as a living symbol of the values and procedure that constitute the political estate" (Buchanan, *The Citizen's Presidency*, 28–29). According to Richard E. Neustadt, "No code of ethics to private life leaves the decision to incinerate a hemisphere, or even to take actions risking such an outcome, in the hands of a mere human, fallible, imperfect. Such things are for God, not for a man or woman. Yet in our public life no Deity has shown a disposition to assume the burden; humans are left to their own devices; so long as their societies allow for such decisions, some person or other has to take responsibility. Why not the President? That's part of what he's paid for. The burden may be inhuman, but somebody must bear it" (Richard E. Neustadt, *Presidential Power and the Modern Presidents* (New York: Free Press, 1990), 209.

28. Thomas Cronin, "The Textbook Presidency and Political Science," in *The American Political Arena*, eds. J. R. Feszman and G. S. Poschman (Boston: Little, Brown and Company, 1972), 294–309. Also see Thomas Cronin, *The State of the Presidency* (Boston: Little, Brown, 1975).

29. John M. Murphy, "The Heroic Tradition in Presidential Rhetoric," *Rhetoric & Public Affairs* 3 (2000): 466–70, 466. "Americans are increasingly finding fictionalized representations of presidents and the presidency in literature, film, and on television. In the 1990s alone, thirty-one films featured presidents or members of their family prominently....These fictionalized presidents, as well as those found in many novels and on television, regularly engage serious issues and define presidential leadership in powerful and meaningful ways, reflecting the cultural preoccupation with this institution and its place in our national culture. But whatever their tone and purpose, such fictionalized depictions of the U.S. presidency provide a commentary on the nature of presidential leadership" (Parry-Giles and Parry-Giles, *The Prime-Time Presidency*, 1–2).

30. Jeffrey C. Alexander, *The Performance of Politics: Obama's Victory and the Democratic Struggle for Power* (New York: Oxford University Press, 2012), 67. "It raises expectations for the office—expectations that were extraordinarily high to begin with. A man who trumpets his ability to protect Americans from economic dislocation, to shield them from physical harm and moral decay, and to lead them to national glory—such a man is bound to disappoint. Yet, having promised much, he'll seek the power to deliver on his promises" (Gene Healy, *The Cult of the Presidency*, 9).

31. Smithsonian National Museum of American History exhibit: "The American Presidency: A Glorious Burden," http://americanhistory.si.edu/presidency/home.html; and Stefan Lorant, *The Glorious Burden* (New York: Harper & Row, 1968).

32. John F. Kennedy, "Television and Radio Interview: After Two Years—A Conversation with the President," December 17, 1962.

33. Andrew Jackson, "Inaugural Address," March 4, 1829, in *The American Presidency Project* [online], eds. John Woolley and Gerhard Peters, http://www.presidency.ucsb.edu/ws/?pid=25810.

34. William McKinley, "Address Accepting the Republican Presidential Nomination," July 12, 1900, in *The American Presidency Project* [online], eds. John Woolley and Gerhard Peters, http://www.presidency.ucsb.edu/ws/?pid=76197 .

35. Neustadt, *Presidential Power*; and Skowronek, *Presidential Leadership in Political Time*, 7.

36. George C. Edwards III, *At the Margins: Presidential Leadership of Congress* (New Haven: Yale University Press, 1989).

37. George C. Edwards III, *On Deaf Ears* (New Haven: Yale University Press, 2002).

38. Samuel Kernell, 2006, *Going Public: New Strategies of Presidential Leadership*, 4th ed. (Washington, DC: CQ Press).

39. Simon, "Public Expectations of the President," 146; and B. Dan Wood, "Presidents and the Political Agenda," in *The Oxford Handbook of the American Presidency*, eds. George C. Edwards III and William G. Howell (New York: Oxford University Press, 2009), 109.

40. Forrest McDonald, *The American Presidency: An Intellectual History* (Lawrence, KS: University Press of Kansas, 1995), 466.

41. Todd Purdum, "Washington, We Have a Problem," *Vanity Fair*, September 2010, http://www.vanityfair.com/politics/features/2010/09/broken-washington-201009.

42. "Sens. Obama and Biden Deliver Remarks in Springfield, Ill.," *Washington Post*, August 23, 2008, http://www.washingtonpost.com/wp-dyn/content/article/2008/08/28/AR2008082803216.html.

43. Jon R. Bond and Richard Fleisher, eds., *Polarized Politics: Congress and the President in a Partisan Era* (Washington, DC: CQ Press, 2000).

44. Barack Obama, "Remarks by the President in Remembrance of Dr. Martin Luther King Jr.," Vermont Avenue Baptist Church, Washington, DC, January 17, 2010, http://www.whitehouse.gov/the-press-office/remarks-president-remembrance-dr-martin-luther-king-jr.

45. George B. Forgie, *Patricide in the House Divided: A Psychological Interpretation of Lincoln and His Age* (New York: W. W. Norton, 1979), 6–12.

46. "To be effective, the presidency must contend successfully with any significant national problem that arises. As a result of a favorable outcome, the country is delivered from threats to its well-being. And if the presidency is to be equal to the task of handling such forbidding problems as war, economic collapse, or the threat of nuclear annihilation, it must be great—great enough to stand on equal terms with such larger than life challenges" (Buchanan, *The Citizen's Presidency*, 26).

47. Skowronek, *Presidential Leadership in Political Time*, 77. "American government and politics are transformed when new interests secure a firm grip on power, when institutional relationships are rearranged to support them, when governmental priorities are durably recast, and when a corresponding set of legitimating ideas becomes the new common sense....Transformational leaders reconstruct American government and politics; they set it operating on (to use the Obama locution "a new foundation." Other presidents have done very important things, but they did not do that. At issue is whether Obama will alter the playing field of national politics, durably, substantially, and on his own terms, whether

he is likely to shift the axis of commitment and conflict so that American government itself is understood differently" (171).

48. Ibid, 28.

49. Curt Nichols, "The Presidential Ranking Game: Critical Review and Some New Discoveries," *Presidential Studies Quarterly* 42 (2012): 295.

50. Alexander, *The Performance of Politics*, 67–68.

51. Ibid., 84.

52. Sean Wilentz, "Worst President in History?" *Rolling Stone* (May 4, 2006): 32–37.

53. On February 10, 2007, Obama officially announced his candidacy in a speech delivered in Springfield, Illinois, a location chosen specifically to reference Lincoln's legacy of presidential leadership. "What's stopped us is the failure of leadership," Obama told the crowd gathered in Springfield, "the ease with which we're distracted by the petty and trivial, our chronic avoidance of tough decisions, our preference for scoring cheap political points instead of rolling up our sleeves and building a working consensus to tackle the big problems of America" (Barack Obama, "Barack Obama Announces Presidential Exploratory Committee," January 16, 2007, American Rhetoric: Online Speech Bank, http://www. americanrhetoric.com/speeches/ barackobamaexploratory.htm). See also David Plouffe, *The Audacity to Win: The Inside Story and Lessons of Barack Obama's Historic Victory* (New York: Viking, 2009), 30–45. Obama routinely linked the nation's burdens to his candidacy throughout the 2007–2008 campaign: the burden of civil rights (March 4, 2007); burdens of Iraq War, bad diplomacy (April 23, 2007); the burden of catastrophic health care (May 2, 2007); the burden of battle and burden of fighting terrorism (August 21, 2007); the burden on the middle class (September 18, 2007); burdens and benefits of the global economy (February 13, 2008); overburdened state of our military (March 19, 2008); the national debt as an unfair burden on our children (March 20, 2008); the terrible burden of losing a home (April 4, 2008); the burden we all bear when workers are abused (April 14, 2008); the burden on Main Street (May 9, 2009); the burden on seniors (June 13, 2008); the military should not bear all the burdens of our foreign policy (July 15, 2008); the burden of gas prices (July 15, 2008); burdens of global citizenship, of development and diplomacy, and progress and peace (July 24, 2008); the unique burden of multiple deployments (August 19, 2008); the burden on struggling homeowners (September 12, 2008); the burden of financial bailout (September 19, 2008); and Americans bearing the burden for the greed and irresponsibility of Wall Street and Washington (September 25, 2008). Finally, his campaign was unique because it was not burdened with old arguments (October 30, 2008).

54. Michael Cabanatuan, "Gas Prices Force Many to Change Holiday Plans," SF Gate, *San Francisco Chronicle* [online], May 23, 2008, http://articles.sfgate.com/2008–05–23/ news/17156363_1_holiday-weekend-travel-weekend-getaway.

55. "Household Incomes Flat during Bush Era," *Washington Times*, Wednesday, August 27, 2008, http://www.washingtontimes.com/news/2008/aug/27/household-incomes-flat-during-bush-administration/.

56. Bob Willis and Rich Miller, "U.S. Unemployment Rate Climbs to 14-Year High of 6.5 percent (Update2)," Bloomberg, November 7, 2008, http://www.bloomberg.com/apps/ news?pid=21070001&sid=aZdisKigEQIE.

57. "U.S. House Prices Suffer Big Retreat in April," CBC News, Business, June 24, 2008, http://www.cbc.ca/money/story/2008/06/24/ushouseprices.html?ref=patrick. net#ixzz11 0KjPrpL.

58. "U.S. Home Foreclosures Hit Another Record," CBC News, Business, June 5, 2008, http://www.cbc.ca/money/story/2008/06/05/ushomes.html.

59. David Henry and Matthew Goldstein, "The Shakeout after Lehman, Merrill, AIG…," *The Economic Times,* September 18, 2008, http://economictimes.indiatimes.com/articleshow/3498583.cms.

60. Victoria Wagner and Daniel E. Teclaw, "A Fannie-Freddie FAQ: S&P Spells out What Investors and Homeowners Need to Know about the Big Bailout," *Bloomberg Businessweek,* September 11, 2008, http://www.businessweek.com/stories/2008-09-11/a-fannie-freddie-faqbusinessweek-business-news-stock-market-and-financial-advice.

61. Steven C. Johnson, "Dow in Record Drop on Bailout Rejection," *Reuters,* September 30, 2008, http://uk.reuters.com/article/businessNews/idUKTRE48S86H20080929.

62. Kate Kenski, Bruce W. Hardy, and Kathleen Hall Jamieson, *The Obama Victory: How Media, Money, and Message Shaped the 2008 Election* (New York: Oxford University Press, 2010); and Michael W. Toner, "The Impact of Federal Election Laws on the 2008 Presidential Election," in *The Year of Obama: How Barack Obama Won the White House,* ed. Larry J. Sabato (New York: Longman, 2010), 149–65.

63. Shailagh Murray and Matthew Mosk, "Under Obama, Web Would Be the Way," *Washington Post,* November 10, 2008, http://www.washingtonpost.com/wp-dyn/content/article/2008/11/10/AR2008111000013.html.

64. John Bentley, "Does Crowd Size Matter? McCain Hopes Not," *CBS News,* October 25, 2008: http://www.cbsnews.com/8301–502443_162–4545511–502443.html.

65. Sasha Issenberg, "Obama-Themed Merchandise Sales Strike it Hot," *Boston Globe,* August 17, 2008, http://www.boston.com/news/nation/articles/2008/08/17/obama_themed_merchandise_sales_strike_it_hot/. See also Lilly J. Goren and Justin S. Vaughn, "Politics and Protest: The Cultural Commodification of the Presidential Image," in *Politics and Popular Culture,* ed. Leah A. Murray (Newcastle Upon Tyne, UK: Cambridge Scholars Press, 2010): 149–65.

66. Nate Silver, "Obama Popular Vote Margin Largest Ever for Non-Incumbent," *Five Thirty Eight: Politics Done Right,* November 26, 2008, http://www.fivethirtyeight.com/2008/11/obama-popular-vote-margin-largest-ever.html.

67. Nicholas Lemann, "Greatness: Presidents Who Really Matter," *The New Yorker,* January 26, 2009, http://www.newyorker.com/magazine/toc/2009/01/26/toc; and Evan Thomas, "Obama's Lincoln," *Newsweek,* November 15, 2008, http://www.newsweek. com/2008/11/14/obama-s-lincoln.html; and Peter Beinart, "The New New Deal," *Time Magazine,* November 24, 2008, http://www.time.com/time/covers/0,16641,20081124,00.html.

68. Rasmussen Reports, "Obama Approval Index History," http://www.rasmussen-reports.com/public_content/politics/obama_administration/obama_approval_index_history; and "In First 100 Days, Obama Meets or Exceeds Expectations: Praise for Obama on

the Economy, Foreign Policy; Criticism on Budgetary Matters," http://www.gallup.com/poll/117853/first-100-days-obama-meets-exceeds-expectations.aspx.

69. Siena Research Institute, "American Presidents: Greatest and Worst," July 1, 2010," http://www.siena.edu/uploadedfiles/home/parents_and_community/community_page/sri/independent_research/Presidents%20Release_2010_final.pdf.

70. Donald R. Kinder, Mark D. Peters, Robert P. Abelson, and Susan T. Fiske, "Presidential Prototypes," *Political Behavior,* 2 (1980): 315–37, 319.

71. Barack Obama, *Dreams from My Father: A Story of Race and Inheritance.* (New York: Times Books, 1995), 51.

72. Shelby Steele, *A Bound Man: Why We Are Excited about Obama and Why He Can't Win* (New York: Free Press, 2007).

73. Thomas Sugrue, *Not Even Past: Barack Obama and the Burden of Race* (Princeton, NJ: Princeton University Press, 2010).

74. Wilbur Rich, "Making Race Go Away: President Obama and the Promise of a Post-Racial Society," in *The Obama Presidency: Change and Continuity,* eds. Andrew J. Dowdle, Dirk C. van Raemdonck, and Robert Maranto (New York: Routledge, 2011), 17–30.

75. Randall Kennedy, *The Persistence of the Color Line: Racial Politics and the Obama Presidency* (New York: Pantheon, 2011).

76. Rich, "Making Race Go Away," 21.

77. Desmond S. King and Rogers M. Smith, *Still a House Divided: Race and Politics in Obama's America* (Princeton: Princeton University Press, 2011).

78. Krissah Thompson, "Cornel West's Criticism of Obama Sparks Debate among African Americans," *Washington Post,* May 18, 2011, http://www.washingtonpost.com/politics/cornel-wests-criticism-of-obama-sparks-debate-among-african-americans/2011/05/18/AFlGTf6G_story.html.

79. King and Smith, *Still a House Divided.*

80. Neustadt, *Presidential Power,* 3.

81. Jeffrey K. Tulis, *The Rhetorical Presidency* (Princeton: Princeton University Press, 1987).

82. Martin J. Medhurst, *Before the Rhetorical Presidency* (College Station: Texas A&M University Press, 2008), 3–11.

83. Robert Hariman, *Political Style: The Artistry of Power* (Chicago: University of Chicago Press, 1995); and Jennifer R. Mercieca, *Founding Fictions* (Tuscaloosa: Alabama University Press, 2010).

CHAPTER 2

A Lighthouse at the Crossroads

Barack Obama's Call for Agonistic Democracy

JAY P. CHILDERS

The 2008 presidential election was widely characterized as being as much about outgoing President George W. Bush as it was about the candidates running for office. With job approval ratings at or below 30 percent in 2008, Bush seemed to have overstayed his welcome in the White House.[1] Regardless of what history eventually makes of Bush's presidency, he was largely seen as excessively partisan by the end of his second term.[2] Bush had, on more than one occasion, suggested that he did not need to listen to or explain his actions to the American people,[3] and his administration had been repeatedly accused of making overtly partisan decisions on matters deemed outside the scope of party politics.[4] Given this context, it was little wonder that Barack Obama campaigned largely on the need for politicians and the American people to rise above partisan divisions. Although such claims are common during campaigns, Obama's ability to position himself above political squabbling during the 2008 election seemed "Teflon-like," in the words of one Republican.[5] Indeed, if Bush was "a divider,"[6] Obama was hailed "a uniter."[7]

Although such labels surely oversimplify both men and overestimate their ability to control American politics, the divider and uniter labels do point to another way of seeing the difference between Bush's and Obama's attitude toward democratic decision making. Indeed, part of Obama's burden entering office was his claim that he could create a more bipartisan, friendly Washington, D.C. Seen through political theory, one can understand such a goal as a shift between two different approaches to political decision making—from aggregative to deliberative democracy. In distinguishing the two models, Iris Marion Young argued the aggregative approach treats democracy as the process of collecting citizen preferences by tallying votes and measuring public opinion.[8] Based on swaying public opinion, aggregative approaches to politics have, however, been criticized as too easily creating antagonistic relationships between citizens. According to Chantal Mouffe, the aggregative model of liberal democracy with its emphasis on the individual fails to take into account and, therefore, prevent the "ever present possibility of the friend/enemy distinction and the conflictual nature of politics."[9] The deliberative approach to democracy, on the other hand, seeks to create open discussion about public issues through which decisions can be agreed upon. Instead of assessing preferences, deliberative democrats hope to help citizens uncover the reasons behind their preferences, leading to greater understanding and more legitimate political decisions.[10] Deliberative democrats assume, moreover, that citizens are universally included as equal, rational individuals. In the aggregative model, citizens vote, answer polling questions, and write letters to their representatives, who then make political decisions based on this information. In the deliberative model, citizens engage in deliberative discussion to reach democratic resolutions collectively.

Many have suggested Obama should be viewed as a deliberative democrat. One of the founders of the modern reemergence of deliberative democracy, Jürgen Habermas, responded to a reporter's question about Obama's victory, for instance, by stating that after eight years of Bush, "Obama has been a great gift."[11] On their Web site, the National Coalition for Dialogue & Deliberation stated that because of "a new presidential administration...2009 has been a whirlwind year of unprecedented opportunity and possibility for the dialogue and deliberation community."[12] Even Obama seemed to have accepted that he was the leader of a deliberative democracy. In a December 2009 interview with ABC's Charles Gibson, Obama responded to a question about the partisan maneuvering in Washington, D.C., over health care reform by stating, "[O]ne of the challenges that we as a country are going to have is that, for our system of government to work, for our *deliberative democracy* to work ... you have to have a sense that occasionally we're willing to rise above party."[13]

Regardless of how many people assumed Barack Obama represented the coming of a new deliberative democracy in the United States, I ask whether such assertions were accurate. Was Obama really the champion of deliberative democracy? Did the system of government and processes of political engagement the president advocated actually adhere to the basic tenets of the deliberative democracy many seemed to believe America was supposed to be? Answering these questions helps to reveal how Obama responded to one central aspect of the presidency's institutional burden—that the nation's chief executive plays a unique role in defining and defending democracy. This is a burden made all the more cumbersome by the deliberative ideal that has long influenced the nation's democratic assumptions. To make sense of how Obama dealt with this particular institutional burden, I turn to the president's own words on how the American people are supposed to engage one another politically in order to, as one group of rhetorical scholars has suggested, pay attention to "the relationship (or lack thereof) between democratic deliberation and political institutions."[14] Although Obama often addressed how the American people ought to act democratically, nowhere did he address this issue more directly than in his 2009 Commencement Address at the University of Notre Dame. Although moments in the speech suggest agreement with the deliberative ideal, I argue that Obama ultimately portrayed the United States as an agonistic democracy—an aggregative model that fully acknowledges that democracy entails sometimes unresolvable conflicts between groups of people with competing beliefs and interests. Through a close reading of his commencement address, I show how Obama presented agonistic democracy as a noble pursuit of political engagement through three narrative exemplars and, ultimately, a mixed metaphor in which every citizen should stand "as both a lighthouse and a crossroads."[15] Before offering the close reading of Obama's speech, I first present the controversy created by Obama's acceptance of Notre Dame's invitation that was the exigency of the speech's content and then present a more developed explanation of both deliberative and agonistic democracy. In the end, I show that Obama responded to the institutional burden of defining and defending democracy in the United States by acknowledging the inherently conflictual nature of politics, a condition ultimately requiring rhetorical struggle.

Obama, Notre Dame, and Controversy

On March 20, 2009, the White House and Notre Dame announced that President Obama would be delivering the commencement address in South Bend, Indiana. In addition, Notre Dame noted Obama would be "the ninth U.S. president to be awarded an honorary degree by the University."[16] The controversy over the upcoming event and honorary degree began almost immediately. The first to respond to the announcement were issue groups, such as Operation Rescue, an antiabortion organization, and The Cardinal Newman Society, who felt Notre Dame was "betraying its Catholic mission." The second wave of criticism came from Catholic laity and clergy.[17] By the time Obama delivered his speech, "71 Catholic bishops—including two cardinals—had denounced the invitation, as ha[d] more than 350,000 Catholics who signed an online petition asking Notre Dame to withdraw it."[18] The third major voice of criticism came from Mary Ann Glendon, former US Ambassador to the Vatican, who was scheduled to receive Notre Dame's highest honor, the Laetare Medal, given each year to recognize a person's outstanding service to the Catholic Church. In a letter addressed to Notre Dame's president and published on numerous news Web sites (e.g., *Newsweek, Boston Globe*), Glendon, a Harvard law professor, declined the honor because she believed that such a situation was not appropriate "for engagement with the very serious problems raised by Notre Dame's decision—in disregard of the settled position of the US bishops—to honor a prominent and uncompromising opponent of the Church's position on issues involving fundamental principles of justice."[19] Regardless of their specific goals, all of these critics at least temporarily forced the difficult issues of abortion and religion into the public sphere.

For its part, the Obama administration had little to say about the controversy, but what it did say largely portrayed the event as a chance for open public discussion about a controversial issue. Indeed, in its comments the White House used terms that echoed how many presidents have dealt with the institutional burden of defending and defining democracy. Just six days after the announcement, White House press secretary Robert Gibbs responded to a question about the controversy by saying, "The President obviously believes in everyone's right to get involved and to exercise their opinion. … And he looks forward to continuing that dialogue in the lead-up to the commencement."[20] In response to Glendon's letter, Obama's spokesperson Jennifer Psaki noted of the president, "While he is honored to have the support of millions of people of all faiths, he does not govern with the expectation that everyone sees eye to eye with him on every position, and the spirit of debate and healthy disagreement on important issues is part of what he loves about this country."[21] When asked about the criticisms at a nationally televised evening press conference three weeks before the commencement, Obama sidestepped the controversy, choosing instead to reiterate his pro-choice views on abortion.[22] Obama ultimately saved his comments about the controversy for the speech itself, a speech that has at its very core the question of how the American people ought to address difference and disagreement in democracy.

Two Models of Democracy

Given that political discourse between peoples with differing value systems and group identities far too often seems to fall into antagonistic constructions of the other, political and communication theorists have struggled with increased vigor in recent years with how best to correct for this tendency to demonize those with whom one disagrees. Recent work on this issue offers us two ways to understand Obama's advice to the graduates at Notre Dame: The first is deliberative democracy; the second is agonistic democracy.

As a corrective to the antagonistic impulse in pluralistic democratic societies, no set of practices has received more attention in recent years than deliberative democracy. Given the popularity of deliberative democracy, it is little surprise that the theoretical construct has taken on divergent and wide-ranging variations. Without constructing a straw person version of deliberative democracy, there are, however, three central concepts that seem to run through much of the current research. Put simply, deliberative democracy is to be universally open to all in such a way that ensures equality, carried out through reasoned or rational discussion, and ultimately lead to decisions founded on either consensus or widespread agreement. Such a definition, although admittedly not universal, does reflect many current attempts to make sense of deliberative democracy.[23]

In response to what they see as the inherent weaknesses of deliberative democracy, a number of scholars have responded by "endorsing a more 'agonistic' model of democratic process."[24] Acknowledging that antagonistic (friend–enemy division) relations are anathema to a healthy democratic public sphere, those advocating agonism (we–they adversaries) argue that deliberative democrats go too far toward attempting to remove conflict and group identity from politics when they advocate for reasoned deliberation between individuals leading to consensus or agreement. Whereas deliberative democrats assume universal equality, agonistic democrats accept that the struggle for equality is inherently part of the conflictual nature of politics.[25] Where deliberative democrats seek to suppress passions and rhetoric in favor of reasoned deliberation in the communicative process, agonistic democrats see such discursive practices as necessary, if not central, to political struggle.[26] When deliberative democrats call for wide-ranging or consensual agreement, agonistic democrats suggest democratic citizens must only accept the political rules and legitimate decisions of aggregation.[27] An agonistic version of democracy is, then, one that understands politics as group conflict without reducing the other to an antagonistic enemy, requiring a multitude of rhetorical practices.

Placed in the context of this debate between deliberative and agonistic democrats, Obama's suggestion for how the American people ought to deal with conflict without demonizing one another can best be understood as an agonistic approach to democratic practices. This is not to propose that one cannot see aspects of deliberative democracy in his address; it does, however, suggest Obama's vision of political disagreement acknowledged deep-rooted conflicts, did not require consensus, refused the impulse to demonize, and incorporated such rhetorical strategies as emotional appeals and personal narrative.

Obama's Agonistic Democracy

Faced with a political controversy concerning an extremely divisive issue, President Obama addressed Notre Dame's 2009 graduating class under the full burden of his institution. His address largely adhered to the basic tenets of epideictic rhetoric in which the speaker makes appeals that attempt to unify the community and also reinforce the community's virtues.[28] Obama attempted to accomplish these epideictic goals, moreover, by carefully constructing a troubled world where the community's values are in a state of uncertain flux and then situating the graduating class as uniquely positioned to respond to such an exigency. The president constructed this rhetorical situation by suggesting early in his speech that of the "one hundred and sixty-three classes of Notre Dame graduates" that had come before, many graduated "during years that simply rolled into the next without much notice or fanfare." According to Obama, the class of 2009 was not graduating in such a year:

> You, however, are not getting off that easy.... Your class has come of age at a moment of great consequence for our nation and for the world—a rare inflection point in history where the size and scope of the challenges before us require that we remake our

world to renew its promise; that we align our deepest values and commitments to the demands of a new age. It's a privilege and a responsibility afforded to few generations—and a task that you're now called to fulfill.

It is difficult to imagine Obama stating the importance of the graduates' burden more powerfully. The class of 2009 faced not merely a turning point, but a "rare inflection point," which in calculus refers to the point when a curve flips from being negative to positive or vice versa. Obama suggested, then, that the class of 2009 was uniquely situated in the moment of a great historical transformation. Given such a profound temporal exigency, it was little surprise that Obama suggested to the graduating class that this moment was nothing short of their calling, invoking religious language for an individual to respond to God's appointed task.

That Obama situated the graduating class of 2009 as uniquely positioned at a moment of great importance was not, of course, particularly unusual for a commencement speech. However, Obama's characterization of this particular exigent instant was illuminating. Obama offered four particularly important aspects of the "inflective" moment: economics, ecology, terrorism, and globalization. The graduating class needed, that is, to "find a path back to prosperity and decide how we respond to a global economy that left millions behind even before the most recent crisis" and "decide how to save God's creation from a changing climate that threatens to destroy it." They needed also, however, to "seek peace at a time when there are those who will stop at nothing to do us harm" and "find a way to reconcile our ever-shrinking world with its ever-growing diversity." This diversity was, according to Obama, the very nexus of the larger historical problem, which he addressed by summing up the list of challenges facing the graduating class by saying, "In short, we must find a way to live together as one human family." It was this last challenge, Obama ultimately suggested, that he would "like to talk about today."

To make way for the possibility of getting people to see themselves as shared members of a single human family, Obama suggested there were external threats to this human family that could only be met with cooperation among and an understanding between diverse others. Obama argued that the "major threats we face in the 21st century—whether it's global recession or violent extremism; the spread of nuclear weapons or pandemic disease—these things do not discriminate. They do not recognize borders ... see color ... [or] target specific ethnic groups." Obama's assertion here can be read as attempting to constitute a shared human identity struggling against outside forces. As these forces were indiscriminate, the president assured his audience that these threats could not be dealt with by isolated groups: "no one person, or religion, or nation can meet these challenges alone." Instead, the very real problems he laid out suggested that "our very survival has never required greater cooperation and greater understanding among all people from all places than at this moment in history." Bringing an end to the world's financial problems, quelling extremists, stopping nuclear proliferation, and fighting disease required an ability to work together and a willingness to at least try to get to know one another.

Getting people to work together to solve problems is at the very heart of democratic politics. Obama clearly understood this difficulty when he quickly noted that neither cooperation nor understanding seemed to be something humans were particularly good at: "Unfortunately, finding that common ground—recognizing that our fates are tied up, as Dr. King said, in a 'single garment of destiny'—is not easy." Calling on King's famous words served multiple purposes. In the first instance, it called forth the memory of the all too often violent civil rights struggle, serving as a reminder of the failure to work together and accept one another as fundamentally equal. Referencing King also pointed toward nonviolent methods of civil disobedience and King's call to love one's enemy. Finally, the use of King's words also reminded many of King's more fleshed out argument about this "single garment of destiny." Although the line is probably best known for its use in King's final sermon at the National Cathedral on March 31, 1968, the basic argument was something King used often in public speeches, even as early as a commencement address he gave in 1958 at Morgan State College. Going further than Obama's institutional burden allowed him, the argument as King delivered it at Morgan State pushed the Golden Rule to its extreme:

> We are caught and involved in a single process. Whatever affects one directly, it affects all indirectly in this world. We are clothed in a single garment of destiny; we are caught in an inescapable network of mutuality....I can never be what I ought to be until you are what you ought to be.[29]

King's words suggest a more fundamental understanding of the inter-connectedness of all humans, a conception of humanity that asserts one's own human potential is inextricably tied to the potential of others. Although such an idea goes beyond the cooperation and understanding Obama advocated, the use of King's words certainly pointed to this deeper conception.

Obama saw two kinds of problems underlying the difficulty of finding common ground. The first reason people seemed to fail at cooperation was that they suffered from "the imperfections of man—our selfishness, our pride, our stubbornness, our acquisitiveness, our insecurities, our egos; all the cruelties large and small that those of us in the Christian tradition understand to be rooted in original sin." Though such innate obstructions to finding common ground are certainly serious, Obama was quick to dismiss them by suggesting "one of the benefits of the wonderful education that you've received here at Notre Dame" allowed one to see one's own flaws and look beyond the individual self. Education was not, unfortunately, enough to deal with a more perplexing problem hindering the human ability to find common ground, which Obama noted by say-ing, "[O]ne of the vexing things for those of us interested in promoting greater understanding and cooperation among people is the discovery that even bringing together persons of good will, bringing together men and women of principle and purpose—even accomplishing that can be difficult." As evidence of this troublesome difficulty, Obama turned to three controversial issues on which people with good intentions might still have difficulty finding a way to work together:

> The soldier and the lawyer may both love this country with equal
> passion, and yet reach very different conclusions on the specific
> steps needed to protect us from harm. The gay activist and the
> evangelical pastor may both deplore the ravages of HIV/AIDS, but
> find themselves unable to bridge the cultural divide that might
> unite their efforts. Those who speak out against stem cell research
> may be rooted in an admirable conviction about the sacredness of
> life, but so are the parents of a child with juvenile diabetes who are
> convinced that their son's or daughter's hardships can be relieved.

With the use of the words *passion, deplore,* and *conviction,* Obama began to push toward his ultimate concern in the commencement address; his point in these examples was to highlight some of the most contentious issues being debated in American society. Although some on both sides of these issues might suggest their views on such value-laden issues are nonnegotiable, Obama suggested that they all shared at least some common ground founded upon their shared humanity.

Although Obama believed common viewpoints were shared by those on both sides of difficult issues, an assumption that is not itself absolutely certain, the president did not believe getting people to see this common ground and use it cooperatively to increase each other's knowledge would be easy. It was at this point, then, in the address that Obama turned to the speech's central topic. He did so by asking four interrelated questions:

> [H]ow do we work through these conflicts? Is it possible for us to join hands in common effort? As citizens of a vibrant and varied democracy, how do we engage in vigorous debate? How does each of us remain firm in our principles, and fight for what we consider right, without ... demonizing those with just as strongly held convictions on the other side?

In these four short interrogatives, Obama suggested that more fundamental than the differences themselves was the question of how a democratic people deals with these differences. He called the struggles over these differences conflicts, vigorous debate, and fights. He wanted, as the last question suggested, to find a way to allow for disagreement that did not force the interlocutors to give up their own values nor castigate one another. Obama waded into, that is, one of the more vigorous and difficult debates in democratic communicative theory. The answer he ultimately offered to his own questions was neither the reasoned conversation of deliberation nor the vitriolic yelling of antagonism. Obama attempted instead to find a middle ground through a model of agonistic democracy.

In many ways, that Obama painted an inherently conflictual picture of American democracy was apparent from the first part of his speech. His reference of the civil rights movement through quoting Martin Luther King Jr., the three examples of well-intentioned people disagreeing over value-laden issues, and the language of the four questions he posed all pointed to a vision of politics as a difficult struggle. In addition to these early depictions of struggle, Obama returned to the conception of politics as conflictual immediately following the four questions that served as the organizing principle of his speech, in order to suggest how these conflicts might avoid falling into antagonistic friend–enemy relations. He did so by referencing the very issue that served as the primary point of controversy over his visit to Notre Dame: "And of course, nowhere do these questions come up more powerfully than on the issue of abortion."

Immediately after naming abortion as the key issue with which to explore the question of how "we work through these conflicts," Obama told the first of three stories that structured the remainder of his speech. In this first story, Obama recounted an e-mail he received while running for the United States Senate "from a doctor who told me that while he had voted for me in the Illinois primary, he had a serious concern that might prevent him from voting for me in the general election." The doctor's concern stemmed from a comment on Obama's campaign Web site referring to pro-life supporters as "right-wing ideologues who want to take away a woman's right to choose." What bothered the doctor, who, Obama noted, "described himself as a Christian who was strongly pro-life," was not that Obama supported a woman's right to choose; the doctor's concern was that Obama would call all pro-life supporters "right-wing ideologues." In relating the e-mail, Obama further described how "the doctor said he had assumed I was a reasonable person…, but that if I truly believed that every pro-life individual was simply an ideologue who wanted to inflict suffering on women, then I was not very reasonable." To make sure the audience did not misinterpret the doctor's complaint, Obama offered his exact words: "He wrote, 'I do not ask at this point that you oppose abortion, only that you speak about this issue in fair minded words.'"

Obama's response to the doctor's e-mail both accepted the conflictual nature of politics and resisted the temptation to demonize those with whom one disagrees. That is, he avoided both the deliberative impulse to treat politics as reasoned, rational argument leading toward consensus or widespread agreement and the antagonistic tendency to treat those with whom one disagrees as enemies. Indeed, Obama continued his story by acknowledging that he wrote the doctor back, thanking him and accepting his views as legitimate. This was a point Obama made explicitly:

> I didn't change my underlying position, but I did tell my staff to
> change the words on my website. And I said a prayer that night
> that I might extend the same presumption of good faith to others
> that the doctor had extended to me. Because when we do that—

when we open up our hearts and our minds to those who may not think precisely like we do or believe precisely what we believe—that's when we discover at least the possibility of common ground.

What Obama called for here in recounting this story was a move away from what Patricia Roberts-Miller calls demagoguery—the "polarizing propaganda that motivates members of an ingroup to hate and scapegoat some outgroup(s)."[30] In calling them "right-wing ideologues," Obama had reduced pro-life supporters to enemies. By naming them in such a way, Obama had excluded them and their ideas from any legitimate consideration. Obama never suggested the doctor's views on abortion changed his own, but he did acknowledge the legitimacy of the doctor's views.

Acknowledging the doctor as a legitimate other, Obama did more than simply make a political calculation. He accepted that some moral and political differences may never be overcome. As he argued a moment later, "I do not suggest that the debate surrounding abortion can or should go away. Because no matter how much we may want to fudge it…the fact is that at some level, the views of the two camps are irreconcilable." Although Obama argued for common ground, he did not assume common ground equals sameness. He did not, that is, seem to believe the conflictual nature of democratic politics could be eradicated. Instead, his narrative's moral echoed Mouffe's acknowledgment that "the antagonistic dimension is always present, it is a real confrontation but one which [can be] played out under conditions regulated by a set of democratic procedures accepted by the adversaries."[31] For Obama, politics was a fight, but it was ultimately to be fought fairly.

Portraying democratic differences as containing within themselves unresolvable moral and political views that must be struggled over leads one to question just how this struggle is to take place. At the risk of oversimplifying the deliberative position, deliberative democrats worry, according to Bryan Garsten, that anything beyond rational, reasoned discussion leads to poor or confused citizen judgments and decision making.[32] Even when some deliberative democrats do attempt to make space for other forms of communicative action, they seem to maintain a basic distinction between reasoned deliberation and passionate rhetoric.[33] Such a distinction is, as Iris Marion Young noted, an attempt by deliberative democrats to "maintain a Platonic distinction between rational speech and mere rhetoric, and in doing so they often denigrate emotion, figurative language, or unusual or playful forms of expression."[34] As Young, Garsten, and a host of rhetoric scholars have repeatedly noted, such denigration fails to understand the nature of human discursive interaction. Although Obama did talk of attempting to "persuade through reason" at one point in his speech, he did not attempt to disparage other rhetorical options. His use of three narratives instead of rational argument to make his case for an agonistic democratic public sphere demonstrated his understanding of the role emotion plays in the communicative process.

Nowhere was Obama's commitment to rhetoric and narrative more obvious than in the second story he told. Laden with emotion, the story was Obama's own religious conversion narrative. Obama began this narrative by acknowledging that although he was not raised in a particularly religious family, he was taught to care for others. This empathic impulse, according to the president, ultimately led him to a life of public service, where he eventually joined forces with "a group of Catholic churches in Chicago" that funded "an organization known as the Developing Communities Project" that "worked to lift up South Side neighborhoods that had been devastated when the local steel plant closed." As Obama described them, this project "was quite an eclectic crew—Catholic and Protestant churches, Jewish and African American organizers, working-class black, white, and Hispanic residents—all of us with different experiences, all of us with different beliefs." These diverse groups of individuals, "bound together in the service of others," came together under the guidance of the Catholic Church and, more specifically, "Cardinal Joseph Bernardin [who] was the Archbishop of Chicago." For Obama, Bernardin was an exemplar for how one engages others in a diverse democracy:

> He stood as both a lighthouse and a crossroads—unafraid to
> speak his mind on moral issues ranging from poverty and AIDS
> and abortion to the death penalty and nuclear war. And yet, he
> was congenial and gentle in his persuasion, always trying to bring
> people together, always trying to find common ground. Just before
> he died, a reporter asked Cardinal Bernardin about this approach
> to his ministry. And he said, "You can't really get on with preach-
> ing the Gospel until you've touched hearts and minds."

As Obama acknowledged that "his heart and mind were touched by" Bernardin and credited him as having played a role in his Christian conversion, this coupling of "hearts and minds" was particularly salient in explaining Obama's vision of persuasion. Obama, that is, did not simply argue that reason (mind) and emotion (heart) are sometimes compatible; he suggested, instead, they were most effective when used together. Democratic persuasion, for Obama, required rhetoric that is both rational and empathetic.

Obama's vision of a rhetorically attuned agonistic democracy was further embodied in the mixed metaphor he used to describe Bernardin and later used to appeal to the graduating class—that of the "lighthouse" at the "crossroads." After finishing the short narrative about Cardinal Bernardin, Obama returned to a view of conflictual democracy, but in this instance he juxtaposed a negative and a positive version. As they left school, Obama warned the graduates that they would "be exposed to more opinions and ideas broadcast through more means of communication than ever existed before." The president then further described these opinions and ideas in negative terms: "You'll hear talking heads scream on cable, and you'll read blogs that claim definitive knowledge, and you will watch politicians pretend they know what they're talking about." By dismissing cable news personalities, political bloggers, and untrustworthy politicians, Obama acknowledged that the democratic public sphere often includes those whose willingness to cooperate or understand one another is limited. Obama offered, however, another option: "Occasionally, you may have the great fortune of actually seeing important issues debated by people who do know what they're talking about—by well-intentioned people with brilliant minds and mastery of the facts." If he was insistent on the role of passion, emotion, and the heart earlier in the speech, Obama now emphasized reason and the mind.

This emphasis on reason, however, turned quickly to a synthesis of passion and reason, conviction and rationality. Obama, that is, told the graduating class to be a "lighthouse" at a "crossroads":

And in this world of competing claims about what is right and what is true, have confidence in the values with which you've been raised and educated. Be unafraid to speak your mind when those values are at stake. Hold firm to your faith and allow it to guide you on your journey. In other words, stand as a lighthouse.

As a lighthouse, the graduates were to have faith in their convictions, in their values. Obama encouraged them not to give up their moral and political worldview for a relativistic democratic position of ethical justice. They were, instead, to hold onto their passion. At the same time, Obama insisted they also be open to the legitimate views and beliefs of others:

> But remember, too, that you can be a crossroads. Remember, too, that the ultimate irony of faith is that it necessarily admits doubt. It's the belief in things not seen. It's beyond our capacity as human beings to know with certainty what God has planned for us or what He asks of us. And those of us who believe must trust that His wisdom is greater than our own.

The president asked the graduating class to hold firm to their faith, allowing it to inform their values and guide their beliefs, but also to accept that their view of the world was not the only one available. He asked, that is, that they not retreat into the comfort of their own particular worldviews where antagonistic impulses might strengthen.

In telling the Notre Dame graduates to be crossroads, Obama rooted their engagement with the other in two important fundamental assumptions that, if nothing else, highlighted a contradiction in the agonistic pluralism of Chantal Mouffe. Mouffe's version of agonistic pluralism requires agreement on the rules of the struggle, which she accepted at one point as those of liberal democracy,[35] but later as ambiguously more fundamental to humanity.[36] Indeed, if one rejects deliberative democracy's faith in the individual, autonomous self acting rationally toward others, and wants to resist the antagonistic friend–enemy relations that lurk about the edges of conflictual politics, then something must compel people to accept each other as legitimate adversaries. What Mouffe failed to answer clearly, Obama answered in two ways. The first part of his answer was alluded to above in his call for the graduates to be crossroads—an intersection between competing worldviews. That is, Obama's agonistic vision required an acceptance of doubt that he claimed was indicative of faith. Faith, for Obama, was to believe in that which cannot be known, to believe in something that cannot be proven. This faith required at least the possibility of being wrong, and this possibility—this doubt—was what Obama suggested demanded one to see those with different views as potentially legitimate.

The second assumption Obama made was that one should accept the legitimacy of the other based simply on the belief that all humans share their humanity. Obama emphasized this shared humanity by arguing what "binds people of all faiths and no faith together... . is, of course, the Golden Rule—the call to treat one another as we wish to be treated. The call to love. The call to serve. To do what we can to make a difference in the lives of those with whom we share the same brief moment on this Earth." In referencing the Golden Rule, Obama did not call for a set of human rights. Instead, as he had done in his widely praised speech on race, "A More Perfect Union," during his presidential campaign, Obama used the Golden Rule, as David Frank has argued, in the "prophetic tradition's insistence on caring for the other."[37] In political terms, this caring for others is "the ethic of reciprocity."[38] Instead of trivializing political difference, Obama has used the Golden Rule to call on a deeper understanding of human mutuality. It was this mutuality that allowed Obama to suggest that the doubt inherent in faith can be combined with the Golden Rule to find common ground—cooperation and understanding.

To illustrate his final point, Obama offered the third story, set during the civil rights movement of the 1960s. After mentioning such contentious events as *Brown v. Board of Education* and freedom rides, Obama then recounted the commission that ultimately led to the Civil Rights Act of 1964. According to Obama, the "six members of this commission" put together by President Eisenhower "worked for two years" through difficult conditions. Ultimately, the commission "reached an impasse in Louisiana." It was then that Father Ted Hasburgh, then the president of Notre Dame, "flew them all to Notre Dame's retreat in Land O' Lakes, Wisconsin where they eventually overcame their differences and hammered out a final deal." When asked years later how he had brokered the final deal, Obama recounted how "Father Ted simply said that during their first dinner in Wisconsin, they discovered they were all fishermen. And so he quickly readied a boat for a twilight trip out on the lake. They fished, and they talked, and they changed the course of history." Obama concluded his speech, then, with the argument that diverse peoples of an agonistic democracy may come to see one another as legitimate because, in the Judeo-Christian language, "in some way we are all fishermen." This shared humanity was the necessary component for getting people with very different worldviews and belief systems to struggle together as democratic citizens without demonizing one another as enemies.

Conclusion

In his 2009 Notre Dame Commencement address, President Barack Obama directly engaged one of the most difficult issues in democratic life—how citizens should deal with their fundamental differences and value-laden disagreements. That the announcement of Obama's visit to Notre Dame touched off a two-month public debate about one of the nation's most divisive issues—abortion—made the topic of his speech perhaps both an appropriate and necessary response. Although some might be tempted to read Obama's speech as advocating for a deliberative democracy, something many have already done in regard to Obama himself, the democratic vision that ultimately arose from the address was, as I have argued in this essay, better understood as an agonistic democracy. The president presented a democratic public sphere that was an inherently conflictual space, filled with the sound of reason and rhetoric that avoids demonizing others. Obama offered an agonistic democracy that walks a middle path between too much passionate antagonism and too much individual rationality. What Obama suggested, then, is best summed up by Mouffe: "Democracy is in peril not only when there is insufficient consensus and allegiance to the values it embodies, but also when its agonistic dynamic is hindered by an apparent excess of consensus, which usually masks a disquieting apathy."[39] That this is a difficult balance to find did not elude Obama; it was, in fact, part of the urgency of his address.

Democratic societies must, of course, continuously deal with the difference and disagreement inherent in any system predicated on liberty and equality. One of the most difficult institutional burdens presidents will continue to carry is the role they play in defining and defending the practices of political engagement. This is a debate that political and rhetorical scholars must continue to pay close attention to if we are to fully understand the complex relationship between the presidency and American democracy.

Notes

1. As Gary Jacobson concluded, Bush's poor job ratings hurt the entire Republican Party. See Gary Jacobson, "The Effects of the George W. Bush Presidency on Partisan Attitudes," *Presidential Studies Quarterly* 39 (2009): 172–209.

2. On Bush's excessive partisanship, see Gary C. Jacobson, *A Divider, Not a Uniter: George W. Bush and the American People* (New York: Longman, 2007); George C. Edwards

and Desmond King, eds., *The Polarized Presidency of George W. Bush* (New York: Oxford University Press, 2007); and Colin Campbell, Bert A. Rockman, and Andrew Rudalevige, *The George W. Bush Legacy* (Washington, DC: CQ Press, 2007).

3. See, for instance, Bush's comment to Bob Woodward, "I'm the commander—see, I don't need to explain—I do not need to explain why I say things. That's the interesting thing about being president" Woodward, *Bush at War* (New York: Simon and Schuster, 2002), 145–46.

4. Although there are many examples of this, the most egregious and widely publicized example was the Bush Administration's firing of US Attorneys. See, for instance, the *Washington Post* editorial that outlined the evidence, "Crossing a Line at Justice; A New Report Lays Out in Breathtaking Detail the Politics Behind the Firing of Federal Prosecutors," *Washington Post*, September 30, 2008, A18.

5. David Jackson, "McCain Plans to Stress Tax Cuts; Seeks to Spark Economic Rally; Obama, Clintons Stump in Ohio, PA," *USA Today*, October 13, 2008, 6A.

6. Gary C. Jacobson, *A Divider, Not a Uniter: George W. Bush and the American People, The 2006 Election and Beyond* (New York: Longman, 2007).

7. Cass R. Sunstein, "The Obama I Know," *The Huffington Post*, March 5, 2008. http://www.huffingtonpost.com/cass-r-sunstein/the-obama-i-know_b_90034.html.

8. See Iris Marion Young, *Inclusion and Democracy* (New York: Oxford University Press, 2000), 18–26.

9. Chantal Mouffe, *On the Political* (New York: Routledge, 2005), 13.

10. Amy Gutmann and Dennis Thompson, *Why Deliberative Democracy?* (Princeton, NJ: Princeton University Press, 2004), 3–4.

11. As reported in the Spanish-language newspaper, *Diario de Navarra*, "Jürgen Habermas afirma que Obama ha supuesto 'un regalo muy grande' para EEUU, tras ocho años de gobierno Bush," *Diario de Navarra*, May 8, 2009: http://www.diariodenavarra.es/20090508/navarra/jurgen-habermas-afirma-obama-ha-sido-regalo-muy-grande-eeuu.html?not=2009050814303441&idnot=2009050814303441&dia=20090508&seccion=navarra&seccion2=campus&chnl=10&ph=7.

12. Sandy Heierbacher, "Obama, Public Engagement, and the D&D Community … An (Extraordinary) Half-Year in Review," National Coalition for Dialogue & Deliberation, July 15, 2009.

13. Transcript: Charles Gibson Interviews President Barack Obama, ABC World News, December 16, 2009, http://abcnews.go.com/WN/charles-gibson-interviews-president-obama-full-transcript/story?id=9345954&page=1.

14. Vanessa B. Beasley, Robert Asen, Diane M. Blair, Stephen J. Hartnett, Karla K. Leeper, and Jennifer R. Mercieca, "Report of the National Task Force on the Presidency and Deliberative Democracy," in *The Prospect of Presidential Rhetoric*, eds. James Arnt Aune and Martin J. Medhurst (College Station: Texas A&M University Press, 2008), 267.

15. All quotes from the commencement address are from, Barack Obama, "Commencement Address at University of Notre Dame," May 18, 2009, *American Rhetoric: Online Speech Bank*, http://www.americanrhetoric.com/speeches/barackobama/barackobamanotredamecommencement.htm.

16. Dennis Brown, "President Obama to Deliver Notre Dame's Commencement Address," ND Newswire, March 20, 2009, http://newsinfo.nd.edu/news/11293-president-obama-to-deliver-notre-dames-commencement-address.

17. The one person who remained silent on the matter was Pope Benedict XVI, which caused some controversy itself. See Amy Sullivan, "The Pope's Stand in Obama's Notre Dame Controversy, *Time,* May 16, 2009: http://www.time.com/time/nation/article/0,8599,1898756,00.html.

18. Robin Abcarian, "Culture Wars Come to Notre Dame," *Los Angeles Times,* May 14, 2009, A11.

19. Mary Ann Glendon, "Declining Notre Dame: A Letter from Mary Ann Glendon," *First Things,* April 27, 2009, http://www.firstthings.com/blogs/firstthoughts/2009/04/27/declining-notre-dame-a-letter-from-mary-ann-glendon/.

20. Robert Gibbs, Press Briefing, March 26, 2009, http://www.whitehouse.gov/the_press_office/Briefing-by-White-House-Press-Secretary-Robert-Gibbs-3-26-09.

21. Mark Murray, "Abortion Foe Declines Notre Dame Award," MSNBC.com, April 27, 2009, http://firstread.msnbc.msn.com/archive/2009/04/27/1910358.aspx?p=1.

22. Barack Obama, News Conference by the President, The White House, April 29, 2009, http://www.whitehouse.gov/the_press_office/News-Conference-by-the-President-4/29/2009.

23. For a good assessment of the different strains of deliberative democracy, see Lawrence R. Jacobs, Fay Lomax Cook, and Michael X. Delli Carpini, *Talking Together: Public Deliberation and Political Participation in America* (Chicago: University of Chicago Press, 2009), 9–10.

24. Young, *Inclusion and Democracy,* 49.

25. See Chantal Mouffe, *On the Political* (New York: Routledge, 2005), 5–19.

26. See Young, *Inclusion and Democracy,* 51–80.

27. Chantal Mouffe, *The Return of the Political* (Brooklyn, NY: Verso, 1993), 63–69.

28. For a similar definition of epideictic rhetoric, see John M. Murphy, "'Our Mission and Our Moment': George W. Bush and September 11th," *Rhetoric & Public Affairs* 6 (2003), 610.

29. Martin Luther King Jr., "Morgan State College Commencement Address," June 2, 1958. http://www.msa.md.gov/msa/speccol/sc5600/sc5604/pdf/afro_speech.pdf.

30. Patricia Roberts-Miller, Democracy, Demagoguery, and Critical Rhetoric, *Rhetoric & Public Affairs* 8 (2005): 462.

31. Mouffe, *On the Political,* 21.

32. For a far more nuanced explanation of these concerns, see Bryan Garsten, *Saving Persuasion: A Defense of Rhetoric and Judgment* (Cambridge, MA: Harvard University Press, 2006), 174–212.

33. Amy Gutmann and Dennis Thompson, *Why Deliberative Democracy?* (Princeton, NJ: Princeton University Press, 2004), 50–51.

34. Young, *Inclusion and Democracy,* 63.

35. Mouffe, *Return of the Political,* 4.

36. Mouffe, *On the Political,* 125–30.

37. David A. Frank, "The Prophetic Voice and the Face of the Other in Barack Obama's 'A More Perfect Union' Address, March 18, 2008," *Rhetoric & Public Affairs* 12 (2009): 187.

38. Robert E. Terrill, Unity and Duality in Barack Obama's 'A More Perfect Union,'" *Quarterly Journal of Speech* 95 (2009): 374.

39. Mouffe, *Return of the Political,* 6.

CHAPTER 3

The "We" in "Yes, We Can"

Obama's Audience, the Audience's Obama, and Consubstantiality

ERIC DIETER

In May 2007, during one of the candidate's first Sunday-morning interviews, George Stephanopoulos asked Barack Obama what "special qualities" he thought he possessed.[1] "I think that I have the capacity to get people to recognize themselves in each other," Obama responded, echoing statements from his 2006 campaign-priming autobiography. "Not so far beneath the surface," Obama wrote in *The Audacity of Hope*, "we are becoming more, not less, alike." He continued, saying that "across America, a constant cross-pollination is occurring, a not entirely orderly but generally peaceful collision among people and cultures."[2] This "peaceful collision" is presented in his autobiography as a congenital characteristic of the American mind, but his response to Stephanopoulos suggests that what is characteristic is not necessarily habitually acted upon. Someone with a "special" capacity, however, can help Americans accomplish these "cross-pollinations," allowing them "to recognize themselves in each other."

Institutional Burdens and American Identities

An incongruity, however, underlies Obama's two claims: Why does someone, specifically a presidential candidate (and then a president), need to provoke Americans to become "more, not less, alike" if they are already predisposed to do so? And even if we can provide an adequate answer for the why, how did a presidential candidate like Obama promote shared identity when the contentious trend of contemporary public discourse suggested that Americans, despite any innate character they may possess, were disinclined "to recognize themselves in each other?" Both questions revolve around what seems like another incongruity, namely the relationship between internal, or intrinsic, senses of identity actually (or assumed to be) held by Americans, and external, or extrinsic, idealized identities urged by US leaders.

Changing those dual strands of identity—persuading Americans either to revise or replace their internal identities with those externally offered and nationally shared—is precisely the sort of "glorious burden" of the presidency that Jennifer Mercieca and Justin Vaughn describe in their introductory chapter to this volume. Of the many "heroic expectations" encumbering the modern presidency, this essay argues that an interesting and complicated one is the reliance of Americans on their president to show them how to be American. More than simply convincing Americans of any particular policy's efficacy, presidents are charged with showing them how to hold an American identity and what identity to hold.[3] As we will see, such modeling is generally done rhetorically, but it is no less a burden of the *institution* of the presidency because it does not deal with overt, constitutionally enumerated economic, diplomatic, legislative, and military powers. And despite the burden of using rhetoric to model American identity for Americans, the modern presidency is also emboldened by this reliance. As Karlyn Kohrs Campbell and Kathleen Hall Jamieson point out, "The U.S. Constitution nowhere refers to 'the presidency' …"; they conclude, "What we now understand as the presidency has come into being as a result of the actions of all our presidents, a process in which rhetorical practices have been of particular importance."[4]

In retrospect, the well-covered (including elsewhere in this volume) popularity of Obama's 2008 campaign and the decisiveness of his victory offer compelling evidence that he was able, at least throughout the heady days of his campaign and inauguration, to find adequate answers to the two questions stated above. This essay offers a way to read how Obama was able to reconcile the incongruity between internal and external identities through his use of rhetoric, and argues that this reconciliation is largely due to avoiding discussions about identity in favor of those either about or enacting identification.

Identification and the Presidency

Indeed, Obama's negotiation of the institutional burden exhibited a comprehension of the rhetorical force found in Kenneth Burke's "identification." Identity suggests fixed selfhood, influenced by, among other things, demographics and psychology, but slow to change on its own and potentially impervious to rhetoric. By contrast, identification, according to Burke, is wholly rhetorical, the persuading of a person "only insofar as you can talk his language by speech, gesture, tonality, order, image, attitude, idea, identifying your ways with his."[5] Identification, by Burke's definition, requires actors purposefully employing rhetorical acts to move identities closer together and further apart, most often for political reasons. Identification involves identity, of course, but identity is not its primary focus. More precisely understood is that the act of unfixing identity, of making it pervious to rhetoric, is the goal of identification. Unfixing identity, as it played out in Obama's 2008 campaign, meant assuring Americans that their "selves" were important to fulfilling the nation's democratic promise. But it meant convincing Americans that that fulfillment also depended on those selves "cross-pollinating" with other American selves, including with Obama himself. Obama's metaphor of pollination seems at first a curious literary flourish, but the choice, viewed through the frame of the institutional burden of the presidency to get Americans to identify with one another, is actually felicitous. Pollination, denoting propagation and growth, is an apt trope for the expectations Americans have of a president's ability, and responsibility, to continually rejuvenate their view of themselves, just as it intimates that these powers of rejuvenation have developed into an almost organic, and definitely enduring, aspect of the presidency.

Obama explained in his autobiography, "Identities are scrambling, and then cohering in new ways."[6] Obama's "scrambling" and re-"cohering" of identities matches Burke's declaration that "The so-called 'I' is merely a unique combination of partially conflicting 'corporate we's.'"[7] For Burke, "corporate" connotes not just a reciprocally social, though not always sociable, relationship between citizens and institutions but also the demonstrable materializations of that relationship as they function in, and perhaps function as, society. That is to say, both citizens and institutions are corporate in the basic etymological sense that they are bodily substantive. They are external to and discrete from each other, and it is the associations between the two that define how a society functions. It is defining and promoting these associations that freight the expectations of presidential uses of identification. It has become part of the president's job, I argue, not simply to garner allegiance and appreciation from the citizens toward national institutions like the presidency but to find a way for citizens to accept that those institutions are actual extensions of themselves. All presidents, but perhaps particularly Obama during his 2008 campaign, can best achieve this acceptance by syllogistically positioning themselves as bridges between the citizens and institutions. Burke describes this process as a "synecdochic form" that "is present in all theories of political representation, where some part of the social body … is held to be 'representative' of the society as a whole."[8] Identification is Burke's prescription for a representationally anemic body politic because "[f]or 'represent,' we could substitute 'be identified with.'"[9] In other words, bridging the discrete corporate substances between citizens and the institutions requires presidents to employ identification whereby citizens are identified with the president, who is identified with the institution of the presidency.[10]

The implication of Burke's theory offers a helpful way to discuss the institutional burdens of the presidency: all presidents are expected not only to maintain explicit and functional social order but also to direct, if not dictate, the character of that order. So, a difficult task for presidents is finding ways to combine the unique individual "I's" that are the internal identities of Americans into a "corporate we" that functions as a shared and ordered national identity. But even more difficult is that, while facilitating the combination of "I's" into "we," presidents must persistently acknowledge that the result of that combination, the "corporate we," is always "partially conflicting." Counterintuitively, it is this conflict that gives identification its value in rhetorical and political spheres. Conflict can be thought of as the moments before and between acts of identification, when citizens are not "talking" each other's "language," not trying to "identify" with each other's "ways." Conflict divides citizens from each other, as each holds—understandably, tenaciously—to his or her fixed identity at the expense of unfixing that identity in the rhetorical sphere in order to "be identified with" fellow citizens. The social body is full of divided parts, Burke insists, but a healthy functioning body's "great emphasis upon division really serves to sharpen our understanding of identification."[11]

Without division, identification becomes unnecessary. In short, "identification is compensatory to division," Burke claims. The "compensatory" aspect allows identification to elide division because its whole mission is to define and then shorten the gap between divided rhetorical entities. As such, identification may help lighten the institutional burden of the presidency by providing a practical rhetorical tool for bridging citizens and institutions. But identification's unavoidable emphasis on "confronting the implications of division" in order ultimately to promote identification quickly reestablishes the weight of the burden, especially when one inevitable division is the exceptional nature of the presidency itself, separating the person in office from the common citizen. The modern presidency requires the burdensome balancing act of simultaneously maintaining the gap between the ethos of the presidency and the citizens, and shrinking it in ways that help Americans identify with not just the person in the office but with the institution of the office itself.

Obama and Consubstantiality

In this view, we can see how Obama's entire 2008 campaign and 2009 inauguration are fairly described as a representational balancing act between the unincorporated and divided substances of the electorate and his own ethos with that "consubstantial" strand of rhetoric that Burke calls "acting-together," a synecdochic transference resulting from the process of, as well as resulting in, acts of identification.[12] Given Burke's expansive view of identification's function in society, and given that what I am arguing is the way Obama embodies that expansiveness in his rhetoric, that which is bodily substantive about citizens and institutions needs to be correspondingly expanded, or at least refined so that we understand substantive to connote (again thinking of root etymology) "a standing for." Though my argument here is rooted in the rhetorical-political world of Burke, the phrase "standing for" will echo in the ears of anyone familiar with the seminal work on political representation by Hanna Pitkin.[13] Of the four genres of representation Pitkin advances, the two that most profitably overlap with Burke's "consubstantiality" are "symbolic" and "descriptive" representations, particularly the symbolic. We can give added significance to the role of symbolic representation in the political sphere if we enhance Pitkin's standing for, which already shelters a rhetorical dimension, with Burke's definition of rhetoric, the essence of which is "the use of language as symbolic means of inducing cooperation in beings that by nature respond to symbols."[14] Such a blending reinforces the notion that consubstantiation is more than a politician acting as representational apotheosis of "who we are," like the flag, the anthem, and the national park, but a persistent, flexible, and mutual symbolic transaction requiring the politician perpetually to seek acceptance from the citizen-audience, and to assess the degree of that acceptance. And of course, politicians also have to maintain, and be judged on, the formalistic, descriptive, and substantive aspects of representation as well, as Pitkin defines them.

The range of representational opportunities available to citizens and institutions—that is, the variety of things that each can usefully and successfully stand for—traces the furthest appropriate margins of their embodiment, defining both their essential substance and their synecdochic substance within the social body. Obama during his campaign and inauguration asked citizens and institutions to stabilize their essential and synecdochic identities in order to participate in society with vim and vigor, and in doing so made palpable the capacity for substance to become mutable, that is, to transfer the fixed identity of the "I" into a "corporate we." Mutable substance explains the power of identification: divided parts of the social body are incorporated during moments of what Burke calls "alchemic opportunity," with Obama's 2008 political campaign as a notable example.[15] Incorporation consists of divided parts being made to stand for other parts, with variable intensities of attachment for variable periods of time, and the omnipresent "synecdochic form" guarantees that each part retains its essential substance while doing representational work. In this spirit, identification, as Gary Woodward usefully summarizes it, "is both a process and an outcome," a summary that makes even more sense if we understand the process of identification and its resulting acts of identification as rhetorical accomplishments concerning substance.[16] When Obama tried to produce identification among various citizen and institutional substances in his rallies and speeches, the rhetorical power came from harnessing the mutability of those substances.

Most pertinent to my argument, then, is that the ethos-driven appeals for consubstantiality found in Obama's invented national narrative and manifested in his campaign slogan tilt closer to an "acting-for" than an acting-together, though both acting-for and acting-together are possible results of consubstantiality.[17] Although the former limits the operative actions of the electorate to the comparatively straightforward and passive acceptance or rejection of the candidate's substance, the latter demands an enduring reciprocal identification of substance. Put broadly, candidates can always grant that their skillful use of ethos does not mean automatic acquiescence by the electorate to either the character of the candidate or any requests for political action. In Obama's case, then, this meant recognizing and promoting the alchemic opportunity for voters, synecdochically, to make "he" stand for "we," which was certainly harder to do than telling his voters how his inspirations translate into their imperatives.

"Acting-Together" on the Campaign Trail

Throughout the 2008 campaign, Obama's rhetoric attempted to carve out space in standard campaign rhetoric where he could offer his presence as ecumenically representative of the Americans' identities. During his pre-inauguration speech in front of the Lincoln Memorial, for example, he confided to his fellow citizens that the "hope" propelling his campaign was "a belief that if we could just recognize ourselves in one another and bring everyone together ... then not only would we restore hope and opportunity in places that yearned for both, but maybe, just maybe, we might perfect our union in the process."[18] The "we" in that sentence quickly enlarges, incorporating not just the campaign's mission of bringing everyone together but also the distinct echo of our foundational national ambition of all citizens singularly working to perfect our union, and Obama suggests that achieving the former means accomplishing the latter "in the process." Obama's success as president would depend on his aptitude and inclination toward using our divisions to sharpen our understanding of our identifications, though it is easy to see the institutional burden such a project engenders. Substantively embodying Americans as he takes the office, he affirms, "[Y]ours are the voices I will take with me every day when I walk into that Oval Office—the voices of men and women who have different stories but hold common hopes."[19]

All of which leads back to the incongruities that opened this essay. "[I]n acting-together," Burke notes, people "have common sensations, concepts, images, ideas, attitudes that make them consubstantial," a "doctrine," he decides, that "may be necessary to any way of life."[20] Woodward's view of identification, as "a rhetorical form of superconductivity that permits a total transfer of emotional energy from one being to another," helpfully overlaps with Burke's definition of acting-together.[21] Taken as a pair they help us to resolve the difference between internal and external identities, essential and synecdochic substances. These identities have less to do with questioning what exists authentically versus representationally, and more to do with the intensity and directionality of the "superconductivity," among citizens; among institutions, especially the presidency; and between the two in any given rhetorical situation. The result is a functional task of developing "a kind of attitudinizing," as Burke puts it, "that may eventuate in the step from an attitude of sympathy with someone to the overt, practical doing of an appropriate kind deed."[22]

Candidate Obama and his campaign showed an exceptional facility at "eventuating," or bringing about, in the electorate the step from sympathetic attitude to appropriate deed, as exhibited by the record number of discrete personal donor contributions, listserv email addresses, and popular votes collected during the 2008 election.[23] Despite the Obama campaign's overachievements, these types of campaign requests, with their consequent audience involvements, are customary modes of campaign identification, where candidates "get out the vote," and voters dutifully oblige the campaign's efforts by donating and voting. Any "superconductivity" here is coursing unidirectionally from candidate to electorate, energizing conventional political tactics and strategies that do not necessarily translate into substantive, consubstantial "acting-together." In other words, within these conventional campaign tasks there is little effort, and little need, to compensate for divisions between the electorate and the elected. There is simply the making of pledges and promises by candidates and either the accepting or rejecting of the same by voters. Saying, for instance, that you are not "the other guy," always a divisive tactic, is often sufficient for garnering the financial and ballot support of voters. So, Obama did not need to initiate his "special quality" of getting people to see themselves in each other in order to convince supporters to give his campaign cash and to cast votes, which is what made his use of consubstantiality conspicuous. Getting Americans to define their involvement in his campaign as *rhetorical* acts with synecdochic dimensions—or cross-pollinations, as Obama puts it—was a much more difficult task than convincing voters that he had the right policy for any particular problem. Obama's unique use of rhetoric as identification during his campaign, however, suggested how he viewed the institutional burden of the presidency to lead through words.

Who Is the "We" in "Yes, We Can"?

Still, despite what we can call his good consubstantial intentions, the risk of over-representing Americans exists. Over-representing would mean obscuring the contributions of Americans to act-together, focusing solely on the candidate's (or president's) ability to stand-for. A small example will suffice to underscore the concern over unidirectionality: when Obama spoke at a February 2007 campaign rally in Austin, Texas, twenty thousand people waited in a cold drizzle for nearly three hours to hear the newly minted presidential candidate.[24] Even Obama was surprised by the turnout: "Unbelievable," he repeated absently into the microphone as he mounted the stage, adding, "I have not seen a crowd like this. I am overwhelmed." He then admitted to feeling similarly overwhelmed during the official announcement of his candidacy two weeks earlier "in front of the old state capitol in Springfield, Illinois," as he put it, "a place where Abraham Lincoln has served and where he delivered his famous speech in which he said that a nation divided against itself could not stand.... [F]or me to be there and see 17,000 people in seven-degree weather was truly an inspiration, and it told me," he continued, "not that people were simply supporting my campaign, but ... that people were ready for a change. That it wasn't just about me." Despite his best efforts to unyoke the campaign from the candidate, as when he entreats those thousands of cold and soggy supporters that their readiness for change "wasn't just about me," Obama ends up embedding himself in a central position apart from the audience, in nonpareil company, when he speaks of standing in the same spot "where Abraham Lincoln has served."

A similar centralizing occurs later in the speech as Obama describes hearing his then-pastor Jeremiah Wright preach about the "audacity of hope." "*I* was inspired by that sermon," Obama related, "not only because *I* thought that it applied to *my* life, [but] because it told *me* that *you* don't have to ignore the problems in the world to be hopeful. *You* simply have to be committed to bringing about change and doing everything *you* can to imagine a better world...." He concluded, "*You* think about it" (emphasis mine). One way to interpret the shift from the first-person singular narrative to the second-person plural imperative is as a grammatical emblem of the probability that candidates, even those who circumspectly avoid trying to do so, often utilize ethos unidirectionally, as a standing-in for the electorate instead of a standing-for them via transdirectional acts of consubstantiation.

We can accept that this utilization is understandable and unavoidable without encouraging candidates and their campaigns to obscure citizen contributions to acting-together. The reality is that for Obama or any presidential candidate, the most practical, appropriate, and kind deed any member of the electorate can do is, unsurprisingly, to vote for him.[25] The politician's influence is exhibited in Obama's response to Stephanopoulos, an agency characterized by an appreciation of how skillfully aware candidates can harness identification's "attitudinizing" force through the use of appeals to their own ethos. Viewed in this ethos-driven vein, the Obama campaign's famous "Yes, We Can" can be read as a highly truncated enthymematic slogan, which in its syllogistic fullness might assert its premises thus: getting Obama elected president is crucial; to achieve his election the electorate must turn their personal attitudinizing into social action in ways dictated by his campaign; because action is a consubstantial endeavor, the electorate must be consubstantial with Obama when they follow the dictates of his campaign; and if Obama and his voters are consubstantial, there must be a "we" acting together.

Obama "knows how to comfort voters with a national narrative of his own invention" writes journalist Jack Shafer, and George Packer adds that he "had figured out how to leave an audience at the peak of its emotion, craving more."[26] Both quotations evince the conventional, and conventionally broad, goal of campaigns to conglomerate as many individuals and their appraisals of the candidate as possible filtered through the singular rhetorical talent and charisma of Obama.[27] Admittedly, even the purposefully interpretative elasticity, particularly with the pronoun "we" and verb "can," of the above enthymeme underlines what scholar Laurinda Porter calls, riffing on Burke, "the desire to transform one's listeners or a situation from a present state or condition to a different (and better) state or condition."[28] After hearing Obama speak, Packer relates, illustratively, "Within minutes, I couldn't recall a single thing that he had said, and the speech dissolved into pure feeling, which stayed with me for days."[29]

Obama's message that "you don't have to ignore the problems in the world to be hopeful. You simply have to be committed to bringing about change and doing everything you can to imagine a better world" is ostensibly a source of genuine acting-together, even for those members of the electorate who disagree with his politics and policies. When, in the wake of comments by Wright taken by some as insensitive and instigative, Obama was pressured in March 2008 to revisit his relationship with his former pastor, that speech crescendoed with the same sense of familiarity introduced two years earlier in his autobiography: "I can no more disown [Wright] than I can disown the black community," he announced, continuing, "I can no more disown him than I can disown my white grandmother, a woman who helped raise me ... but a woman ... who on more than one occasion has uttered racial or ethnic stereotypes that made me cringe." He ends, "These people are part of me. And they are part of America."[30] "[I]n the faces of all the men and women I'd met," he recalled in *The Audacity of Hope*, "I had recognized pieces of myself." "In them," he continues, "all of it felt familiar."[31] It is only after describing this emergent "sense of familiarity" that Obama proposes his theory of peaceful collisions and cross-pollinations. Another way, then, to interpret the grammatical shift from the narrative "I" to the imperative "you" in the portion of Obama's Austin speech treating Wright's sermon is to view it as an attempt to do for the electorate a kind deed. Specifically, that deed is an opening up of his candidacy so that the electorate and the candidate can be identified with each other in a constructive and coequal consubstantial manner.

Obama's impulse to determine the extent to which each individual is a part of the whole is the same prescription offered by Burke, again emphasizing "division" in order "to sharpen our understanding of identification." What Obama's campaign offered is an acting-together where consubstantiality itself was the ambition. The overt, practical, and appropriate kind deed that the Obama campaign attempted to "eventuate" in the electorate was the holding of an attitude of empathy, regardless of partisanship, as antecedent goal for more sophisticated and inclusive acts of identification that would be especially productive after he took office. In short, what "we" "can" do for Obama, according to Obama, is to become consubstantial and use that consubstantiality to act together, in situations ideological and legislative. Viewed in this familiarity-driven vein, the Obama campaign's "Yes, We Can" can be read as a quite different kind of enthymematic slogan, where the unstated premise still acknowledges that getting Obama elected is important but pushes the campaign's purpose beyond getting out the vote toward creating in the electorate a comprehension of the ways citizens and institutions interact in rhetorical situations. If we agree that developing such comprehension is civically worthwhile, then we accentuate the need for an authentic acting-together, and because acting-together can be authentic only if there exists a consubstantial "we," we are charged with creating that consubstantiality.

The Limits of "Acting-Together" as a Burden of the Presidency

But it is important to admit that this is a "charge;" as ambitious and admirable as it may be, it is not a guarantee. For reasons intricate yet obvious, national "acting-together" in a genuine, durable way could prove an improbable, though we should not assume impossible, achievement. At the heart of its improbability is the fact that, as one of this volume's editors suggests, "America's democratic style is primarily ironic" because it "figuratively negates its literal political theory," allowing "politicians to occupy the realm of democratic appearances by eliding the fact that the American government is a republic."[32] Political scientist Robert Dahl is similarly skeptical of balancing republican representation and democratic ideals, though he does offer some comfort: "As a means for helping to democratize the governments of national states, representation can be understood both as a historical phenomenon and as an application of the logic of equality to a large-scale political system."[33] In the end, then, even if we do increase the centrality of the symbolic representation of politicians by emphasizing the symbolic nature of the rhetorical transactions required to obtain citizen-audience acceptance, the question remains: What then? Theoretically, what sorts of substantive actions are consequent of a particular set of accepted symbolic representations, and how can we be certain that a fundamental irony is not constantly eroding our ability to judge the appropriate political action required from a symbolic action? Practically, and more pressing perhaps, what sort of administrative *modus operandi* are required to maintain acceptance gained during the election? These are the questions that seem to have haunted the Obama administration as they transitioned from campaigning to governing.

Obama's 2008 campaign, with its "Yes, We Can" slogan insinuating identification, used familiar campaign tactics and strategies to advance a type of consubstantial political conversation that fully and fairly incorporated voters, a commendable goal that, given his election, must have, to some genuine extent, resonated with voters. After his inauguration, what became less clear was whether "Yes, We Can" would continue to resonate, particularly in the wake of hyper-partisan intractability, vocalized mistrust of government, historic economic and environmental obstacles, and White House victories resulting not from acting-together, but from the throwing of sharp political elbows. In short, although it was clear that Obama could satisfy the institutional burdens of identification enough to get elected, it was unclear whether his presidency would be thwarted by the contextual burdens of the office. Journalist and media critic Eric Alterman, citing Mario Cuomo's saying that "Candidates campaign in poetry but govern in prose," explained that, since the election, "Obama supporters have been asked to swallow some painfully 'prosaic' compromises," not least of which is the creeping notion that, despite grassroots rhetoric of the campaign, the Obama administration is "clearly happier with a top-down approach."[34]

There is also the nagging suspicion, succinctly expressed by well-known social activist Naomi Klein, that Obama's consubstantial ambition was little more than a well-intentioned feint to revitalize the American image, with Klein arguing that Obama, who she labels "the first U.S. president who is also a superbrand," was "the most successful rebranding campaign of all time."[35] Obama, Klein charges, "favors the grand symbolic gesture over deep structural change every time."[36]

What is more clear, then, is Obama's institutional burden, the overarching task of his presidency: not only did he need to create opportunities for discrete identities to consubstantially act-together—simultaneously emphasizing the significance and functionality of both division and identification—but he needed to do so in a way that his citizen-audience accepted as more than empty symbolism. Journalist Sasha Abramsky, announcing that his "can be no ordinary presidency," offered this reading of the Obama presidency: "He has changed America and created expectations for more change," Abramsky writes, shifting "how America understands itself," and in the process heightened the rhetoric of presidential expectations.[37] Obama's presidency was not ordinary, in part because he championed consubstantiality, an ambition that admittedly may be as philosophically dense as it is practically difficult. However some, like Alterman, are willing to accept that the compromises the Obama campaign made with the Obama administration were merely a pragmatic "playing for time." "Obama is taking the best deal on the table today," Alterman speculated, "but hopes and expects that once he is re-elected in 2012—a pretty strong bet, I'd say—he will build on the foundations laid during his first term to bring on the fundamental 'change' that is not possible in today's environment." In the meantime, meeting the institutional challenges Obama set for himself may mean that Americans will gain new understandings of themselves, understandings that may permanently change their attitudes and actions in rhetorical situations.

Notes

1. *This Week,* ABC, May 13, 2007.

2. Barack Obama, *The Audacity of Hope: Thoughts on Reclaiming the American Dream* (New York: Crown, 2006), 51.

3. To be clear, presidents have always had the power to use rhetoric to define what is "American," so I do not mean to overemphasize this power as a purely modern phenomenon. For historical examples of presidential rhetoric in action, a good starting point is

many of the volumes from Texas A&M University Press's "Presidential Rhetoric Series," particularly Jim Aune and Martin Medhurst, *The Prospect of Presidential Rhetoric* (College Station, 2008) and Leroy Dorsey, *The Presidency and Rhetorical Leadership* (College Station, 2002). For examples of presidential rhetoric in inaction, please see Martin Medhurst, *Before the Rhetorical Presidency* (College Station, 2008). That said, I do contend that the modern presidency is particularly attentive to identity, its effects on political discourse and policy, and vice versa—the presidency's effects on identity. Obama's 2008 campaign and inaugural year in office may be the apex of the nation's attentiveness.

4. Karlyn Kohrs Campbell and Kathleen Hall Jamieson, *Presidents Creating the Presidency: Deeds Done in Words* (Chicago: University of Chicago Press, 2008), 1–2. They go on to say, "The Constitution permits varying levels of discretionary power in rhetorical action and provides for varying degrees of rhetorical effect" (5). What they have in mind is more concerned with exercise of rhetoric as direct action, for example, the appropriateness of a pardon, the effectiveness of a veto, and so on, and less concerned with the way presidents use the presidency to shape something as protean as American identity.

5. Kenneth Burke, *A Rhetoric of Motives* (Berkeley: University of California Press, 1969), 55. For some additional commentaries about Burke's identification and consubstantiality, see Bryan Crable, "Distance as the Ultimate Motive: A Dialectical Interpretation of *A Rhetoric of Motives*," *Rhetoric Society Quarterly* 39, (2009): 213–39; Robert L. Ivie, "Democratic Dissent and the Trick of Rhetorical Critique," *Cultural Studies Critical Methodologies* 5, no. 3 (2005): 276–93; Jeffrey W. Murray, "Kenneth Burke: A Dialogue of Motives," *Philosophy and Rhetoric* 35, no.1 (2002): 22–49; Laurinda W. Porter, "Identification and Consubstantiation in the 1988 California Primary Campaign Rhetoric of Jesse Jackson: A Burkeian Approach," paper presented at the Annual Meeting of the Speech Communication Society Association, Atlanta, GA, November 2, 1991; and Theodore F. Sheckels, "The Rhetorical Success of Thabo Mbeki's 1996 'I Am an African' Address," *Communication Quarterly* 57, no. 3 (2009): 319–33.

6. Obama, *Audacity,* 51.

7. Kenneth Burke, *Attitudes Toward History* (Berkeley: University of California Press, 1984), 264.

8. Kenneth Burke, *A Grammar of Motives* (Berkeley: University of California Press, 1969), 508.

9. Burke, *Grammar,* 508.

10. This prescription, not incidentally, is the one Burke most frequently offers, because identification is "hardly other than a name for the function of sociality." Burke, *Attitudes,* 266.

11. Burke, *Rhetoric,* 150.

12. Burke, *Rhetoric,* 20–22.

13. See especially chapters 4 through 6 of *The Concept of Representation* (Berkeley: University of California Press, 1972), which was subsequently expanded by, among many others, Samuel L. Popkin, *The Reasoning Voter: Communication and Persuasion in Presidential Campaigns* (Chicago: University of Chicago Press, 1994); Iris Marion Young,

Inclusion and Democracy (New York: Oxford University Press, 2002); Jane Mansbridge, "Rethinking Representation," *The American Political Science Review* 97, (November 2003): 515–28; and Andrew Rehfeld, *The Concept of Constituency: Political Representation, Democratic Legitimacy, and Institutional Design* (New York: Cambridge University Press, 2005).

14. Burke, *Rhetoric, 43.*

15. Burke, *Grammar,* xix. Notable because of the controversial Bush administration that preceded it, the economic and military consequences of Bush's presidency, and because of Obama's race.

16. Woodward, Gary C., *The Idea of Identification* (Albany, NY: State University of New York Press, 2003), 5. "Substance evolves from and is absorbed by the agonistic struggle among discourses," Robert Wess asserts, adding that for Burke, "[N]o rhetoric is more powerful than the rhetoric of substance." *Kenneth Burke: Rhetoric Subjectivity Postmodernism* (New York: Cambridge University Press, 1996), 154–55. Because substance is always, according to Burke (*Grammar,* 29, 51), "existing both in itself and as part of its background," an "ambiguity of substance affords a major source of rhetoric."

17. Fran Lentricchia highlights in Burke a similar "ambiguity" when he draws a distinction between "identification of" versus "identification with" a substance, the former being less rhetorical and less "mediating," though no less influential, than the latter. *Criticism and Social Change* (Chicago: University of Chicago Press, 1983), 148–50.

18. *Pre-Inauguration Address at Lincoln Memorial,* January 18, 2009.

19. Small manifestations of these "voices in the Oval Office" are the ten letters from citizens that Obama is reported to read every day. For more, please see Eli Saslow, *Ten Letters: The Stories Americans Tell Their President* (New York: Doubleday, 2011); and *Inside the White House: Letters to the President,* YouTube, https://www.youtube.com/watch?v=eG00mM8QEGk .

20. Burke, *Rhetoric,* 21.

21. Woodward, x.

22. Burke, Kenneth, *Dramatism and Development* (Barre, MA: Clark University Press, 1972), 23.

23. A *Washington Post* postelection (November 20, 2008) breakdown, based on interviews with the online operation arm of Obama's campaign, claims that "3 million donors made a total of 6.5 million donations online adding up to more than $500 million. Of those 6.5 million donations, 6 million were in increments of $100 or less. The average online donation was $80, and the average Obama donor gave more than once." Jose Antonio Vargas, "Obama Raised Half a Billion Online," *Washington Post,* http://tinyurl.com/274rxmc. According to the US Federal Election Commission (FEC), Obama raised $246,110,054 from contributors donating "$200 and under." The same FEC page lists Obama's total individual contribution receipts for 2008 at just under $659 million; by comparison, Bush and Kerry's *combined* total receipts for the 2004 presidential election were approximately $722 million. "2012 Presidential Campaign Finance: Contributions to Obama, Barack by State Through 09/30/2009," FEC, http://tinyurl.com/67ceun. The same *Post* article claims that "Obama's e-mail list contains upwards of 13 million addresses,"

and that "[o]ver the course of the campaign, aides sent more than 7,000 different messages," noting, by comparison, that previous Democratic presidential nominee Senator John Kerry had three million emails in 2004, whereas Governor Howard Dean had just six hundred thousand during his presidential primary campaign in 2000. And according to the US Electoral College portion of the US National Archives and Records Administration (NARA) Web site, Obama gained 69,297,997 popular votes (52.9 percent of the total cast in 2008), topping George W. Bush's previous record from 2004 by over seven million votes. "2008 Presidential Election: Popular Vote Totals," U.S. Electoral College, NARA, http://tinyurl.com/2ctbdep; and "2004 Presidential Election: Popular Vote Totals," U.S. Electoral College, NARA, http://tinyurl.com/20wfva.

24. "Sen. Barack Obama's Austin Speech Transcription," YNN News [online], February 27, 2007, http://austin.ynn.com/content/186045/sen--barack-obama-s-austin-speech-transcription. He announced his intentions to run for president on February 10, 2007.

25. On this point Burke (*Grammar*, xx) is blunt: "We may think of voting as an act, and of the voter as an agent," he writes, evoking his language of dramatism and the pentad; "yet votes and voters both are hardly other than a politician's medium or agency; or from another point of view, they are part of his scene."

26. Jack Shafer, "How Obama Does That Thing He Does," *Slate Magazine*, February 14, 2008, http://www.slate.com/id/2184480/; and George Packer, "The Choice: The Clinton-Obama Battle Reveals Two Very Different Ideas of the Presidency," *The New Yorker*, January 28, 2008, http://tinyurl.com/yvm65z.

27. Charisma was clearly a significant part of Obama's rhetorical and political successes (and failures, perhaps), clearly related to ethos, and potentially a threat to consubstantiation; a longer version of my essay would engage this concept more fully, but for now, to both support and trouble the claims of my argument, particularly the dutiful relationships between rhetors and audiences, please see, as a starting point, Max Weber, *On Charisma and Institution Building*, S. N. Eisenstadt, ed. (Chicago: University of Chicago Press, 1968), particularly chapters 1 and 2.

28. Porter, 3. Jeffrey Walker, who deepens the common view of Aristotelian enthymematic *techne* by reaffixing to it antecessor sophistic understandings, claims that it is "the rhetorical move *par excellence* for guiding an audience's inference-making and attitude-formation in a particular direction" Jeffrey Walker, "The Body of Persuasion: A Theory of the Enthymeme," *College English* 56, (January 1994): 46–65, 53.

29. Packer, "The Choice: The Clinton-Obama Battle, The New Yorker online, http://www.newyorker.com/reporting/2008/01/28/080128fa_fact_packer.

30. *A More Perfect Union*, March 18, 2008. For more about this important speech, particularly its engagement with race and identity, please see T. Denean Sharpley-Whiting, ed., *The Speech: Race and Barack Obama's "A More Perfect Union"* (New York: Bloomsbury, 2009).

31. Obama, 51.

32. Jennifer R. Mercieca, "The Irony of the Democratic Style," *Rhetoric & Public Affairs* 11, no. 3 (Fall 2008): 441–49. See also Jennifer R. Mercieca, *Founding Fictions* (Tuscaloosa,

AL: The University of Alabama Press, 2010), especially chapter 1.

33. *Democracy and Its Critics* (New Haven, CT: Yale University Press, 1989): 215, but see chapter 2.

34. Eric Alterman, "Kabuki Democracy: Why a Progressive Presidency Is Impossible, for Now," *The Nation,* July 7, 2010, http://tinyurl.com/35zk9ar.

35. Naomi Klein, "No Logo at Ten," In *No Logo: Taking Aim at the Brand Bullies,* Tenth Anniversary Edition (New York: Picador, 2009), xxiii.

36. Ibid., xix, xxvi.

37. Sasha Abramsky, *Inside Obama's Brain* (New York: Portfolio, 2009), 7. Abramsky's position, that Obama's campaign was so transformative and disruptive that its effects must necessarily spill over into his presidency, is typical. For variations on the same approbative theme, please see Jonathan Alter, *The Promise: President Obama, Year One* (New York: Simon and Schuster, 2010); Dan Balz and Haynes Johnson, *The Battle for America 2008: The Story of an Extraordinary Election* (New York: Viking, 2009); David Plouffe, *The Audacity to Win: The Inside Story of the Lessons of Barak Obama's Victory* (New York: Viking, 2009); and David Remnick, *The Bridge: The Life and Rise of Barack Obama* (New York: Knopf, 2010).

CHAPTER 4

Overcoming Institutional Burdens

President Obama's Rhetorical Leadership in His First Year

BRANDON ROTTINGHAUS

There is ongoing debate about whether presidents can lead public opinion. To address this debate in the context of the themes of this volume, this chapter investigates how, when, and under what conditions presidents succeed at leading public opinion on public policy. Specifically, in this chapter I investigate how President Obama's early efforts to lead on Afghanistan, health care, and stimulus legislation were affected by institutional burdens and how his rhetoric reflected his attempts to engage and transcend those burdens. To accomplish this, I build on previous work to outline a theoretical story about how presidents might lead public opinion, and highlight the specific time periods, political conditions, communication tactics, and levels of public information that should enhance or detract from the president's ability to lead public opinion.

This theoretical and empirical foray into President Obama's first year in office explores the tension between the president's institutional burdens and his ability to persuade the public. Although elected with a good deal of promise, after revolutionizing the way campaigns are run and won in the United States, President Obama came into office facing some of the gravest individual political and policy challenges the nation had ever faced.[1] Collectively, these challenges posed a major burden to successful leadership from his (or any) White House. Recognizing these barriers to success, in his first State of the Union message President Obama railed against the "politics of 'no'" and appealed to an end to the "tired old battles" that divided the country and stalled his legislative agenda on Capitol Hill.[2] Yet it is not just these specific elements faced by the Obama administration that contribute to the burden of leadership for modern presidents. Presidents must now deal with, among other political impediments, a twenty-four-hour news media clamoring for conflict, a highly polarized public unwilling to listen to his messages, and party coalitions fraying in the legislature. Any leadership success in navigating these contextual burdens would require expert strategic timing and delivery.

Divergent Findings on Presidential Leadership

As noted in the previous section, there is debate about the degree to which presidents can lead public opinion in a modern political environment. Presidents have not been shy about using the "bully pulpit" to carry their messages to the American public, believing it to be important to their policy success while in office, their political legacy after they leave office, and the future success of their party.[3] Yet despite lofty expectations for this tactic, some scholars find that presidents are generally unsuccessful at opinion leadership as an instrument to advance their policy agenda.[4] Scholars argue that presidents fail at moving public preferences for a number of reasons, typically in combination with each other, such as shrinking audiences, media message screeners, the political partisanship of citizens, and a lack of public attention to the news.[5] Several authors claim that the rise of television (and the rise in the diversity of viewers) challenges the president's ability to lead public opinion.[6] Specifically, that viewers today have increased choices—and that many are exercising this choice by turning to likeminded news sources—means that the president's ability to consistently lead public opinion has been limited.[7] Less attention is paid to presidents, even in venues and on issues that traditionally afforded the president a great deal of coverage, such as foreign policy. Declining trust in government is also to blame.[8]

Given the argument that the presidency (and some individual presidents) is too institutionally weak and situationally disadvantaged (as identified by its institutional burdens) for its occupant to effectively use the bully pulpit, many prominent studies find little success for presidents in moving public opinion to the president's preferred policy outcome.[9] One classic example of failed presidential leadership is Woodrow Wilson's exasperating (and eventually fatal) trip across the nation to drum up support for the League of Nations.[10] Likewise, George Edwards's *On Deaf Ears* establishes a compelling argument for recent presidential ineffectiveness in leading public opinion.[11] The outdated and inconsistent tools presidents have to accomplish these tasks may not be up to the job.[12] By this logic, presidents are "doomed to failure" because public expectations are out of step with the realities of presidential ability.[13]

Yet, despite recent studies indicating less than significant public opinion movement after policy speeches, there are many documented instances where presidents do successfully lead public opinion. If one includes all works in history, communication, sociology, public policy, and other related fields, there are many moments that demonstrate "presidential leadership." Indeed, because many case studies describe how presidents can lead public opinion in particular circumstances, there is a need for a broader study of the multiple conditions that may foster successful presidential leadership. Previous research has demonstrated that Kennedy,[14] Reagan,[15] and Clinton[16] each successfully led the public. Interestingly, evidence shows presidents are also successful at motivating positive perceptions of the economy, a potentially powerful tool in a dour economy.[17] Likewise, several scholars find that presidents achieve leadership success by "mobilizing support from their party base, interest groups, and select localities."[18] In addition, although there is not consensus on when presidents are able to lead opinion on domestic policy, there is consensus that presidents can generally lead public opinion successfully on matters of foreign policy or military intervention.[19]

A Theory of Conditional Presidential Leadership of Public Opinion

To address this debate, and claim ground to a middle position, I present a theory to predict the conditions under which presidents may succeed in leading public opinion. Generally, this occurs when they make consistent, solid, and unwavering attempts to do so. Of course, a president's leadership ability does not exist in a vacuum. Presidents must operate within institutional and contextual burdens, including *constraining elements* and *constraining agents*. Constraining elements are those events or conditions that are beyond the president's control that disrupt the ability of the president to convey his or her message credibly or truthfully. These elements include low popularity (or low credibility), economic troubles (perhaps also signaling low credibility and encouraging dissent), or "lame duck" status that manifests in second terms. Constraining agents are those individuals or groups that intentionally challenge the president's message or actively discount what he is saying so that the president's message retains less credibility. Examples include an unpersuadable public or publics (such as out-group partisans or groups that traditionally ally with the opposition party), divided government (where the president's political opponents obscure the strength or veracity of the president's message), or the media that challenges the president's message.[20]

The greater the number or impact of these countervailing elements, the less likely presidents are to lead public opinion. Not surprisingly, presidents are significantly disadvantaged by the presence of at least one (but often more) of these countervailing elements. It is the rare moment, therefore, when presidents are able to lead public opinion, because there are simply so many different ways in which presidential messages can be obscured and comparatively few in which they are adequately and completely received by the public. As a result, scholars generally find few moments where presidents are able to lead public opinion.[21] This theory, which allows for the conditions shaping presidential difficulty in leading public opinion to be understood as both input and output, reveals why presidents generally fail at leading public opinion. But when such contrary voices are more silent or the president's voice is more resonant, the opportunities for presidential leadership are greater.

Several specific techniques employed by presidents demonstrate how this works. For instance, when presidents made the same argument two days in a row, they were able to move public opinion. Communication tactics involving television also demonstrate success in leading public opinion. Grouped together, all presidents find success at leading public opinion with a "major address" tactic (where presidents deliver televised addresses from Washington, D.C.). The effect is impressive, with an 8 percent change in opinion.[22] This suggests that presentations that are more White House–driven (where the White House has more control over the format and message) are more suitable venues for successful presidential leadership, rather than those events where the president must be reactive to questions or explain a policy through other kinds of individual speeches. Likewise, an increase in the percentage of the public registering "don't know" to a policy question presents more opportunity for presidential leadership,[23] suggesting that the more the public learns about a topic or the more certain they become about an issue, the more easily (but modestly) the president is able to lead them.

President Obama and Leadership of Public Opinion

Given the general precepts of how and when presidents should find success in leading public opinion, to what degree was President Obama successful in his first year in office? The burden of presidential leadership in the United States has certainly not improved—it seems clear that presidents face a political environment for opinion leadership that has gotten worse, not better. For instance, the media is more ubiquitous; the sources of media are more prolific; political partisanship has intensified as the "center" of American politics has disappeared; and audiences are more segmented in their consumption of political information.[24] Success or lack of success during the Obama administration is a telling story about how these factors affect prospects for presidential leadership. The next section examines the presidency of Barack Obama in order to identify specific trends in his leadership tactics and the success or failure of these efforts.

STIMULUS PACKAGE

First on President Obama's agenda was a push for a multibillion-dollar economic stimulus package designed to jump-start the sluggish US economy. Among other items, the stimulus package included targeted tax cuts (rebates, an education tax credit, and homebuyers tax credits); additional spending on public roads, bridges, and schools; funding to modernize health care records; and investment in alternative energy—a total spending package of almost $800 billion.[25] Even with the president's calls for bipartisanship, selling the plan to Republicans would be a challenge. The president began his push with five short television interviews (sit-downs with the network news anchors). Although the president stressed the importance of his plan and answered critics who argued the spending priorities were misplaced or not needed, his message was detoured by the surprise withdrawal of Tom Daschle as the nominee designate for the Department of Health and Human Services due to nonpayment of taxes.[26]

The cornerstone of the administration's push for passage of key legislation was Obama's first prime-time press conference, a rare event for recent presidents.[27] Although the president chose to take his message to the public through a press conference, three elements of that press conference helped to overcome the otherwise minimal effect of press conferences on public leadership. First, the president combined his press conference with a "barnstorm" trip to Elkhart, Indiana, a city that had been hard hit by the economic slump. President Obama began the press conference with a narrative about the hurting city and linked the policies from his economic stimulus proposal to ways in which the citizens of Elkhart (and others) would be helped by investment in education, infrastructure, and social benefits. Second, following the press conference, the next day the president departed for several states, including Florida, Virginia, and Illinois, to continue to stump for the plan and talk about the need for the spending proposed by the legislation.[28] A barnstorm tactic by itself is a positive enhancer of the president's ability to lead public opinion, especially if the president is popular (which President Obama was, with 66 percent of the public approving his job performance).[29] Third, the president took only fourteen questions in the hour-long press conference, spending a majority of his time answering questions with lengthy speeches, each of which allowed him to stay on message and control the floor. By controlling the content more carefully, the president was able to use the press conference to his advantage. In addition, the questions were not all focused on the contentious stimulus package legislation: several reporters asked the president about foreign affairs (Iran and Afghanistan) and Department of Defense policies regarding the photographing of returning flag-draped coffins of killed soldiers, and one asked about New York Yankees baseball player Alex Rodriguez's admission to steroid usage. These temporary diversions from President Obama's main message did not help him, but also did not hurt him as much as negative or probing questions on his core agenda might have.

Working against the president, according to the general leadership findings documented above, were the higher salience of the issue (along with concurrent criticism from putative opponents); the short (or nonexistent) "honeymoon" of recent presidents; the fact that the president did not sell his proposals by using the medium of a nationally televised address, which the White House could control; and that the president attempted to use a press conference as a vehicle to lead public opinion. Yet working in the president's favor were his popularity and the issue's salience—a potent combination when taken together; the public's being "persuadable" in that they were less informed or certain about the impact of the stimulus package (in part due to its complexity); and that the president pressed the issue in public for several consecutive days.[30]

The president's full court press worked. A majority of the public approved of the stimulus plan in late January and early February (52 percent), and after his press conference (February 9) and barnstorm during the following two days, the percentage of the public who approved of the plan rose to 59 percent.[31] This 7 percent movement toward the president's position occurred even with the presence of stiff opposition from the Republican Party. Further, the percentage of the public who responded "Don't know" to the question fell from 11 percent in late January to 8 percent in mid-February, suggesting that the public became more informed about the issue because of the amount of coverage and because of the president's public relations efforts. The legislation passed both houses of Congress, although the bill only attracted three Republican votes in the Senate (where an additional 56 Democrats and 2 Independents voted in favor and 36 Republicans voted against) and no Republican votes in the House (where 246 Democrats in the House voted in favor and 183 Republicans voted against). Still, the opposition was muted enough to provide smooth passage of the legislation through Congress.[32]

AFGHANISTAN

As a candidate for the presidency, Obama made an issue of the languishing conflict in Afghanistan almost as often as he did the ongoing conflict in Iraq. As he assumed the presidency, and "Bush's War" became "Obama's War," President Obama struggled to find the proper course of action in winning the "dismally complex and intractable" Afghanistan conflict.[33] With little fanfare, President Obama announced in mid-February 2009 that he was sending an additional seventeen thousand troops to aid those already there in the conflict. He argued "in a written statement that the increase was 'necessary to stabilize a deteriorating situation in Afghanistan, which has not received the strategic attention, direction and resources it urgently requires.'"[34] The president defended his decision with a justification that the war was one "of necessity" because threats from al-Qaeda were omnipresent.[35] Additional decisions on the long-term strategy of the conflict, including the prospect of additional military service personnel, would follow in the coming months.

The president may have had limited time to "sell" the public on his course of action on Afghanistan—early in his first term the public was growing impatient about the course of the conflict.[36] Indeed, by early October 2009, a majority of Americans (57 percent) opposed the war in

Afghanistan.[37] The association of the ongoing war with the conflict in Iraq and the Bush administration as well as the public's thinning patience for international conflict, contributed to declining support for continued hostilities. Yet this does not suggest that the public could not be convinced to accept specific changes, especially with regard to protecting the United States against a terrorist attack or quickly ending the role of the United States in the conflict. Presidents generally have additional persuasive capability under certain conditions, especially when talking about foreign policy issues.

Yet the evidence suggests that the president had early trouble moving the public's positions on either his "handling" of the conflict or in increasing its support of sending additional military personnel. Figure 4.1 graphs the percentages of the public approving and disapproving of the president's handling of the conflict in Afghanistan. There is a fairly steady decline from March, when the approval was very high at 67 percent, to October, when approval of his speeches fell to less than a majority of the public at 42 percent. The frequency of his speeches seems to have an inverse effect on the approval of his handling of the situation. The approval of his handling of Afghanistan dropped during polling periods when the president gave more speeches in the two weeks prior to the date of the poll (April 5, August 28, and September 23). Although causality cannot be determined from these data, it seems clear that the president's speeches did little good in positively influencing the public's opinion of his handling.

Why? Like other instances of lack of presidential persuasion, the problem was a communication problem. The president seemed reluctant to address the issue in public, especially in the United States. Between his announcement to increase troop levels in February and April 2009, the president only spoke substantively of the issue *abroad,* primarily in relation to helping to foster the commitments of other nations to the cause. A majority of the speeches in which he spoke of the issue (twenty-four of the forty-seven, or 51 percent) were delivered abroad. Likewise, his announcement of troop increases in February 2009 was done through a statement issued by the White House, *not* spoken by the president. Even on a major policy speech to the United Nations General Assembly, a speech designed to recapture the positive image of the United States abroad, President Obama said nothing about Afghanistan. Because such a widely reported and televised speech would have been an excellent platform from which to persuade the public, the president appears to have intentionally kept the issue off the

FIGURE 4.1.

Approval of President Obama's handling of Afghanistan

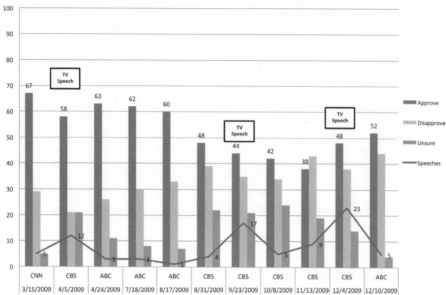

agenda—perhaps because the White House needed the public's attention on the health care debate; the issue was not popular (and growing more unpopular); and the White House had yet to formulate a long-term plan.

However, later gains made up some of the ground the president lost early after his February 2009 announcement. Table 4.1 charts the public's preferences on increasing or decreasing the level of troops in Afghanistan. Multiple polls indicate growing support for increasing the number of troops on the ground, including an 8 percent gain in a poll released on February 18 and an additional overall gain of 12 percent across the three polls conducted in late summer/early fall polls (i.e., those released on August 27, September 19, and October 5). At the last polling date in October, support and opposition seemed to have crystallized into pro-Obama and anti-Obama camps—almost equally identical percentages of the public support increases (37 percent) and support decreases (38 percent) in the level of troops, and the percentage supporting "keeping the same" number fell to 17 percent. But when directly posed the question about favoring or opposing a decision by President Obama to send more troops to Afghanistan, the percentage of the public favoring this decision rose from 41 percent in late September to 48 percent in early October.[38]

TABLE 4.1
Support for Changes in Troop Levels in Afghanistan (2009)

"From what you have seen or heard about the situation in Afghanistan, what should the United Stated do now? Should the U.S. increase the number of U.S. troops in Afghanistan, keep the same number of U.S. troops in Afghanistan as they are now or decrease the number of troops in Afghanistan?"

	Increase	Keep Same	Decrease	Unsure
January 11	34	28	26	12
February 18	42	23	24	11
April 1	39	18	33	10
August 27	25	23	41	11
September 19	29	27	32	12
October 5	37	17	38	8
November 13	32	20	39	9

"Do you strongly support, somewhat support, somewhat oppose, or strongly oppose increasing troop levels in Afghanistan?"

	Strongly Support	Somewhat Support	Somewhat Oppose	Strongly Oppose	Unsure
September 17	19	25	20	31	5
October 22	28	19	15	28	10
December 11	30	25	15	24	6

Source: Data in the top panel were taken from CBS News polls. Data in the bottom panel were taken from the NBC/Wall Street Journal Poll. Dates signify the start of the polling window period.

As the president began to defend the strategy more in public, the public followed along. In early September, the White House shifted its rhetorical strategy, arguing that the war would not "turn into another Vietnam" and that the conflict was necessary to continue to pursue and quell the possible rise of terrorism in the region. This renewed public effort at persuasion seems to coincide with pressure from Congress, especially Democrats, to explain the administration's goals and justify current (and future) funding for the conflict.[39] It is also, not surprisingly, associated with the politics of the 2010 midterm elections. The president's political opposition threatened that Obama had to "[b]e hawkish on foreign policy or risk letting your party be painted as weak in next year's midterm elections."[40] Leaks about future requests of additional troops, which seem to temporarily rally the public, and elections in Afghanistan, which were argued by experts to stabilize the government,[41] seemed to have rallied the public behind the president, albeit modestly.

The public's approval of the president's handling of the Afghanistan issue dipped while he decided on a course of action in late 2009. Yet after the president decided on a course of action, the public's estimation of his handling of the situation rebounded. For instance, in Figure 4.2, additional speeches pertaining to the conflict (including a televised address in December devoted to the topic) led to an increase in the public's approval of his handling of the situation from 38 percent to 48 percent, to 52 percent. Likewise, the bottom panel of Table 4.1 demonstrates increasing support for the president's proposed troop increases for Afghanistan after the president's announcement. The percentages of the public favoring troop-level increases rose from September 19 (where 19 percent strongly supported increasing troop levels) to December 30 (where 30 percent strongly supported increasing troop levels). Further, in the days following the televised address, asked directly whether they favored the president's plan or not, 51 percent of the public approved, whereas 43 percent disapproved.[42] A more active president as communicator-in-chief seems to have paid off.

HEALTH CARE

As a signature agenda item in the president's first term, health care reform was a major campaign promise and an issue whose success or failure could define the Obama presidency. Diverging from President Clinton's strategy of crafting health care legislation internally and delivering it to Congress for ratification, the Obama administration largely sketched the broad contours of his vision for reform and let Congress, primarily the Senate Finance Committee led by conservative Democrat Max Baucus of Montana, hammer out the details.[43] The president's plans called for near universal coverage, expansion of Medicare, efficiencies in federal health spending and, perhaps most controversially, a government-run health care plan to compete with private insurance plans. Despite concerns that the nation's economic doldrums would limit the amount of health care reform possible, President Obama pressed ahead.[44]

This process can be divided into two phases. Phase I (January 21–June 6, 2009) primarily focused on agenda setting and issue framing. During this initial phase, the president's messages were not getting through to the public effectively. Criticism of the president was rising during this time period, and the public began to doubt the president's stimulus and health care plans would have the intended positive effect on the economy.[45] Likewise, the administration was still linking the health care and economic stimulus package policies. Indeed, thirty speeches in the 129 days during this time period referenced health care in relation to the federal stimulus package (compared to only four times in the second phase's 131 days). According to the edicts above, presidents will be able to move public preferences more easily if they narrowly focus on a single issue and continuously press it in public. In Phase II, the White House switched tactics.

In Phase II (June 7–October 18, 2009) the administration made a more concerted effort to lead public opinion. According to Stolberg, "After months of insisting he would leave the details to Congress, President Obama has concluded that he must exert greater control over the heath care debate and is preparing an intense push for legislation that will include speeches, town-hall-style meetings and a much deeper engagement with lawmakers."[46]

FIGURE 4.2.
Approval of Obama's handling of health care

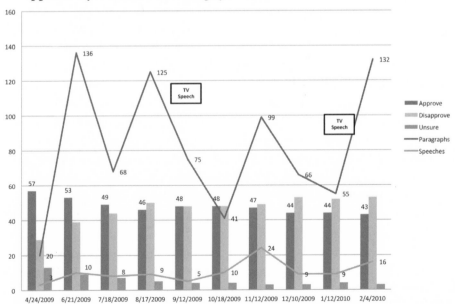

The president used several tactics here, including "a series of question-and-answer sessions in public forums, a prime-time address to a joint session of Congress, campaign-style rallies and a number of television interviews."[47] This "all-the-time carpet bombing" strategy has been shown to be effective.[48] The president was also more attentive to pitching his message to key states with "swing" senators (including Maine, Nebraska, Arkansas and Florida).[49] Figure 4.2 tracks the total number of speeches delivered by President Obama in which he mentioned health care, the total number of paragraphs spoken, and poll questions querying support for President Obama's "handling" of health care.[50] The data from Figure 4.2 pick up these accelerated public relations trends and show a significant increase in the number of paragraphs devoted to health care reform in June of 2009.

According to the findings from Figure 4.2, there appears to be an inverse relationship between the number of paragraphs spoken and the approval of the president's handling of the health care. For instance, in the June 21 and August 17 poll, more time in speeches devoted to health care seemed to drive down the percentage of the public approving of the president's handling of the policy. One reason for this inverse relationship is that the process began to become politicized, and the result was that the president's message was not always fully received. During the early August recess, lawmakers met vocal opposition in town hall meetings largely organized by conservative lobbying groups.[51] Widening criticism from the Republican Party, whose Chairman labeled the plan "socialism," also limited the president's reach.[52] The White House was largely taken aback by these increasingly negative developments, yet perhaps they should not have been surprised. Dissonance on the issue was increasing with the silence from the White House and the increasing partisan debate in Congress.[53] President Obama's message during an Address to a Joint Session of Congress in late September, his first prime-time address on health care reform, competed for attention in the media with Representative Joe Wilson's (South Carolina) shouting, "You lie!" at the president while he addressed health care coverage for illegal immigrants.

Efforts to pursue his health care reform agenda also stalled in the early part of 2010. After losing a filibuster-proof majority in the Senate (with the special election of Scott Brown to replace Edward Kennedy in Massachusetts), the White House seemed adrift and changed their strategy to one of compromise and accommodation rather than persuasion. One significant moment came when President Obama gave a speech and took

FIGURE 4.3.

Support for the "public option" and Obama speeches

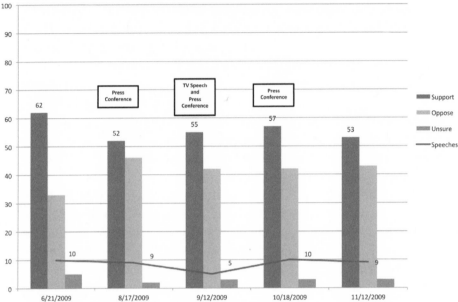

questions at the House Republican Conference in the days following his State of the Union Address. Although the address was well received, the president was asked some very tough questions from the Republican members of the House. Although this interaction was supportive of bipartisan policy making, it distracted the public and hurt the president's ability to clearly convey his message. Figure 4.3 demonstrates this—the president gave more speeches about health care reform between January 12 and February 4, 2010 (the dates the polls were taken), and dedicated a significant portion of the State of the Union to it, but the percentage of the public approving of his handling of health care reform declined in each instance. The president's focus had waned; his message was not presented as being important (as happens with a litany list during a State of the Union); and his message was beginning to be drowned out by other actors.[54]

Yet even though public polling showed an initial loss and only modest rebound from the start of Phase II, support for the public option grew during this time. Figure 4.3 charts similar trends as Figure 4.2 but focuses on Phase II of the president's public relations plan and specifically on the favorability of the "public option."[55] Table 4.2 confirms these findings and demonstrates a modest movement of opinion to a position more favorable to the opinion that the public option was "necessary" to health care reform. Two findings related to the president's tactics are important here. First, more speeches on the issue from President Obama tended to increase support for the public opinion in the June 21 and October 18 polls. The president mentioned the issue almost daily from August to October and did so on consecutive days four times during this period (averaging two to three days in a row). The president effectively combined the momentum inherent in the strategies of constant communication and major national exposure by traveling to several states to hold public meetings in the days before his national address.[56] The president also "saturated" the television talk shows in the days following his health care address to Congress (see below), and on these occasions he dispelled erroneous criticism and tried to build support for his reform plans.[57]

Second, the text boxes above the bar graph at each polling date (representing press conferences and major addresses) show that the president was more willing to take his case to the public in the form of press conferences or national addresses to the nation. In particular, the president's address on September 10 seems to have had the effect of rallying the public behind the public option (and his handling of the issue, as seen in Figure 4.2) because we see an increase in Figure 4.2, Figure 4.3, and Table 4.2 in the percentage supporting President Obama or his policies. The president's prime-time press conferences proved effective here as well, similar to the effect achieved when he was selling the economic stimulus plan. Although these trends were temporary, many observers gave the administration credit for leading the public.[58] In fact, because the data described above track short-term trends and the argument is that presidents can temporarily move public opinion under these circumstances, these findings make sense. But as his communication focus became unfocused after October, support of the policy again fell (see Figure 4.3).

Trends in Obama's Leadership

The results from examining current political trends and tactics pertaining to "Obama's burden" demonstrate the unique institutional burdens faced by President Obama early in his first term. First, President Obama successfully navigated his first leadership challenge on some issues related to policy in a time period where the previous findings suggested he should not succeed. Perhaps the nature of the president's victory prompted a resurgence of the presidential honeymoon, replete with less opposition and less critical media coverage. Majorities in both houses of Congress allowed for fewer critics than those faced by past presidents, who found their honeymoons very short. Several observers suggested that, although the difficult economic situation may have warranted a halt to any further big ticket–spending item, the White House was wise to act quickly before the president's "honeymoon" was over.[59]

Similar to this trend, the president's press conference of February 9, 2009, did little to stifle the momentum of the White House's public relations efforts, again suggesting that the nature of press coverage is important to presidents and that President Obama may have been the recipient of enough positive coverage (or absence of negative coverage) to mitigate the otherwise deleterious effects of presidential press conferences. Further, President Obama tended to control the questioning well in these press conferences, responding directly to criticism. For instance, in consecutive individual interviews on September 20 with George Stephanopolous, David Gregory, John King, and Bob Schieffer, the president responded to nearly identical questions about the amount of tax increase for the health care plans, the need to include public opinion in the health care plans, and a timeline for withdrawal from Afghanistan. By using these press conferences to tackle and diffuse tough questions, the president was apparently able to succeed where other presidents have not.

Several other trends demonstrate how the Obama administration overcame the twin concerns of its institutional and contextual burdens. First, the combination of a highly salient issue and a very popular president provided a boost to the president, especially given the depth of the crisis and the aversion of Congress to do nothing to forestall the crisis. The president was often more popular than his policies, which provided for a White House advantage. Specifically, on health care reform, as charges about "socialized medicine" and "death panels" mounted, the president was able to use his popularity (and the coverage that followed) to address and quell these charges. Although the Obama White House's plan was to have Congress take the lead on the specifics of a health care plan, more guidance from the president may have been warranted. Democrats in Congress acknowledged that "the bully pulpit" is powerful, but the president needed to shore up support for a specific policy earlier.[60] The president's public appeals were credited with assisting Democratic leaders with passing health care reform in Congress.[61]

Second, several presidential communication tactics were effective in leading public opinion. Specifically, a presidential "barnstorm," talking about the issue for consecutive days, and a major address to the nation had a positive effect on presidential leadership, again confirming that presidents who actively and continually press their message with the public are more likely to achieve public persuasion. Also as expected, criticism from opponents in the health care debate also limited the president's message, causing him to "steer the health debate out of the capital" and take his message to the public.[62] The use of a major televised address, though not to date the preferred method of utilizing the bully pulpit of the Obama White House, appeared to be as potent as expected.

Similarly, the higher the degree of public learning or the larger the increase in public certainty about an issue, the greater the ability of the president to lead public opinion. On a complicated, interconnected, and vastly large issue like the Obama administration's stimulus package, the potential for public confusion was significant. Yet the White House, in using the "bully pulpit" to explain its position to the public (as well as to counteract opposing voices), was able to educate the public and convince them to be more certain about the need for the plan. The same was true for public preferences on increasing the troop levels in Afghanistan—the president seemed to be able to persuade those who were "unsure" and gain momentum toward his preferred policy. One interesting exception is that the public grew more supportive of the "public option" for health care reform without necessarily lowering the percentage of the public more certain about their opinions (see Figure 4.3). Convincing the public to undertake major changes in health care would be a challenge because the policy is connected to taxes, insurance, doctor pay, and possible future Medicare benefits.[63] By the end of Phase II (described above), the public seems to have converted their opinions from opposing to supporting.

The flip side of this is that the president's less clear and focused communication efforts decreased his ability to lead public opinion. By the beginning of the president's second year in office, he faced greater public scrutiny and a more crowded media environment. The president found himself defending his policies while reaching for victory on several policies. The burden of leadership was increasing. The president reached out for bipartisanship and effectively allowed his spotlight to be shared with opposing messages. The White House admitted that it did not handle the political onslaught well—reports indicated that the "president's communications team had not taken the initiative often enough and had allowed drawn-out debates in Congress, and relentless criticism by Republicans, to drown out his message."[64] This was especially true on health care reform, where the message from the White House was presented (at various times) as a cost-containment measure, a restraint on greedy insurance companies, security for middle-class families, and a moral imperative.[65] As argued above, persuading the public in a crowded media environment is an arduous task. This task is multiplied in difficulty when the White House is pushing several agenda items at the same time.

Leadership and President Obama's Institutional Burdens

As argued above, several recent studies have suggested that presidential leadership of public opinion is an unsound strategy as it generally fails, challenging conventional political wisdom that presidents effectively employ the "bully pulpit" to lead the public. Scholars suggest presidents struggle with opinion leadership in a dense political environment, crowded with a truculent media, a narrowing public, and partisanship from both political parties.[66] Put another way, modern presidents are overwhelmed by the "glorious burdens" of their offices. Yet this is not to imply that opinion leadership is a bankrupt strategy—quite the contrary. Opinion leadership is simply poor as a *general* strategy but can be excellent as a *specific* strategy. Based upon the findings in this chapter and related prior work, the "bully pulpit" is largely *provisional* for modern presidents. The descriptions from this chapter indicate that presidents are successful at leading opinion when they continuously push the issue in public, while delivering speeches on television from the seat of presidential power, when the public is persuadable as well as under several other contingencies.

In both the health care and Afghanistan debates, the president was unable to move the public's perceptions of his "handling" of the situation, but he was able to move *substantive* opinion on the public option and troop increases on each respective policy. The partisan nature of responses to the "handling" questions, as well as the president's effectiveness in communicating his message to the public, establish these differences. This does not suggest that the White House will find success on every important issue on which it attempts to convince the public, but it does suggest that President Obama has some control over the conditions argued to be effective in communicating his ideas and the White House can therefore use the "bully pulpit" provisionally.

That the White House can strategically use its communication resources to its advantage *and* that the president is more effective in persuading the public on substantive matters than on political matters (such as the "handling" questions) suggests that it is important to understand not just *that the president spoke* on an issue (or the number of times he spoke about it), but what the president *says*. Thus, the premature reports of the "death" of the president's rhetorical ability are, to borrow a phrase from Mark Twain, "exaggerated." A substantive debate can benefit presidents, especially on issues where they can find some political traction in the public or in Congress. On the issues explored here, the president seems uniquely able to frame issues to his advantage on matters of public policy, both foreign and domestic, and this framing helps the president gain an advantage in terms of getting his message through to the public. The key for the White House is to focus on the specifics of a policy rather than a more generic "need for reform." In a sense, this relates to the difficulty President Clinton faced when he attempted to lead public opinion on his universal health care policies. Clinton's rhetoric was too broad and generic, offering his plan as a solution to all problems. President Obama, on the other hand, discussed the advantages of the key precepts of the plan, ultimately building support for each.

The tension between President Obama's institutional burdens illustrates that presidents face tremendous challenges in attempting to lead public opinion. Tackling some of the most pressing and controversial problems the nation faced in a generation (two wars, financial disaster) served up rare leadership burdens. A congested and calamitous political environment now seems the norm. Indeed, the data from my previous work demonstrate that later presidents are afflicted with several more negative conditions than earlier presidents. These factors demonstrate that as presidents face more constraints on their leadership (in the form of countervailing elements or agents), their ability to communicate with the public (and therefore lead the public) declines. Yet, as the preceding discussion uncovers, President Obama has overcome many of these barriers to success by acutely realizing the limitations of presidential leadership and navigating around them.

Notes

1. Kate Kenski, Bruce W. Hardy and Kathleen Hall Jamieson, *The Obama Victory: How Media, Money and Message Shaped the 2008 Election* (Oxford: Oxford University Press, 2010).

2. Sheryl Gay Stolbert, "Obama Says Nation Can't Afford the Politics of No," *New York Times,* January 28, 2010, A1.

3. George C. Edwards III. *On Deaf Ears: The Limits of the Bully Pulpit* (New Haven: Yale University Press, 2003).

4. Benjamin I. Page, Robert Y. Shapiro and Glenn Dempsey, "What Moves Public Opinion?" *American Political Science Review* 81 (1987): 23–44; and Jeffrey E. Cohen, *The Presidency in the Era of 24-Hour News* (Princeton: Princeton University Press, 2008).

5. Joel Aberbach and Bert Rockman, "Hard Times for Presidential Leadership? (And How Would We Know?)" *Presidential Studies Quarterly* 29 (1999): 757–78; and Edwards, *On Deaf Ears.*

6. Reed L. Welch, "Presidential Success in Communicating with the Public through Televised Addresses," *Presidential Studies Quarterly* 33 (2003): 347–65; Reed L. Welch, "Was Reagan Really a Great Communicator? The Influence of Televised Addresses on Public Opinion," *Presidential Studies Quarterly* 33 (2003): 853–76; and Garry Young and William B. Perkins, "Presidential Rhetoric, the Public Agenda, and the End of Presidential Television's 'Golden Age,'" *Journal of Politics* 67 (2005): 1190–205.

7. Samuel Kernell and Laurie L. Rice, "Cable and the Partisan Polarization of the President's Audience," *Presidential Studies Quarterly* 41 (2011): 693–711.

8. Joel D. Aberbach and Bert A. Rockman, "Hard Times for Presidential Leadership? (And How Would We Know?)" *Presidential Studies Quarterly* 29 (1999): 757–778.

9. Richard E. Neustadt, "The Weakening White House," *British Journal of Political Science* 31(2001): 1–11.

10. Kernell, *Going Public.*

11. Edwards, *On Deaf Ears.*

12. Bert A Rockman and Richard W. Waterman, "Two Normative Models of Presidential Leadership," in *Presidential Leadership: The Vortex of Power,* ed. Bert A. Rockman and Richard W. Waterman (New York: Oxford University Press, 2008).

13. Theodore Lowi, *The Personal Presidency: Power Invested Promise Unfulfilled* (Ithaca, NY: Cornell University Press, 1985).

14. Andreas Wenger and Marcel Gerber, "John F. Kennedy and the Limited Test Ban Treaty: A Case Study of Presidential Leadership." *Presidential Studies Quarterly* 29 (1999): 460–87.

15. John W. Sloan, *The Reagan Effect: Economics and Presidential Leadership* (Lawrence: University of Kansas Press, 1999).

16. Lawrence R. Jacobs and Robert Y. Shapiro, "The Rise of Presidential Polling: The Nixon White House in Historical Perspective." *Public Opinion Quarterly* 59 (1995): 163–95.

17. B. Dan Wood, *The Politics of Economic Leadership: The Causes and Consequences of Presidential Rhetoric* (Princeton: Princeton University Press, 2007).

18. Jeffrey Cohen, *Going Local* (New York: Cambridge University Press, 2010), 2. Andrew W. Barrett and Jeffrey S. Peake, "When the President Comes to Town: Examining Local Newspaper Coverage of Domestic Presidential Travel," *American Politics Research* 35 (2007): 3–31; Matthew Eshbaugh-Soha, "Local Newspaper Coverage of the Presidency," *International Journal of Politics/Press* 13 (2008): 103–119; and Matthew Eshbaugh-Soha and Jeffrey S. Peake, "'Going Local' to Reform Social Security," *Presidential Studies Quarterly* 36 (2006): 689–704.

19. Brandice Canes-Wrone, *Who Leads Whom? Presidents, Policy and the Public* (Chicago: University of Chicago Press, 2006). Lee Sigelman, "Disarming the Opposition: The President, the Public, and the INF Treaty." *Public Opinion Quarterly* 54 (1990): 37–47. Alan J. Rosenblatt, "Aggressive Foreign Policy Marketing: Public Response to Reagan's 1983 Address on Lebanon and Grenada." *Public Behavior* 20 (1998): 225–40.

20. Matthew Baum and Tim Groeling, "What Gets Covered?" in *In the Public Domain*, eds. Lori Cox Han and Diane Heith (Albany: State University of New York Press, 2005).

21. See Edwards, *On Deaf Ears;* and Cohen, *The Presidency in the Era of 24-Hour News.*

22. Rottinghaus, "Strategic Leaders."

23. Rottinghaus, "Strategic Leaders."

24. Cohen, *The Presidency in the Era of 24-Hour News.*

25. William Branigin and Michael D. Shear, "Senate Passes Economic Stimulus Bill," *Washington Post,* February 10, 2009, A1.

26. Anne E. Kornblut and Michael D. Shear, "Obama Says He Erred in Nominations," *Washington Post,* February 4, 2009, A1.

27. Martha Joynt Kumar, *Managing the President's Message: The White House Communications Operation* (Baltimore: Johns Hopkins University Press, 2007).

28. The President also gave an exclusive interview with ABC's *Nightline* that aired the evening of his visit to Fort Myers.

29. A three-day rolling Gallup Poll; the question asked: "Do you approve or disapprove of the way Barack Obama is handling his job as president?" The poll was conducted February 6–8, 2009. Twenty-one percent disapproved. See Rottinghaus, *The Provisional Pulpit.*

30. Jeff Zelney, "Already Back on the Trail, Now to Sell a Stimulus Plan," *New York Times,* February 8, 2009, A1.

31. The poll was a *USA Today*/Gallup Poll taken January 27, February 4, and February 10, 2009. The poll question asked, "As you may know, Congress is considering a new economic stimulus package of at least 800 billion dollars. Do you favor or oppose Congress passing this legislation?"

32. David M. Herszenhorn, "Recovery Bill Gets Final Approval," *New York Times,* February 13, 2009, A1.

33. Alessandra Stanley, "Situation Report: The Dilemma of Afghanistan," *New York Times,* October 13, 2009, C1.

34. Helene Cooper, "Putting Stamp on Afghan War, Obama Will Send 17,000 Troops," *New York Times,* February 18, 2009, A1.

35. Sheryl Gay Stolberg. "Obama Defends Afghanistan as a 'War of Necessity,'" *New York Times,* August 18, 2009, A6.

36. Graham Bowley, "How to Sell a War: First, Start to Win," *New York Times,* October 11, 2009, WK4.

37. Associated Press Poll, October 6, 2009. "Do you favor or oppose the war in Afghanistan?"

38. Poll was a *USA Today*/Gallup Poll taken on September 23, 2009, and October 6, 2009. The question asked: "Would you favor or oppose a decision by President Obama to send more US troops to Afghanistan?"

39. Scott Wilson, "On War, Obama Could Turn to G.O.P.," *Washington Post,* October 1, 2009, A1.

40. Peter Wallsten, "G.O.P. Targets Obama's Foreign Policy," *Los Angeles Times,* October 2, 2009, A 21.

41. Peter Baker and Dexter Filkins, "Obama to Weigh Buildup Option in Afghan War," *New York Times,* September 1, 2009, A1.

42. The *CBS News/New York Times* Poll asked, "As you may know, Barack Obama announced that an additional 30,000 US troops will be sent to Afghanistan in the coming months. Do you approve or disapprove of sending additional troops to Afghanistan?" Six percent responded "unsure."

43. Matt Bai, "The Insiders," *New York Times Magazine,* June 7, 2009, 12.

44. Robert Pear and Jackie Calmes. "As Obama Pushes Health Issue, Cost Concerns Arise," *New York Times,* June 16, 2009, A1.

45. Jeff Zeleny and Dalia Sussman. "Obama Poll Sees Doubt on Budget and Health Care," *New York Times,* June 18, 2009, A1.

46. Sheryl Gay Stolberg, "Obama to Forge a Greater Role on Health Care," *New York Times,* June 7, 2009, A1.

47. Sheryl Gay Stolberg, "Obama Takes a Health Care Hiatus," *New York Times,* October 21, 2009, A13.

48. Peter Baker, "Obama Complains About the News Cycle but Dominates It, Worrying Some," *New York Times,* July 24, 2009, A6.

49. Katharine Q. Seeyle, "President's Approach to Selling Health Care Becomes More Focused," *New York Times,* October 11, 2009, A1.

50. The data are from ABC/*Washington Post* polls. The question asks: "Do you approve or disapprove of the way Obama is handling health care?"

51. Ian Urbina, "Health Debate Turns Hostile at Town Hall Meetings," *New York Times,* August 8, 2009, A1.

52. Brian, Knowlton, Kevin Sack and Robert Pear, "Obama Making Push on Health as G.O.P. Steps up Criticism," *New York Times,* July 21, 2009, A1.

53. Michael Shear and Ceci Connoly, "Debate's Path Caught Obama by Surprise," *Washington Post,* August 19, 2009, A1.

54. Kent Tedin, Brandon Rottinghaus, and Harrell Rodgers, "When the President Goes Public: The Consequences of Communication Mode for Opinion Change across Issue Types and Groups," *Political Research Quarterly* 64 (2011), 506–19.

55. The data are from ABC/*Washington Post* polls. The question asked, "Would you support or oppose having the government create a new health insurance plan to compete with private health insurance plans?"

56. Sheryl Gay Stolbert, "Obama Rallies Supporters on Health Care," *New York Times,* September 8, 2009, A1.

57. Jeff Zeleny, "Hitting Talk Shows, Obama Defends Health Care Agenda," *New York Times,* September 21, 2009, A1.

58. Sheryl Gay Stolbert, "Obama Takes a Health Care Hiatus," *New York Times,* October 21, 2009, A1.

59. Jackie Calmes, "A Policy Debacle and its Lessons," *New York Times,* September 6, 2009, A1.

60. Sheryl Gay Stolberg and Jeff Zeleny, "Obama Moves to Reclaim the Debate on Health Care," *New York Times,* July 23, 2009, A1.

61. Carl Hulse and Robert Pear, "Sweeping Health Care Plan Passes House," *New York Times,* November 8, 2009, A1.

62. Sheryl Gay Stolberg, "Obama Steers Health Debate Out of Capital," *New York Times,* June 30, 2009, A1.

63. David Leonhardt, "Challenge to Health Bill: Selling Reform," *New York Times,* July 22, 2009, A1.

64. Michael D. Shear, "White House Revamps Communication Strategy." *Washington Post,* February 14, 2010, A1.

65. Dan Blaz, "For Obama, A Tough Year to Get the Message Out," *Washington Post,* January 10, 2010, A1.

66. See Edwards, *On Deaf Ears: The Limits of the Bully Pulpit;* Matthew Eshbaugh-Soha, *The President's Speeches: Beyond "Going Public"* (Boulder, CO: Lynne Rienner Publishers, 2006); and Cohen, *The Presidency in the Era of 24-Hour News.*

CHAPTER 5

Where's the Media?

President Obama, the Public, and News Coverage

MATTHEW ESHBAUGH-SOHA

Presidential leadership of public opinion is a central topic of debate in the presidential studies literature. On the one hand are those who argue that presidential rhetoric is an effective and important tool of presidential leadership.[1] Presidents may speak to improve their job approval ratings,[2] set the public's agenda,[3] influence media coverage,[4] or even alter the "national conversation" on important policy issues, including people's perceptions and beliefs about government and politics.[5] That rhetoric is vital to an effective presidency is also concomitant with what Samuel Kernell calls "going public." When presidents go public, Kernell argues, they appeal directly for public support, which puts pressure on legislators to support the president's policies.[6]

On the other hand are those who question the expectation that presidential rhetoric will move public opinion. George C. Edwards III's critical treatise on the president's rhetorical leadership of public opinion, in particular, shows that two of the most rhetorically-gifted presidents—Reagan and Clinton—could not move public opinion on their top policy priorities.[7] Even earlier claims that national addresses increased the president's public job approval ratings[8] appear time-bound[9] and are an ineffective means to move public opinion for recent presidents.[10] Edwards has long called into question the benefits of presidential rhetoric, arguing that although it appears to have the potential to affect the public's opinion, evidence that rhetoric actually does affect public opinion is lacking.[11]

What is missing from this larger debate is the role that the news media play in the president's prospects for rhetorical leadership, that is, their ability to move public opinion through public speeches. Without question, the presidency has an immense institutional apparatus resourced to affect news coverage.[12] But the complications of presidential leadership of the public are confounded in the new media age.[13] Presidents have more opportunities to reach the public, whether through Twitter, YouTube, or the White House's official Web page, yet their efforts are undermined simultaneously by a corresponding depression in newspaper readership and network news audiences, and an increase in available channels and outlets that presidents must reach to communicate to the American people. Presidents have fewer opportunities to speak directly to large prime-time audiences with national addresses and also have to contend with often negative and superficial news coverage of their administrations.[14] Thus, the president's success at rhetorical leadership depends ever more on his ability to first lead news coverage.[15]

To his credit, President Obama was well aware of the institutional burden that the new media environment placed on his presidency. In an interview with George Stephanopoulos on January 20, 2010, the president reasoned that:

> In this political environment, what I haven't always been success-
> ful at doing is breaking through the noise and speaking directly to
> the American people in a way that during the campaign you could
> do. You know I'd just get...I wouldn't be here and I wouldn't be
> bogged down with how are we negotiating this provision or that
> provision of a bill. I could speak directly to people and hear from
> them.

Whether the president's failures to change the tone in Washington, increase public support for health care reform, or improve the economy can be reduced to a failure of communication,[16] President Obama recognized the central difficulties faced by presidents in the current political environment. This "noise," the endless rambling of the twenty-four-hour news cycle, Internet, and countervailing opinions in a more partisan media and government environment, makes public leadership even more difficult than it may have been in previous political eras.[17] One might surmise that of anyone, President Obama, as he transitioned from campaigner to president, had the oratory skills to penetrate this "noise" and reach the American people. Whether President Obama did so, given his institutional burden of overcoming a news media focused on the superficial and negative rather than substance, is the focus of this essay.

Obama's Campaign and First-Year News Coverage

The general perception of Barack Obama's relationship with the news media throughout his campaign and first year in office was that it was overwhelmingly positive. As the first African American nominated by a major party as its presidential candidate, Obama provided an obvious story line and ample opportunity for abundant news coverage throughout the 2008 presidential campaign. The political context at the president's inauguration, including an economic recession and two wars, provided him with the opportunity to build a transformative presidency.[18] But with his historical election and opportunity also came heightened expectations to lead the nation. Although the general perception of favorable news coverage persisted during the campaign[19] and his first few months in office, it appears as if heightened expectations and the president's institutional burden to generate favorable news coverage contributed, ultimately, to less favorable news coverage, especially on his major policy initiatives.

According to the Project for Excellence in Journalism (PEJ), candidate Obama enjoyed more positive television news coverage overall, by a margin of 36 percent to 14 percent, than his opponent, Senator John McCain, during the 2008 general election campaign.[20] Even so, Obama still received far less than a majority of positive campaign coverage. And although his positive coverage was much higher than Democratic candidate Al Gore's 13 percent positive coverage in 2000 (compared with 24 percent positive for Bush), it was on par, nevertheless, with PEJ's 34 percent tally of positive news coverage for Senator Kerry in 2004 (compared with 15 percent positive for President Bush). What is more telling, the PEJ reports that 55 percent of all news coverage of the 2008 campaign was on the horse race, but only 25 percent concerned policy. Because Barack Obama led in the polls for much of the campaign, it is no surprise that horse race–dominated coverage would be mostly positive for him. However, the assumption that the media were uncritically supportive of Obama would have led one to believe that he received overwhelming positive *policy* coverage from the news media, as well.[21]

As president, Obama enjoyed considerably more news coverage than either of his two predecessors during each president's first fifty days in office. The three network news programs devoted 1021 stories, at 27 hours and 44 minutes to Barack Obama, with a daily average of seven stories and 11 minutes. In contrast, they devoted only 7 hours and 42 minutes to the George W. Bush presidency during early 2001, down from the 15 hours and 2 minutes of coverage that Bill Clinton received during his first 50 days in 1993.[22] President Obama actually received the most coverage from FOX News's *Special Report with Brett Baier* with 1789 stories—762 more than the highest amount of network news coverage on NBC. Alas, very little of this coverage had to do with his policies.[23] What is more, the president's daughters (Sasha and Malia) received more news coverage (37 and 35 stories, respectively) than two-thirds of the president's cabinet, White House Chief of Staff Rahm Emanuel, and the Director of the CIA![24]

President Obama's news coverage also began positively, at least when his policies were not the story. During his first fifty days, Obama's overall news coverage was approximately 58 percent positive, compared with 44 percent and 33 percent positive coverage for Presidents Clinton and George W. Bush early in their administrations. Yet he received only 39 percent positive coverage of his policies, with much positive coverage devoted to personal issues and the historical significance of his election victory. Although Obama received a majority of positive coverage for 2009 (52 percent), the tone of his policy coverage was only 39 percent positive. Moreover, his coverage became more negative throughout his first year in office. His fourth quarter in office ended with only 39 percent positive coverage, which is 1 percentage point lower than George W. Bush during the fourth quarter of his first year in office.[25] Coverage of President Obama on Fox News was much worse, with 79 percent negative coverage overall and 85 percent negative coverage of his policies.

These numbers denote that President Obama's first year in office was the most newsworthy in a generation. However, being on the news is insufficient for presidents to convey the message *they wish to convey* to the public. As the Fox News example illustrates, even a substantial amount of news coverage can be mostly negative—noise that obstructs the president's path to public leadership. Moreover, Obama's positive coverage plummeted throughout his first year in office, much as we would expect for all presidents,[26] and he never received a majority of positive coverage of his policies. Unfortunately, this is the reality—and burden—that worked against the president's prospects for effective public leadership.

Expectations for Obama's Public Leadership

Given the historical significance of President Obama's election and the president's initially voluminous news coverage, expectations mounted that he would be a more successful leader than other modern presidents, on par with presidential greats of the twentieth century. He enjoyed a landslide victory in the Electoral College—being the first Democratic president to receive over 50 percent of the popular vote since 1976—and came into office the beneficiary of popular enthusiasm and with the institutional advantages of super majorities in both Houses of Congress. Numerous early popular comparisons of President Obama to FDR (depicted on the November 24, 2008, cover of *Time* magazine with an FDR-styled cigarette and 1930s-era suit and hat) and JFK[27] further fed expectations.

Especially given his political advantages, Obama was in a unique position to command the attention of the American people through his public rhetoric. All presidents wield the power of the bully pulpit, after all, generating the most news exposure of any American politician. The bully pulpit may enable presidents to marshal a vast array of institutional resources to communicate their policy preferences to the American people. Even so, successful rhetorical leadership—the president's ability to move public opinion through his speeches—is only likely to occur under certain circumstances. First, the available means of communication matters. When presidents can speak on national television, they communicate directly with the American people and often without an opposition response, which is likely to increase public support for the president's position.[28] Because presidents can generate news for their domestic travels,[29] they succeed by "barnstorming"—relentlessly promoting their messages, not the opposition's—which can increase public support for the president's policy preference as well.[30]

The second condition may be an even more compelling and a potentially more predictive element of effective rhetorical leadership. Put simply, the more malleable the public's preferences are on an issue, the greater the president's opportunity to shift the public's support in his favor. It is not that presidents cause myriad Americans to flip their policy preferences from supportive to opposed, or vice-versa. Rather, presidents may lead those who are uncertain of their policy preferences or who have not thought enough about an issue to form a clear preference.[31]

A third, but often neglected condition is the state of the media environment. Even if the president chooses the right public forums in which to speak and has a sizeable undecided population to more easily persuade, he must contend with a media environment that is motivated more by profit, entertainment, and conflict than acquiescence to the president's message. Obama's media environment especially, one characterized by more channels, fragmented audiences, and the "echo chamber" of conservative media[32] may have hurt his leadership success both by limiting the prospects for effective leadership through otherwise favorable speeches and reducing the number of undecided (and persuadable) hearers on key issues.

The president certainly attempted to maximize his prospects of leading the public by holding several primetime addresses and traveling frequently around the nation. His comments during his fourth prime-time presidential news conference, that the arrest of Professor Henry Louis Gates Jr. of Harvard was "stupid," illustrate one of the difficulties in relying on media to lead the public, however. It was this response, not his answers to questions about health care reform, which drove the week's news. Partisan media confounded the president too. The Tea Party Express, fueled by conservative media, guided a partisan voice against the president,[33] helping to reduce the percentage of the population open to persuasion. Below I elaborate upon the interrelationship among the president, the news media, and the public, using two key examples from Obama's first twelve months in office.

Two Cases of Obama's Public Leadership

Whether one contends that rhetorical skill is central to effective presidential leadership of the public[34] or leadership likelihood is conditional upon speech type and public salience,[35] scholars who debate these arguments often neglect the dominant role that the news media play in the possibility of the president leading the public. Perhaps we should not be surprised that recent presidents have had no significant impact over public opinion given the array of news and other entertainment options on cable television and the Internet. The prospects suggest, nevertheless, that when presidents can penetrate the filter of the news media—when they can speak directly to the American people—then, given an uncertain public and other favorable conditions, presidents may be able to lead public opinion. When presidents do not have this luxury, then presidential rhetoric is likely to remain ineffective.

I examine two cases from the Obama administration to explore these considerations—the president's 2010 State of the Union Address and his efforts to lead on health care in fall 2009. Using these examples, I contend that the media environment at once confounded the president's leadership efforts through his State of the Union address and also contributed to uncertainty surrounding the president's health care policies. Both of these conditions contributed to a lack of effective rhetorical leadership. I selected the 2010 State of the Union address given its proximity to the president's one-year anniversary in office and because it was the first major address after Democrats lost a filibuster-proof majority control in the Senate, forcing the president to consider first, and on national television, his diminished political standing and a more burdensome institutional environment. I examine health care reform because it was the centerpiece of the president's discretionary domestic policy agenda, one characterized by intense media coverage and high expectations.

2010 STATE OF THE UNION

On January 27, 2010, President Barack Obama delivered his first official State of the Union address before joint session of Congress. The president had hoped to use this forum to claim credit for reforming health care, one of his central campaign promises. On the heels of a Republican senatorial victory in the normally dark-blue state of Massachusetts, however, the fate of health care reform remained tentative. President Obama used the address instead to remind Americans of the "big and difficult challenges" that the country faced. He reached out to unemployed Americans, offering a jobs bill with both spending for small business loans and tax incentives for businesses to create jobs. He offered a spending freeze and a promise to reduce the budget deficit by $1 trillion over ten years. Additionally, he renewed the call for health care reform when he said: "Here's what I ask Congress: Don't walk away from reform. Not now. Not when we are so close. Let us find a way to come together and finish the job for the American people. Let's get it done. Let's get it done."

Americans responded warmly to this address, according to the data compiled from a *CBS News/Knowledge Networks* Poll in Table 5.1. Among those who watched the address, an overwhelming 83 percent supported the proposals that the president outlined in the speech.[36] The president scored gains across the board, averaging a 16 percentage point improvement in his handling of the major issues of the speech, including Afghanistan, the economy, jobs, and even health care.[37] Nevertheless, the president was unable to convince a majority of viewers that he would actually be able to accomplish his goals.[38]

This is exactly what many expect from presidential State of the Union

TABLE 5.1.

Public Opinion before and after 2010 State of the Union Address

Question	Before	After
Shares Priorities	57%	70%
Plan for Creating Jobs	40	59
Approval Dealing with:		
Health Care	54	67
Afghanistan	58	74
Economy	55	76

Source: *CBS News/Knowledge Networks Poll, January 27, 2010.*

addresses in general and especially from a president with the oratory skills of Barack Obama. But is this an example of rhetorical leadership? Perhaps. Clearly, the president scored improvements on each question *among those who watched the address* and should be given credit for reaching these viewers positively and in the short term. Yet, Obama wanted to lead the entire population, not just those who watched his speech. Therefore, knowing that 48 million Americans watched the president's address, according to Nielsen, is important. Although this pales in comparison to the viewership presidents enjoyed during the 1970s, it is on par with what both Presidents Bush and Clinton received in their 2002 and 1997 State of the Union addresses, respectively, and is about the number of viewers who watched the president's first Address to a Joint Session of Congress on the economic stimulus bill, February 9, 2009. Even so, there are approximately 230 million American of voting age, meaning that only 21 percent of the adult voting population watched the president deliver his address, with an even smaller percentage supporting the president's policies.

The rest of the population, if they even heard of the president's speech and his policy proposal at all, would have received their information through the news media, which may or may not have reported on the substance of the address. Indeed, the new media environment presented a paradox to President Obama's leadership capacity. On the one hand, the president has reached vastly different audiences with weekly Internet (not radio) addresses, answered questions from citizens on YouTube, and appeared on *The Daily Show with John Stewart* to engage young voters in a more relaxed and humorous setting. On the other hand, just as sensationalism in the news has increased, so too has the number of news stories without any mention of public policy,[39] which limits the president's ability to communicate his policy preferences through the news. Cable television and its news channels may undermine presidential management of the news by concurrently reducing the number of accidental viewers of the president's speeches,[40] while further isolating partisan conservatives to the echo chamber of anti-Obama rhetoric.[41] It appears that new media compound the president's institutional burden. For example, just as social media provided the president with an opportunity to reach young voters during the 2008 presidential election, so too did social media fail to motivate campaign followers to support health care reform.[42]

For this reason, the media's reaction to the speech becomes paramount to the prospects for presidential leadership of the public. In other words, the president's policy rhetoric is only as good as the news coverage he receives for those citizens who did not watch the speech live or online. As expected, the State of the Union Address, according to the Project for Excellence in Journalism (PEJ), occupied about 19 percent of the news hole for the week. Yet the economy, at 18 percent, and the Haitian earthquake, at 11 percent of the news hole, restricted the president's singular access to the mainstream media. PEJ's "new media index," moreover, did not register the State of the Union Address in the top five stories for the week of the address, January 25–29, 2010. A limited audience and limited news coverage should undermine the durability of the public's response to the president's address.

Furthermore, public opinion data recorded after the speech revealed no continued benefit for the president. Although slightly more respondents supported the president's health care reform efforts one-week after the speech, the percentage of the public who approved of the president's handling of health care dropped to its lowest point, at 43 percent.[43] President Obama gained a couple of points on his approval ratings after the address, according to Gallup's daily tracking poll. But this too faded to pre-speech numbers only one week after the address. Although the public generally supported his position on gays and lesbians in the military, this should not be considered an example of presidential leadership because the public had held this position for a decade.[44]

HEALTH CARE REFORM

Although the State of the Union Address provides limited direct and short-term evidence of presidential rhetorical leadership, perhaps this is not the best test case. After all, only short-term leadership of the public is likely through the State of the Union Address.[45] Thus, a better test case may be concerning the president's efforts at health care reform. If President Obama succeeded in leading the public and news media on health care reform, an issue that divided Americans throughout 2009 and 2010, then this would be a glowing example of effective rhetorical leadership, especially given the burdensome media environment the president faced.

On September 9, 2009, President Obama delivered a national address specifically on health care reform, a valuable opportunity to generate news coverage and lead public opinion. Unfortunately for the president, public support for the president's health care reform policies changed little. Those who felt Obama had explained his health care position nudged from 31 percent to 32 percent.[46] Although more Americans approved of Obama's handling of health care after (47 percent) than before (40 percent) his address,[47] this was still less than a majority,[48] which is a necessary threshold for presidents to use public support to move Congress to act. These numbers provide little evidence that the president's September address to the nation was a leadership success.

National addresses are not the only weapon in the president's rhetorical arsenal, however. Presidents can also attempt to influence public opinion by sustained attention to an issue through numerous speeches. A majority had supported the public option, and to the president's credit, more of the public supported the idea as the president "barnstormed" his health care reform ideas in October 2009. Nevertheless, support was highest in June before Obama turned his full attention to health care reform and the public option in the summer of 2009.[49] If Obama had led the public, then we would expect to see an increasing trend throughout the summer, not an initial decline. Moreover, presidential rhetoric may require a focused message for presidents to be effective leaders. But the president's public rhetoric took a conciliatory tone, in which he did not demand a public option but surmised that it was but one part of overall health care reform. Therefore, it is difficult to attribute the increase in support for the public option as a response to President Obama's lukewarm endorsement of it. Besides, more of the public thought the public option to be "necessary" just as Obama began to say that it was not vital to a comprehensive reform bill![50] Over the long haul, moreover, public support declined, even as the president spoke consistently about health care reform and the public option.[51] We see a similar trend in support for the president's handling of health care reform.[52]

A striking feature of public opinion on health care reform is the percentage of those who remained undecided about reform (see Table 5.2).[53] Just as the public's predispositions drive opinion, this uncertainty provided presidents with the opportunity to lead because those who are uncertain are more persuadable.[54] Yet despite ample effort—a national address, numerous speeches, interviews by the president and White House staff—the president did not move the undecideds to support his policy. What is more, the public was unequivocally "confused" about health care reform in the summer of 2009, even after much of the president's public relations efforts.[55]

These numbers suggest that President Obama failed to lead despite having the potential to do so. Theoretically, the president's speeches provided more information to the public, which should have reduced its uncertainty about health care reform and perhaps encouraged support of the president's position. Yet when the public is uncertain about something—in this case whether they supported the public option and, perhaps, whether the president did—they are more likely to oppose it.[56] These conflicting possibilities for presidential leadership suggest that if presidents are unable to shift those who are unsure about a policy even after providing them with more information, there must be something that is preventing the president from reaching the public. Although much research on the question of uncertainty and public preferences focuses on election campaigns, it is still instructive for my assertions. Simply, more media exposure can increase uncertainty about a candidate, and more uncertainty increases opposition.[57] In other words, it is likely that media coverage of health care reform increased uncertainty surrounding the president's position.

TABLE 5.2.

Public Support for Health Care Reform

Date	Favor	Oppose	Unsure
1/28–31/10	40%	51%	12%
11/19–22/09	34	46	20
10/29–11/1/09	39	49	12
10/1–5/09	40	42	18
8/27–31/09	40	45	15

Source: *Ipsos/McClatchy Poll, "As of right now, do you favor or oppose the health care reform proposals presently being discussed?"*

The media environment in the summer of 2009 speaks to this very point as it clearly exacerbated the president's difficulty in expressing his policy message to the American people. During the congressional recesses, many members of Congress held town hall–styled meetings in their districts. The primary topic, still being debated in congressional committee, was health care reform. The opposition was fierce, concentrated in what the new media called "Town Halls Gone Wild."[58] Aided by conservative news reports that described health care reform as a government takeover or socialized medicine, the newly emboldened Tea Party effectively organized opposition to the reform effort. The cornerstone of opposition was that the proposal would subject elderly Americans not only to cuts in their Medicare benefits, but also to "death panels," which stoked fear that the government would stop treating the critically ill to save costs. Recall that most Americans were unclear about the president's positions on health care reform, even after his prime-time July press conference on this subject. This uncertainty did not lessen amid news coverage that focused on the few negative, but also entertaining, shouting matches that occurred at congressional town hall meetings.

The data support the idea that the tenor of news coverage affected public support for health care reform. According to Figure 5.1, opposition to the public option increased through the month of August and then declined. This tracks closely and inversely with news coverage, which during August 2009 focused almost exclusively on the negative and raucous shouting matches at town hall meetings. According to the PEJ, nearly 35 percent of all network news and 65 percent of cable news stories in mid-August 2009 covered health care. When Congress returned to session and news coverage shifted to other issues, such as Afghanistan and the more mundane policy process in Washington, opposition lessened, and support for the public option began to rebound toward where it had been at the beginning of the summer. In fact, health care reform garnered only 39 percent positive coverage through 2009.[59] Simply put, heightened negative news coverage increased uncertainty about health care reform policy, which helped to depress public support.

Not only was negative news coverage problematic for the president, so too was the superficial coverage that occurred after President Obama's national address on health care reform. Although most of the news coverage during the week of the president's speech focused on health care reform, it did not center on the implications of the president's policy. It

FIGURE 5.1.

News coverage and support for the public option, 2009

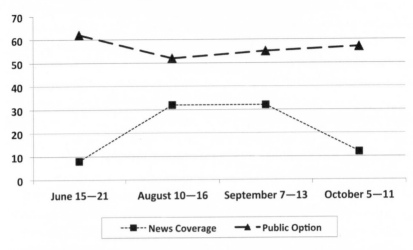

Sources: *ABC/*Washington Post *poll: Would you support or oppose having the government create a new health insurance plan to compete with private health insurance plans? Project for Excellence in Journalism, News Coverage Index.*

focused instead on the political strategy of the address and Representative Joe Wilson's "You lie!" outburst during the address from the House floor.[60] The PEJ reports that health care reform garnered about a third of the total coverage for the week of September 7–13, 2009, on network television news and over 45 percent of the coverage on cable news channels. It also notes that most of the health care coverage focused on the strategy of the speech, its political impact, and Wilson's outburst. For presidents to be effective policy leaders in the new media age, even as they deliver major addresses and barnstorm their policies before the American people, they need positive and at least substantive coverage to reduce uncertainty among the public. Yet both were absent during the peak of the health care reform debate in the late summer and early fall of 2009, a function of a more sensational news environment.

Recall Obama's remarks about the "noise" of news coverage. That the president could not reach through negative and superficial news coverage to make his point to the American people may be one reason why he fretted that his failures were products of ineffective communication.

That presidents must penetrate this noise to lead public opinion, however difficult it may be to overcome this institutional burden, is clearly borne out by this discussion. Ironically, it appears that the president was in his strongest position to do this as the amount of news on health care reform declined. As opposition to health care reform became less newsworthy after August 2009—when news coverage shifted from the grass-roots versus AstroTurf, or orchestrated, nature of the town-hall exchanges[61] to the president's barnstorming tour—then the president may have been more likely to garner coverage on the news, and his voice, at least relatively speaking, may have been more forceful in the absence of the sustained noise of the opposition.

Even if we seek to credit Obama with a leadership success after accounting for news coverage of the public option, we should still seek alternative explanations for what drove news coverage during October 2009. Although it may have served to benefit the president, other non-presidential influences may have driven news coverage during the resurgence of support for the public option. According to the PEJ, the "health care narrative was driven, at least in part, by the news that the so-called public option could be enjoying something of a revival" for the week October 19–25, 2009. At the same time, "the NewsHour reported on a push by liberal groups and labor unions to re-open the battle for the 'public option' that was not in the Senate Finance bill"[62] (October 12–18, 2009). If the efforts that generated positive news coverage for the public option can be attributed to Obama's rhetoric, then we can infer that the president had a modest, indirect impact on the public by altering news coverage. The evidence presented here is too thin to maintain that the president was successful overcoming the institutional burden of the news media, and only future research can substantiate these claims further.

Conclusion

If the foundation of modern presidential power is rhetorical leadership, then the presidency is faced with increasing powerlessness over assuaging perhaps its greatest institutional burden: the news media. Although relatively positive news coverage may have helped candidate Obama's presidential election campaign, it may have also heightened the public's expectations for pronounced and immediate policy change. Driven by mostly negative policy news coverage, media did not help the president meet these expectations. What is more, news coverage did not facilitate passage of the president's economic stimulus or health care reform policies, leading me to conclude that the president's difficulty in leading public opinion was only exacerbated by this institutional burden he faced.

This essay recognizes that presidential leadership of the public has become even more challenging in the new media age and a more burdensome media environment. This perspective contrasts directly with those who would surmise that effective presidential leadership rests with the president's ability to make an emotional connection with the American people and, in so doing, inspire them to follow the president's vision for the United States.[63] It is not a lack of an emotional connection that has burdened the president's leadership. Instead, that Barack Obama's story of public leadership appears to track those of earlier presidents serves to confirm that even an inspirational president will produce no more movement among public preferences than any other, less gifted speaker, absent a less burdensome news environment.

Just as President Obama conceded that new media "noise" complicates his leadership effectiveness, he remained insistent that this is a burden that presidents can and should be able to overcome. That is, if he could just do a better job communicating, his presidency would look much different. Responding to a question on January 20, 2010, by an *ABC News* correspondent, the president replied:

> And, you know, if there's one thing that I regret this year, is that we were so busy just getting stuff done and dealing with the immediate crises that were in front of us, that I think we lost some of that sense of speaking directly to the American people about what their core values are and why we have to make sure those institutions are matching up with those values. And that I do think is a mistake of mine.

If the president is correct, then a change in strategy may have encouraged different judgments by the news media and the court of public opinion. But Obama held a prime-time press conference on health care reform, delivered a national address on the subject, and stumped frequently about it. If he still failed to drive news coverage and move public opinion after these efforts, what else could he have done? Speak more? Deliver another national address? It seems unlikely that more effort was needed or that more carefully crafted words would have swayed the public. Thus, the president's greatest burden—not just Obama's, but all presidents' perhaps—may be to overcome the institutional burden of the media environment that confounds successful leadership of the public. That many Americans were unsure about health care reform cannot be blamed solely on the president's inability to communicate. But rather, news coverage of public policy is likely to undermine and inhibit the president's effectiveness in leading public opinion, rendering the new rhetorical presidency prisoner to a decentralized and increasingly fragmented new media, one that may have been initially supportive of the Obama presidency, but one that was never enthusiastic about his policies.

Notes

1. Craig Allen Smith and Kathy B. Smith, *The White House Speaks: Presidential Leadership as Persuasion* (Westport, CT: Praeger, 1994); and David Zarefsky, *Lincoln, Douglass, and Slavery: In the Crucible of Public Debate* (Chicago: University of Chicago Press, 1990).

2. Paul Brace and Barbara Hinckley. *Follow the Leader* (New York: Basic Books, 1992).

3. Jeffrey E. Cohen, "Presidential Rhetoric and the Public Agenda," *American Journal of Political Science* 39 (1995): 87–107.

4. Jeffrey S. Peake and Matthew Eshbaugh-Soha, "The Agenda-Setting Impact of Major Presidential TV Addresses," *Political Communication* 25 (2008): 113–37.

5. Roderick P. Hart, "Thinking Harder about Presidential Discourse: The Question of Efficacy," in *The Prospect of Presidential Rhetoric,* ed. James Arnt Aune and Martin J. Medhurst (College Station: Texas A&M University Press, 2008).

6. Samuel Kernell, *Going Public: New Strategies of Presidential Leadership,* 3rd ed. (Washington, DC: CQ Press, 1997).

7. George C. Edwards III. *On Deaf Ears: The Limits of the Bully Pulpit* (New Haven, CT: Yale University Press, 2003).

8. Brace and Hinckley, *Follow the Leader.*

9. Edwards, *On Deaf Ears,* 30–32.

10. Reed L. Welch "Presidential Success in Communicating with the Public through Televised Addresses." *Presidential Studies Quarterly* 34 (2003): 347–65.

11. George C. Edwards III. "Presidential Rhetoric: What Difference Does it Make?" In *The Future of the Rhetorical Presidency,* ed. Martin J. Medhurst (College Station: Texas A&M University Press, 1996).

12. Martha Joynt Kumar, *Managing the President's Message: The White House Communications Operation* (Baltimore, MD: The Johns Hopkins University Press, 2007).

13. Jeffrey E. Cohen, *The Presidency in an Era of 24-Hour News* (Princeton, NJ: Princeton University Press, 2008).

14. Ibid.

15. Matthew Eshbaugh-Soha and Jeffrey S. Peake. *Breaking through the Noise: Presidential Leadership, Public Opinion, and the News Media* (Palo Alto, CA: Stanford University Press, 2011).

16. Edwards, *On Deaf Ears.*

17. Whereas former President George W. Bush complained of the filter of mainstream news, Hartnett and Mercieca maintain that the president fostered this "white noise" as a way to "confuse public opinion, prevent citizen action, and frustrate deliberation." Stephen Hartnett, Stephen John, and Jennifer Rose Mercieca, "'A Discovered Dissembler can Achieve Nothing Great'; or, Four Theses on the Death of Presidential Rhetoric in an Age of Empire," *Presidential Studies Quarterly* 37 (2007): 599–621.

18. Steven E. Schier, ed. *Transforming American: Barack Obama in the White House* (Lanham, MD: Rowman & Littlefield, 2011).

19. Melissa K. Miller, Jeffrey S. Peake, and Brittany Boulton, "Testing the *Saturday Night Live* Hypothesis: Fairness and Bias in Newspaper Coverage of Hillary Clinton's Presidential Campaign," *Politics & Gender* 6, (2010): 169–98.

20. Coverage for a sample of all media collected between September 8 and October 16, 2008.

21. In its more limited examination of the three networks, the Center for Media and Public Affairs shows much more positive coverage, at 68 percent for Obama and 33 percent for McCain. It also reports much less horse race coverage and much more positive policy coverage for Obama (52 percent positive). Fox News Channel's *Special Report with Brett Baier* produced only 37 percent positive coverage for Obama.

22. Donald Rieck, "Media Boost Obama, Bash his Policies," *Center for Media and Public Affairs*, April 27, 2009, http://www.cmpa.com/media_room_4_27_09.htm.

23. "White House Watch: Obama's First Year," *Media Monitor*, 24, (2010), http://www.cmpa.com/pdf/media_monitor_q1_2010.pdf.

24. Ibid.

25. Ibid.

26. Michael Baruch Grossman and Martha Joynt Kumar, *Portraying the President: The White House and the News Media* (Baltimore, MD: The Johns Hopkins University Press, 1981).

27. David Greenberg, "Playing the Tolerance Card: How Obama is like JFK," *Slate*, April 20, 2007, http://www.slate.com/id/2164662.

28. Brandon Rottinghaus, *The Provisional Pulpit: Modern Presidential Leadership of Public Opinion* (College Station: Texas A&M University Press, 2010).

29. Matthew Eshbaugh-Soha and Jeffrey S. Peake, "The Presidency and Local Media: Local Newspaper Coverage of President George W. Bush," *Presidential Studies Quarterly* 38, (2008): 609–30, and "The Contemporary Presidency: 'Going Local' to Reform Social Security," *Presidential Studies Quarterly* 36, (2006): 689–704.

30. See Brandon Rottinghaus, chapter 4, in this volume.

31. Bailey, Sigleman, and Wilcox show not that presidents can change Americans'

dichotomous preferences for policies, but rather that President Clinton was able to shift the intensity of the public's support for his position on the military's "Don't ask, don't tell" policy through his public pronouncements on the matter. Michael Bailey, Lee Sigelman, and Clyde Wilcox, "Presidential Persuasion on Social Issues: A Two-Way Street?" *Political Research Quarterly* 56, (2003): 49–58.

32. Kathleen Hall Jamieson and Joseph N. Cappella, *Echo Chamber: Rush Limbaugh and the Conservative Media Establishment* (New York: Oxford University Press, 2008).

33. Theda Skocpol and Vanessa Williamson, *The Tea Party and the Remaking of Republican Conservatism* (New York: Oxford University Press, 2012).

34. Zarefsky, *Lincoln, Douglass, and Slavery.*

35. Rottinghaus, *Provisional Pulpit.*

36. "In general do you approve or disapprove of the proposal the President made in his speech tonight?"

37. Rotating these topics, the question asks: "From what you have seen or heard, do you generally approve or disapprove of the Barack Obama's plans for dealing with…"

38. Only 42 percent responded positively to this question: "Do you think President Obama will be able to accomplish all the goals he set out in his speech tonight?"

39. Thomas E. Patterson, "Doing Well and Doing Good," *John F. Kennedy School of Government, Faculty Research Working Paper Series,* December 2000.

40. Markus Prior, *Post-Broadcast Democracy: How Media Choice Increases Inequality in Political Involvement and Polarizes Elections* (New York: Cambridge University Press, 2007).

41. Jamieson and Capella, *Echo Chamber.*

42. George C. Edwards III. *Overreach: Leadership in the Obama Presidency* (Princeton, NJ: Princeton University Press, 2012).

43. ABC News/*Washington Post* Poll, February 4–8, 2010.

44. "Do you favor or oppose allowing openly gay men and lesbian women to serve in the military?," *USA Today*/Gallup Poll: 69 % favor (5/7–10/09); 63 % favor (11/19–21/04).

45. Cohen, "Presidential Rhetoric and the Public Agenda"; Hill, Kim Quaile. "The Policy Agendas of the President and the Mass Public: A Research Validation and Extension." *American Journal of Political Science* 42, 4 (1998): 1328–34.

46. Do you think Barack Obama has clearly explained what his plans for health care reform would mean, or hasn't he clearly explained that? (August 27–31, 2009 and September 19–23, 2009) *CBS News* Poll.

47. Do you approve or disapprove of the way Barack Obama is handling health care? (August 27–31, 2009 and September 19–23, 2009) CBS News/*New York Times* Poll.

48. By December 4–8, 2009, this number had dropped to 44 percent (CBS News/*New York Times* Poll).

49. See Rottinghaus, chapter 4, in this volume.

50. Ibid.

51. The numbers continue to trend downward, dropping to 53 percent support in a November 12–15, 2009, ABC News/*Washington Post* Poll.

52. The numbers continue to trend downward, dropping to 44 percent support in a January 12–15, 2010, ABC News/*Washington Post* Poll.

53. One might infer that these numbers are inflated and thus unrepresentative. It is correct that the percentage of "Don't Knows" in several ABC News/*Washington* Post polls do not reach double digits, hovering instead between 5 and 7 percentage points. Yet the Pew Center, in response to its question concerning support or opposition to health care reform, also reports "Unsure" numbers in line with this poll. Moreover, the movement in support, without subsequent variation in those who claim to be unsure, in itself suggests a good deal of uncertainty about public support.

54. R. Michael Alvarez and John Brehm, *Hard Choices, Easy Answers* (Princeton University Press, 2002).

55. "Do you think you understand the health care reforms under consideration in Congress, or are they confusing to you?" CBS News/*New York Times* Poll. In two polls conducted in August 27–31, 2009, and September 19–23, 2009, 67 percent and 59 percent, respectively, reported that they were confused.

56. R. Michael Alvarez, *Information and Elections* (Ann Arbor: University of Michigan Press, 1998).

57. Ibid., 101, 104, and 220. Alvarez's media exposure results vary by election, with a few elections (1976 and 1988) lead to an inverse relationship between media exposure and voter uncertainty.

58. Alex Isenstadt, "Town Halls Gone Wild," *Politico,* July 31, 2009.

59. Donald Rieck, "Obama's Media Image—Compared to What?" *Center for Media and Public Affairs,* January 25, 2010, http://www.cmpa.com/media_room_press_1_25_10.html.

60. For those who do not remember, Joe Wilson, a Republican from South Carolina, claimed that the president was lying when he stated that illegal immigrants would not be covered under his plan to reform existing health care law. One of the factors that likely contributed to Representative Wilson's uncertainty—and the public's confusion about what was actually in the bill—was that several bills were being considered by multiple committees in the Senate at the time of the president's speech. Moreover, the Internet—and e-mail, especially—was a particularly useful tool for those opposed to the reform effort to spread information, which also increased uncertainty about what the bill would or would not do.

61. Mark Jurkowitz, "Town Hall Showdowns Fuel Health Care Coverage," August 3–9, 2009, *Journalism.org,* Pew Research Center, http://www.journalism.org/node/17089.

62. Mark Jurkowitz, "Health Care Re-emerges and 'Balloon Boy' Takes Flight," *Journalism.org,* Pew Research Center,, October 12–18, 2009, http://www.journalism.org/print/17954.

63. George Packer, "One Year: Obama Pays the Price," *The New Yorker,* January 20, 2010, http://www.newyorker.com/online/blogs/georgepacker/2010/01/one-year-obama-pays-the-price.html.

CHAPTER 6

The United States and the World

The Rhetorical Dimensions of Obama's Foreign Policy

DAVID ZAREFSKY

Barack Obama campaigned for the presidency at a time when the place of the United States in the world was under review. The war in Iraq had become unpopular. Indeed, one of Obama's strengths as a candidate was that he had been an early and persistent opponent of that war. For many, however, Iraq was not an isolated case but a reflection of attitudes of very long standing. They were summed in the term *American exceptionalism*, often understood as signifying that the United States is qualitatively different from, and superior to, any other nation on Earth, and hence that it is entitled to behave as it wishes. For Obama, that trajectory had run its course, meeting its demise on the deserts of Iraq, and had become counterproductive to the goal of global leadership. He sought instead to emphasize the special responsibilities of the United States to help in creating partnerships on an equal basis with other nations sharing similar values.

But if the traditional ideal of American exceptionalism had fallen out of favor abroad, it was still very much alive and well at home. In many quarters, to suggest that there were limits on Americans' ability to have their way was little short of treasonous. The Iraq war, in this view, was an aberration, not a challenge to basic premises of foreign policy or a call for its reorientation.

Obama came to office facing a dilemma. The nation's foreign policy message needed to change (in order to appeal to a global audience), and yet it appeared that it could not (because of the constraints of the domestic audience). Negotiating this difficult terrain required a sophisticated rhetoric that somehow satisfied both parts of the tension.

What follows is an exploration of the contextual burden that the moment placed on the man. The argument proceeds in four stages: a review of the long trajectory of American exceptionalism, explication of the moment facing Obama, analysis of speeches in 2008 and 2009 in which the president tried to work out a new vision, and finally a discussion of a possible alternative path.

The Trajectory of American Exceptionalism

It was Obama's contextual burden that he came to office when a rhetorical trajectory of American exceptionalism was coming to an end although many Americans did not realize it. This trajectory rests in the belief that our exceptional status derives from God, who has given us the mission of being the "saving remnant" that will purify the evil nations of the world by spreading democracy to them. This mission and its source mean that the historical experience of other nations is not necessarily relevant to the United States because they suffered limitations we do not share. God, superior to any human rules, grants dispensation to His people when doing so will achieve His purposes.

It is almost impossible to overstate the resonance of this belief system throughout the American experience. It can be traced back to the colonial period, when it was sincerely held, but also strategically useful. How better to overcome the fear of the unknown, the separation from one's community and culture, the discomforts of a long voyage, the likelihood of privation, and the risk of death than to console oneself with the knowledge that one was on an errand for the Lord? On board the *Arbella* before the Puritans landed at Massachusetts Bay, John Winthrop delivered a lay sermon exhorting his companions to make their new settlement "a model of Christian charity." He declared that if the people kept their covenant with God, then "the Lord will be our God and delight to dwell among us, as His own people, and will commend a blessing upon us in all our ways," so that the community would be "as a city upon a hill, the eyes of all people are upon us."[1] Winthrop's argument was conditional: *if* the colonists met their responsibilities and kept their covenant, *then* God would bestow His mercy upon them and make them His chosen. The Massachusetts Bay Colony witnessed continued conflict between those who maintained that the Puritans *had* fulfilled their part of the bargain and those who warned that the community was backsliding and daily risking the loss of God's favor. The widening gap between these two positions eventually doomed the Puritan experiment.

Shorn of its explicit theological rationale (though not of religious analogies), exceptionalism also helped to justify the American Revolution. In *Common Sense,* Thomas Paine's Biblical analogy was explicit: "We have it in our power to begin the world over again. A situation, similar to the present, hath not existed since the days of Noah until now."[2] As God showed favor to the descendants of Noah, He will enable the American colonists to establish a new nation that ultimately will rebuild civilization. Paine's argument also was conditional: *if* we overcome our misplaced affection, our fear of failure, and our unwillingness to act, *then* we can experience the rewards of chosenness.

The unlikely success of the Revolution provided sign evidence that divine blessing indeed had been showered upon Americans. And there were many other signs, including the availability of George Washington for national leadership just when he was most needed, the miraculous acquisition of Louisiana which doubled the nation's territory, the improbable victory of Andrew Jackson in New Orleans, the simultaneous deaths of John Adams and Thomas Jefferson on the jubilee of American independence, and the emergence of Abraham Lincoln as the savior of the Union.

The effect of all these signs was to remove the conditional nature of the exceptionalist argument. The blessings the nation enjoyed *proved* that we had acted virtuously and therefore deserved them. Never mind that this "proof" committed the logical error of affirming the consequent (we might just have been lucky or there might be other causes of our good fortune); the accumulation of sign evidence made the claim of virtuous American conduct compelling. The statement that Americans are God's chosen became not the *conclusion* of a conditional argument aiming to motivate us, but the *premise* of a pragmatic argument aiming to license us. Instead of being a potential reward for virtuous behavior yet to be performed, it was taken as an already-received gift that could legitimize whatever we did. The trajectory of this new argument would be long and its power would not be seriously weakened until the age of Obama.

What the belief in American exceptionalism implied for foreign policy was laid out in George Washington's Farewell Address. To maximize our freedom of action, we should not embroil ourselves in European quarrels; nor should we form permanent alliances with European powers.[3] In his First Inaugural Address, Thomas Jefferson codified this warning into the principle of "no entangling alliances."[4] From the first principle that the United States had no need to become involved in European quarrels, two other beliefs quickly followed. One was that, by the rule of reciprocity, European nations had no business involving themselves in American affairs—a belief that was codified in the Monroe Doctrine. The second was that the United States should act alone in its relations with other countries.

The Monroe Doctrine is also an early illustration of the choice to act alone. Invited by Britain to issue a joint statement warning continental powers against recolonizing the Western Hemisphere, the United States chose a unilateral declaration instead. With few exceptions, European nations did, indeed, leave the Americas alone. A neutral observer might attribute this result to the fact that the British navy controlled the seas, deterring aggression by other nations and providing the United States with "free security."[5] But it was easier for Americans to explain the result as the effect of our promulgating the Monroe Doctrine. Events "proved" that there was power in our words when we acted alone. That power obviously emanated not from military strength but from something even better: our status as God's chosen.[6] The Monroe Doctrine became a sacred text and gave rise to corollaries asserting American rights to military intervention to prevent interference in the Western Hemisphere by another nation. The Doctrine was invoked as recently as 1983 when Ronald Reagan used it to justify American intervention to prevent communist subversion of Grenada.

When the United States annexed Texas, knowing that this act probably would precipitate war with Mexico, and then used military victory to justify the acquisition of vast additional territory to the west, all this was seen as the working out of God's plan. It was America's "manifest destiny" to span the continent.[7] "Such a 'conquest,' stigmatize it as you please," editorialized the *Boston Times,* "must necessarily be a great blessing to the conquered."[8]

When the United States briefly flirted with imperialism during the 1890s, similar arguments were employed. Those favoring imperialism maintained that it was high time for God's chosen to take their place among the great empires of the world, holding colonies in faraway places. Opponents insisted that we demonstrated our exceptional status by *not* occupying territories permanently nor making colonies of them but instead liberating them, teaching them to live by the precepts of American democracy. As these examples illustrate, American exceptionalism could justify a wide range of action. We could act alone because we were not like other nations; we could take pre-emptive action because we were merely carrying out God's plan. We could make declarations of our wishes, knowing that there was power in our divinely inspired words. Favorable results confirmed our exceptional status. The occasional setback could be understood as a test of our commitment or our will.

American exceptionalism also helps to explain ambivalence in attitudes about war. We resist becoming involved, following Washington's advice. When we do become a belligerent, we want quick and decisive results, since that is what a war for the Lord should produce. We are impatient with long and inconclusive wars, whether the American Civil War or the wars in Iraq and Afghanistan.[9] And what justifies our resort to military force is not the desire for conquest or economic supremacy, but the vindication of a moral principle. Perhaps the clearest example is World War I. American involvement was warranted by Woodrow Wilson's claim, after neutral rights were violated, that "the world must be made safe for democracy."[10] The assumption was that our way of life was naturally best and that our responsibility was to create conditions under which it could flourish in all lands.

The discourse of exceptionalism was easily adapted to new geopolitical realities after 1945. Now the United States was a superpower, with the military and economic might to match its pretensions to chosenness. In a bipolar world under the shadow of nuclear weapons, there were limits to what we could do. Once we had lost the nuclear monopoly, we could not use the bomb without risking annihilation. But we could not acknowledge that fact lest nuclear weapons lose their deterrent power or lest our commitment to come to other nations' defense ring hollow. So in lieu of nuclear weapons, we committed conventional forces to limited wars, thinking that these commitments would signal our willingness to use the ultimate weapon in response to the ultimate threat. Vietnam undermined the credibility of that rationale.

Even more than small-scale wars, though, the United States issued declarations, statements of our policy and goals that we, as God's messengers, expected to be carried out. During the 1950s, Americans called for a "rollback" of the Iron Curtain, adopted the Captive Nations Resolution encouraging the peoples of eastern Europe to rise up against their Soviet masters, and announced the "unleashing" of Chiang Kai-shek so that he could recapture the mainland if he so chose. We promulgated "doctrines"—the Eisenhower Doctrine, the Nixon Doctrine, the Carter Doctrine. If we were firm and resolute enough, these declarations would have the same force as military might because there was power in the American word. Sometimes there were setbacks, such as the Bay of Pigs fiasco; these proved that we were not firm enough, but as President Kennedy warned at the time, "Our restraint is not inexhaustible."[11] Sometimes there were successes, such as the Cuban missile crisis, when American statements and symbolic actions were thought to prompt Soviet withdrawal; these proved that if we were clear and firm in our resolve, we could have our way. When Ronald Reagan in 1987 called upon Mikhail Gorbachev to "tear down this wall," and two years later the wall came down and the Cold War ended, and then two years after that the Soviet Union collapsed, these events were widely taken as proof that America had "won" the Cold War.

Of course, the end of the Cold War did not make the world safe for democracy. Long-simmering ethnic rivalries erupted in Europe, Africa, and Asia. The United States faced wrenching decisions about whether, when, and how to intervene, with inconsistent and unsatisfying results. In the 1990s and with even greater urgency in the new millennium, Americans faced the threat of global terrorism. But if this threat was new, the rhetoric by which we understood and responded to it was readily at hand. Indeed, replacing the word "communist" with the word "terrorist" made much of the Cold War rhetoric of American exceptionalism readily serviceable. In his address to Congress after the attacks of September 11, 2001, President Bush proclaimed that terrorists hate us because of our freedom, but that we will defeat them because "God is not neutral" between freedom and fear.[12] In his Second Inaugural Address, his most expansive justification for exporting democracy, Bush explicitly rejected the claim that we could assume we are God's chosen.[13] But his rhetorical stance throughout his presidency, and his willingness to make decisions with great confidence regardless of military realities, American public opinion, or the criticism of allies, are more easily explained by that assumption than by any other. For Bush, the war on terror was another struggle between good and evil in which Americans were doing God's work. Critics of Bush's policies who demonized him or doubted his intellectual capacity missed the point. His administration marked only the latest step in the evolution of the rhetoric of American exceptionalism, though perhaps the step that, in Kenneth Burke's phrase, took this cosmic frame to "the end of the line."[14]

Exceptionalism at the End of the Line

The dominant mind-set of American exceptionalism is captured in public discourse about the role of the United States in the world, which displays characteristics about which we are largely unaware because we do not stop to examine them.[15] First, policy discussions take on a moral tone. They are not about realism and national interest, prudence and *realpolitik,* but about good and evil and what other nations must do to be worthy of favor. The role of the United States in this discourse becomes lecturing and exhortation. Second, it is very hard to compromise on divinely inspired moral commitments. Others may see the refusal to compromise as arrogance or closed-mindedness on our part, and it is true that in taking moral positions we do not give ourselves much room to negotiate. But we do not need to, secure in the knowledge that our position is right and possessing faith that others eventually will see the light or suffer the consequences. Third, the belief that God is acting in the world to show us favor gives believers a teleological explanation for events. God has vouchsafed to them knowledge of how the story will come out. This situation inspires confidence; we are able to put setbacks and delays into their proper context. Fourth, the place for self-reflection, self-doubt, and second thoughts is minimized because, after all, this is not about human agency; when we act in the world we are carrying out God's plan. Finally, the knowledge that one is among the chosen reduces the need to justify a course of action to other audiences. If one is carrying out the Lord's dictates, God after all has His own reasons.

These characteristics are ingrained in the discourse of American foreign policy; they comprise its frame of reference. As Burke notes, though, a cosmic frame tends to be stretched until it finally cracks. It no longer can encompass everything—reality undermines its premises—and it collapses of its own weight. This is what Vietnam did for the frame of Cold War liberalism. If doing battle with communism in order to protect the free world meant supporting a tyrannical government, engaging in a war without end, undermining the dollar abroad, and alienating allies to whom we were trying to prove our credibility, then perhaps something was wrong with the paradigm itself. In like manner, the administration of George W. Bush saw the cracking of the cosmic frame of American exceptionalism, at least in its dominant manifestation. If, in order to protect ourselves, we claimed the rights to engage in preemptive war in

Iraq, to torture prisoners, and to sacrifice civil liberties, if the result was to embroil us in a long and inconclusive war, and if our efforts failed to mobilize a true global alliance but instead aroused unprecedented hostility, then perhaps something was wrong with our basic assumptions. Certainly Obama thought so; he had opposed the war in Iraq from the start. And although it is unlikely that they reasoned this way, a majority of Americans came to oppose the war too.

The frame did not just collapse of its own weight; its demise was hastened by external events. One was the mounting international debt of the United States, the result of financing the wars in Iraq and Afghanistan, the Bush tax cuts, and the Medicare prescription benefit through deficit spending. As Cohen and DeLong make clear, American influence over other nations, especially China, is weakened when the United States is beholden to those nations to carry its debt. Simply put, Americans cannot invoke claims to exceptionalism when they are dependent on the good will of others.[16]

In a similar vein, Andrew Bacevich has argued that the asymmetry of power exposes "the end of American exceptionalism." Although the United States possesses great military might, it is very difficult to quash an attack that takes unconventional form, does not come from a nation-state, and that is carried out in stealth. Efforts to do so are particularly likely to encounter unintended consequences that will make the implementation of policies messier than their conception. Meanwhile, we adopt expedients that sacrifice democracy to an imperial presidency at the very time we are trying to export democracy to other lands.[17]

Likewise, Fareed Zakaria argues that other nations, such as China, India, and Brazil, are on a trajectory of economic growth and geopolitical prominence.[18] The bipolar world of the Cold War and the period since 1989 when the United States was the sole superpower are about to be replaced with a world of multiple centers of power and influence, a world in which no single nation will be able credibly to claim exceptionalist status. This will be, as his title suggests, "the post-American world."

Approaching the 2008 presidential campaign, Barack Obama recognized these elements of the shifting scene. His opposition to the Iraq war was not an isolated spark of good luck in 2002; it was part and parcel of an alternative worldview. In a speech in October 2007, he had said, "The election is about ending the Iraq war, but even more it's about moving beyond it. And we're not going to be safe in a world of unconventional threats with the same old conventional thinking that got us into Iraq."[19] Exceptionalism as commonly described had become "old" and no longer serviceable.

Barack Obama's Foreign Policy Discourse

Obama gave voice to his vision in a series of speeches, most of them delivered abroad. These speeches have several similar elements that reveal how Obama constructed an alternative to the traditional rhetoric of American exceptionalism. He rejected the unilateralist emphasis by stressing the interdependence of nations and the need for joint action. He acknowledged American mistakes. And he rejected the focus on American uniqueness by articulating connections between the United States and other nations, sometimes using his own biography to make his point. Often he added urgency to his appeal by stressing the kairotic nature of the moment, the growing seriousness of the challenges, and the possibility that opportunities will be lost if they are not seized now.

Taken together, these features depart from the frame of American exceptionalism. They see foreign policy as being not about good and evil, but about living safely and comfortably with others. They find power not in unilateral declarations, but in cooperative action. They reveal flexibility and openness to compromise. And they find justification in more universal warrants than American uniqueness. These aspects of Obama's discourse will be traced through seven of Obama's speeches during 2008 and 2009.

THE BERLIN SPEECH

Obama spoke in Berlin in 2008 largely to offset the allegation that he was naïve and inexperienced in foreign affairs. The adulation he received suggested that Europeans were not concerned.[20] Obama built the Berlin speech around the themes of the airlift and the wall. The former, whose sixtieth anniversary came in 2008, was a symbol of rebirth after World War II and a symbol of German-American cooperation barely three years after the end of bitter hostilities. The collapse of the wall symbolized interdependence. As the candidate said, with the collapse of the Berlin wall, "walls came tumbling down around the world." Lowering of these walls makes it clear how much nations depend upon one another and have common aspirations despite diverging circumstances. This is a source of hope, but also of danger—precisely because the world is so interconnected, an attack in any particular place could threaten an entire international order. And these dangers, including poorly secured nuclear material, heroin, terrorism, and the genocide in Darfur, have spread "faster than our efforts to contain them."[21]

Obama acknowledged frankly that many in Europe find America to be part of the problem, but he offset this observation by noting also, "In America, there are voices that deride and deny the importance of Europe's role in our security and our future." These are both dangerous misconceptions. In place of the walls being torn down, we must "build new bridges across the globe." But doing this requires "constant work and sustained sacrifice." And that in turn requires "allies who will listen to each other, learn from each other, and, most of all, trust each other." Obama argues *a fortiori* that "if we could create NATO to face down the Soviet Union," then surely "we can join in a new and global partnership" to dismantle terrorist networks. But we must seize the moment and "reject the Cold War mindset."[22]

Obama ended by acknowledging American failings and imperfections.[23] This was not an "apology" but was clearly a move away from exceptionalist claims of chosenness. "We've made our share of mistakes," he said, "and there are times when our actions around the world have not lived up to our best intentions."[24] Such an acknowledgment, Obama apparently believes, will help to move beyond mutual posturing and to address the pressing new problems of the era of interdependence.

THE INAUGURAL ADDRESS

The treatment of international relations in the Inaugural Address was brief, because the primary audience was domestic, and the most immediate concern was economic recovery. But the same rhetorical moves are evident. Obama emphasized the ties connecting Americans and other peoples, and he affirmed American readiness to act multilaterally: "to all the other peoples and governments who are watching today, from the grandest capitals to the small village where my father was born, know that America is a friend of each nation, and every man, woman, and child who seeks a future of peace and dignity."[25] He did not limit his concern to nations that fashion their political system in the American image.

Elsewhere in the Inaugural Address, Obama criticized overreliance on

US military power alone. He said that those who "faced down fascism and communism" understood that military power has limits. Attributing to previous generations this acknowledgment of limits enabled Obama to portray his abandonment of exceptionalist thinking as less radical a departure than it really was. Likewise, he said, "As for our common defense, we reject as false the choice between our safety and our ideals."[26]

THE PRAGUE SPEECH

In Prague, Obama talked specifically about the danger posed by unsecured nuclear weapons that remain even after the end of the Cold War and the collapse of the Soviet Union. "In a strange turn of history," the president mused, "the threat of global nuclear war has gone down, but the risk of a nuclear attack has gone up." He therefore stated "clearly and with conviction America's commitment to seek the peace and security of a world without nuclear weapons."[27] This is a significant shift from the belief that, as a sign of its exceptional status, the United States could justify the maintenance of a nuclear arsenal while calling on other nations to forego or abandon their own.

THE CAIRO SPEECH

The Cairo speech had been billed as an effort to open productive conversations with the Muslim world. Perhaps no other opening would better signal a break with the past—a rejection not just of the Bush policies but of an American exceptionalist worldview "in which Muslim-majority countries were too often treated as proxies without regard to their own aspirations" while "the sweeping change brought by modernity and globalization led many Muslims to view the West as hostile to the traditions of Islam."[28]

As in other addresses, Obama sought to define the relationship with the Muslim world as interactive rather than antagonistic. The first step in such a definition is to make clear that America and Islam were not discrete categories, but overlapping. They shared ideals and they also shared membership: "since our founding, American Muslims have enriched the United States." Next, there needs to be more open conversation between the United States and the Muslim world. This is inherently a two-way street, with neither party claiming a privileged or exceptionalist position, nor relying on stereotypes. Obama acknowledged that "part of my responsibility as President of the United States [is] to fight against negative stereotypes of Islam whenever they appear," but immediately called for reciprocity, saying, "that same principle must apply to Muslim perceptions of America. Just as Muslims do not fit a crude stereotype, America is not the crude stereotype of a self-interested empire."[29]

As in other speeches, Obama urged the transcendence of even deep-seated cultural differences by recognizing the need to address shared problems. Referring to the need to secure nuclear weapons, combat a flu epidemic, prevent the acts of violent extremists, and solve the humanitarian crisis in Darfur, he insisted that we can meet the needs of people around the world only "if we understand that the challenges we face are shared, and our failure to meet them will hurt us all."[30]

This general perspective was applied to the most obvious example of significant tension, the conflict between Israel and the Palestinians. Balancing support for Israel and acknowledgment of Palestinian aspirations, Obama called for a larger view of the conflict that recognizes the legitimacy of both sides. If both Israelis and Palestinians surmount their postured positions, they should be able to acknowledge publicly what many say privately: "[M]any Muslims recognize that Israel will not go away. Likewise, many Israelis recognize the need for a Palestinian state. It is time for us to act on what everyone knows to be true."[31] But the United States cannot impose this result and possesses no unique or superior insight.

The Cairo speech, then, followed the same pattern as the other speeches, even as it spoke to a particularly volatile situation. Obama acknowledged that American perceptions and actions must change, even as he called for change from others. He emphasized the need for multilateral actions and he stressed the need to surmount differences with recognition of common goals and values and the need for coordinated action in an interdependent world.

THE UNITED NATIONS SPEECH

The 2009 speech to the United Nations General Assembly struck the same themes. If international relations are seen as adversarial, then we are blinded to the fact that we face common problems: "the interests of nations and peoples are shared." Accordingly, rather than envisioning competing power blocs, "we must embrace a new era of engagement based on mutual interest and mutual respect." Important corollaries followed about the nature of power. It "is no longer a zero-sum game. No one nation can or should try to dominate another nation. No world order that elevates one nation or group of people over another will succeed. No balance of power among nations will hold."[32] These were stated as universal principles, but they represented significant changes from the dominant tradition of American exceptionalism.

As in the Cairo speech, Obama pivoted from his announcement of changes in thinking made by the United States to calls for appropriate changes by others. He did so not from a stance of American superiority, but from the recognition that "the old habits, the old arguments, are irrelevant to the challenges faced by our people....They build up walls between us and the future that our people seek, and the time has come for those walls to come down."[33]

THE TOKYO SPEECH

The speech in Japan was delivered not long after the election of Yukio Hatoyama as Prime Minister. Like Obama, he had been elected on the theme of change. To many, that meant change in the relationship between Japan and the United States—a relationship in which Japan, at best, seemed to be the junior partner.

Explaining the future of the US–Japan relationship, Obama again emphasized the interconnection among peoples. He said that the US–Japan alliance endures "because it reflects our common values...that made possible the election of both Prime Minister Hatoyama and myself on the promise of change." As he did at the United Nations, Obama announced that this approach required change by the United States as well. Acknowledging that the United States has been disengaged from many multilateral initiatives, he said, "So let me be clear: Those days have passed." The president also made clear that he does not see power as a zero-sum game. "In the 21st century," he said, "the national security and economic growth of one country need not come at the expense of another."[34] He applied these general principles to the specific case of the emergence of China as a world power.

THE OSLO SPEECH

The announcement in October 2009 that Obama had been awarded the Nobel Peace Prize came as a surprise to many. He had been in office only a short time; his aspirations exceeded his achievements to date. What he had done was to modify other nations' views of the United States and of the prospects for peace by conveying a new message about America's place in the world. Regardless of their views on the merits of Obama's selection, rhetorical critics should be encouraged by the Nobel committee's recognition that discourse makes a difference.

Ironically, Obama's Nobel Prize Acceptance Speech came shortly after he had ordered an additional 30,000 US troops to Afghanistan. He addressed this exigence directly, noting that war is sometimes necessary because there is evil in the world. He made this point "because in many countries there is a deep ambivalence about military action today, no matter what the cause."[35] A commitment to avoid war under any and all circumstances does not lead to peace, he was suggesting; it is more likely to lead to the triumph of evil.

But the speech was not a strident defense of American military action. Obama did not say that the people whose countries we invade will welcome us as liberators, or that right necessarily accompanies America's might, or that America as the sole superpower should or could act alone, or that because of our exceptional status the rules governing the conduct of others did not apply to us. Rather, while acknowledging the necessity sometimes of war, he developed claims that are strikingly similar to those in his other foreign-policy speeches: that Americans must ground their policies in their ideals, that nations and people have common interests, that the United States cannot act alone, and that multilateral efforts must be genuine partnerships and not coalitions in which other nations are recruited to be our junior partner.

For example, Obama stated that neither America nor any nation "can insist that others follow the rules of the road if we refuse to follow them ourselves." This is a sharp break not just from the approach of his immediate predecessor but from the long tradition of American exceptionalism. There is a pragmatic reason: when we employ a double standard, "our actions appear arbitrary and undercut the legitimacy of future interventions, no matter how justified."[36] Obama here recognized that an important dimension of American foreign policy is the message it communicates.

Although there will be differences of interest and occasional justifications for war, they would be less likely if nations and people recognized how much they held in common. This has been a theme in Obama's other speeches and he repeated it here. "Even as we respect the unique culture and traditions of different countries," he pledged, "America will always be a voice for those aspirations that are universal." Later he said, "As the world grows smaller, you might think it would be easier for human beings to recognize how similar we are; to understand that we're all basically seeking the same things, that we all hope for the chance to live out our lives with some measure of happiness and fulfillment for ourselves and our families."[37]

There is a fine line, of course, between appealing to universal values and seeking to universalize American values. It is worth noting that Obama appealed to basic human desires rather than to the achievement of American-style democracy or, for that matter, any political value. This is reminiscent of President Kennedy's American University speech, in which he said, "We all breathe the same air. We all cherish our children's future. And we are all mortal."[38] Like Kennedy, Obama was implying that if we built our understanding of our role in the world from points of underlying commonality, we would be less likely to confront the circumstances that lead to war. Finally, as in other speeches, Obama expressed his belief in coordinated, multilateral action. His statement here is quite brief: "[I]n a world in which threats are more diffuse, and missions more complex, America cannot act alone."[39]

SUMMARY

In these seven speeches, Obama acknowledged errors and imperfections on everyone's part, including America's; he stated that the United States cannot and should not work its will unilaterally; he urged other nations to be genuine partners; he advocated support for international organizations; and he found points of connection between the United States and other nations, and among peoples around the world. He articulated a rhetorical vision that departed in significant ways from the vision of American exceptionalism that arguably had reached the end of the line during the administration of President George W. Bush. But impressive as this achievement was, it was not enough. It did not fully meet Obama's contextual burden.

Complicating the Rhetorical Problem

Except for the Inaugural Address, these speeches were delivered abroad or to a primarily international audience at the United Nations, and they did not receive significant attention within the United States. Alter regards them as intended to change the tone of American discourse, not to solve policy problems.[40] It is not apparent that Obama's rhetorical vision was widely understood by the American people or that it would be widely supported if it had been.[41] And even though the president enjoys far greater prerogative in foreign affairs than in domestic, still his ability to act depends on approval of at least the broad contours of his approach by the American people.

Certainly one cannot regard the fact of Obama's election by itself as evidence of popular agreement with his vision, because foreign policy received little sustained attention during the 2008 campaign. Public opinion polls registered growing dissatisfaction with the war in Iraq, but to use Obama's distinction, opposition to the Iraq war was not the same as opposition to the mind-set that got us into the war. It might reflect frustration with the length of the war, or a belief that it is not the best front against terrorism, more than the conviction that the effort is not genuinely multilateral, the judgment that America has no right to be there, or the renunciation of American exceptionalism. As recently as 2004, after all, Americans responded positively when President Bush disparaged multilateral action as "seeking a permission slip"[42] to use military force.

Perhaps reflecting these cross-pressures, Obama moved less forthrightly than many of his supporters would have wished. He retained some of the unilateral presidential powers to which he had objected, such as indefinite detention and extraordinary rendition, although he promised to use them more sensibly. His plan to phase out nuclear weapons "has run up against powerful resistance from officials in the Pentagon and other US agencies," challenging his ability to enact the change about which he spoke in Prague.[43] He did not fulfill his promise to close the military prison at Guantánamo within one year. More generally, Garry Wills argues that Obama's administration has not seriously arrested many of the trends about which it had complained.[44] And even the moves he did undertake were condemned by critics as unjustified American apologies.[45]

With this backdrop in mind, Barack Obama's contextual burden can be stated more starkly. For the sake of America's role in the world, he needed to abandon or at least strongly attenuate claims to American exceptionalism, which for the sake of his domestic audience he must reaffirm. This rhetorical problem, which confronted him upon assuming office, continued to bedevil him during his presidency. Without addressing it, he could not hope to persuade Americans to accept his foreign policy vision. Yet how could he reconcile these seeming opposites?

Paradoxically, a return to the origins of American exceptionalism itself might furnish a solution. Although it has become a proud boast, the premise of an argument that we can do what we want, the idea of exceptionalism began instead as a burden and a challenge. Winthrop argued that God had singled out the Puritans for the heavy responsibility of living out their covenant on earth. The context of the reference to the city on a hill was that, as God's elect, they would be highly visible, so if they failed to keep their part of the bargain, the world would know it; they had no place to hide. This realization should prompt humility, not hubris. The seriousness of the task should inspire community and motivate people to meet their responsibilities. Far from giving them reason to gloat, Americans' exceptional status would add to their burdens and tasks.

Across the sweep of history, this clearly has been a recessive strain in the discourse of American exceptionalism. But it sometimes has been used to warrant restraint rather than intervention, reminiscent of John Quincy Adams's statement that America "goes not abroad in search of monsters to destroy."[46] The argument has been that America's role is to serve as an example, "the beacon on the western shore," and that we can perform that role effectively only if our own society is secure, strong, and healthy. Obama might usefully sound this call. It would not require him to *abandon* American exceptionalism, so he could appeal to a broad domestic audience. But he clearly would *redefine* exceptionalism, bringing it into line with the views of a broad international audience and with the demands of world politics.

Appealing to *this* strain of exceptionalism should not harm Obama abroad. What would it matter to other nations if he used the claim that Americans were special in order to challenge them to live up to their own ideals? Doing this would not undercut his acknowledgment of past American errors, his emphasis on the interconnectedness of the world and the increasingly shared aspirations of its people, or his clear preference for multilateral rather than unilateral responses to emerging problems.

Students of the work of Chaim Perelman and Lucie Olbrechts-Tyteca will recognize here the elements of dissociation.[47] The term "exceptionalism," which has a single dominant meaning at present, can be dissociated into the exceptionalism of boast and the exceptionalism of challenge, with the latter gradually displacing the former as the understanding of what exceptionalism "really" is. This dissociation would allow Obama to tap into Americans' deep-seated belief that they are different from other nations because imbued with a special mission, while smoothing the very rough edges that that claim, as currently understood, presents for much of the world.

Obama did not strike this theme during his early months in office, or for that matter during his first term. Could it have worked? Possibly so, but it is hard to know. For most Americans, the continuing economic distress precipitated by the collapse in the housing and financial markets trumped all other considerations of public affairs, and the highly polarized state of American politics counseled pessimism about the prospects of an appeal for shared commitment and action. The danger was that Obama's speeches articulating a new view of America's place in the world would be consigned to the genre so often popularly labeled "empty rhetoric." The bold pledges and announcements of change then could be disregarded by international audiences if those audiences came to believe that there is nothing standing behind them on the part of the United States. That is the risk Obama faced as he assumed office and governed throughout his first term.

But if Obama temporized, he received little gain from doing so. Supporters were impatient, whereas critics condemned his statements as apologies for America. For example, well before declaring his presidential candidacy, in 2010 Mitt Romney published a book lamenting the tendency to acknowledge weakness or error.[48] Projection of strength was what would earn respect. That recognizing past mistakes is widely considered weakness per se is a sign of the continuing influence of exceptionalism in the American political imaginary, even though the trajectory has run its course in world politics.

The opportunity to reclaim and reinterpret American exceptionalism, however, remained available and offered Obama the chance to realign both American foreign policy and American public opinion with what he and others see as the new realities of international politics. Doing so would be necessary if Obama were to overcome his contextual burden.

Notes

1. The text of Winthrop's sermon may be found in Ronald F. Reid and James F. Klumpp, eds., *American Rhetorical Discourse,* 3d ed. (Long Grove, IL: Waveland, 2005), 24–36.

2. Thomas Paine, *Common Sense* (1776; rpt. New York: Penguin, 1986), 120.

3. The text of Washington's Farewell Address can be found in Reid and Klumpp, 186–202.

4. For the text of Jefferson's First Inaugural Address, see Reid and Klumpp, 203–207.

5. C. Vann Woodward, "The Age of Reinterpretation," *American Historical Review* 66 (1960), 1–19.

6. See Dexter Perkins, *A History of the Monroe Doctrine* (Boston: Little, Brown, 1963) for further development of this idea.

7. The term *manifest destiny* was coined by journalist John L. O'Sullivan. See his 1845 editorial, "The Great Nation of Futurity," reprinted in *The People Shall Judge* (Chicago: Univ. of Chicago Press, 1949), vol. 1, 717–19.

8. Cited in Rush Welter, *The Mind of America, 1820–1860* (New York: Columbia University Press, 1975), 69.

9. The outstanding exception to this generalization is the Second World War. Although long, it was not inconclusive; the momentum of the war was reasonably clear by the end of 1943. Moreover, World War II was justified on the basis of moral principles that commanded nearly universal assent.

10. From Woodrow Wilson's War Message of April 2, 1917, which can be found in Stephen E. Lucas and Martin J. Medhurst, eds., *Words of a Century: The Top 100 American Speeches, 1900–1999* (New York: Oxford Univ. Press, 2009), 73–79. In a recent essay, David M. Kennedy argues that Wilson was really a realist politician and that his concern was not with the export of democracy but with making the world safe for it—that is, creating the conditions under which it could emerge if it was appropriate to local circumstances. See David M. Kennedy, "What Would Wilson Do?" *The Atlantic,* January/February 2010, 90–94.

11. John F. Kennedy, "Speech to the American Society of Newspaper Editors, April 20, 1961," *Public Papers of the Presidents: John F. Kennedy, 1961* (Washington: US Government Printing Office, 1962), 304.

12. The text of this speech may be found in Reid and Klumpp, 805–10. The quotation is on page 810.

13. George W. Bush, "Second Inaugural Address," Washington, DC, January 20, 2005, *Presidential Rhetoric*.com, http://www.presidentialrhetoric.com.

14. In his "definition of man," Burke includes the phrase "rotten with perfection," which he describes as a tendency to follow frames of reference or their linguistic manifestations to their ultimate conclusion, the "end of the line." See Kenneth Burke, *Language as Symbolic Action* (Berkeley: University of California Press, 1966), 3–20. The "end of the line" phrase appears in several of Burke's writings.

15. For a fuller discussion, see David Zarefsky, "The U.S. and the World: Unexpressed Premises of American Exceptionalism," *Proceedings of the Sixth Conference of the International Society for the Study of Argumentation,* eds. Frans H. van Eemeren, J. Anthony Blair, Charles A. Willard, and Bart Garssen (Amsterdam: Sic Sat, 2007), 1567–71.

16. Stephen S. Cohen and Brad DeLong, *The End of Influence: What Happens When Other Countries Have the Money* (New York: Basic Books, 2009).

17. Andrew J. Bacevich, *The Limits of Power: The End of American Exceptionalism* (New

York: Henry Holt/Metropolitan Books, 2008). On a similar theme, see David S. Mason, *The End of the American Century* (Lanham, MD: Rowman & Littlefield, 2009).

18. Fareed Zakaria, *The Post-American World* (New York: Norton, 2008).

19. Quoted in Spencer Ackerman, "The Obama Doctrine," *The American Prospect,* April 2008, 13.

20. See, for example, "Going into Battle," *Newsweek,* November 17, 2008, 82; John Heilemann and Mark Halperin, *Game Change* (New York: HarperCollins, 2010), 329–32; and David Plouffe, *The Audacity to Win* (New York: Viking, 2009), 271–82.

21. Barack Obama, "A World That Stands as One," Berlin, Germany, July 24, 2008, *Huffington Post,* http://www.huffingtonpost.com/2008/07/24/obama-in-berlin-video-of_n_114771.html, paragraphs 18, 23.

22. Ibid, paragraphs 24, 30, 29, 29, 31, 34.

23. This would become a common feature of Obama's addresses abroad, probably aimed to remove the argument that the United States was acting hypocritically. See Jonathan Alter, *The Promise: President Obama, Year One* (New York: Simon and Schuster, 2010), 226. Obama's domestic critics often characterized this move as apologizing for US policies.

24. Obama, "A World That Stands as One," paragraph 43.

25. "President Barack Obama's Inaugural Address," *The White House Blog,* http://www. whitehouse.gov/blog/inaugural-address, paragraph 18.

26. Ibid, paragraph 17.

27. "Remarks by President Barack Obama," Hradcany Square, Prague, Czech Republic, April 5, 2009, *The White House,* http://www.whitehouse.gov/the_press_office/Remarks-By-President-Barack-Obama-In-Prague-As-Delivered, paragraphs 23, 27.

28. "Text: Obama's Speech in Cairo," *New York Times,* June 4, 2009, http://www.nytimes.com/2009/06/04/us/politics/04obama.text.html?pagewanted=all&_r=0, paragraph 2.

29. Ibid., paragraphs 9, 10, 11.

30. Ibid., paragraph 15.

31. Ibid., paragraph 40.

32. "Obama's speech to the United Nations General Assembly," *New York Times,* September 23, 2009, http://www.nytimes.com/2009/09/24/us/politics/24prexy.text .html?pagewanted=all, paragraphs 4, 6, 19.

33. Ibid., paragraph 20.

34. "Remarks by President Barack Obama at Suntory Hall," Tokyo, Japan, November 14, 2009, *The White House,* http://www.whitehouse.gov/the-press-office/remarks-president-barack-obama-suntory-hall, paragraphs 8, 21, 17.

35. Obama, "Remarks by the President at the Acceptance of the Nobel Peace Prize," Oslo City Hall, Oslo, Norway, December 10, 2009, *The White House,* http://www.white-house. gov/the-press-office/remarks-president-acceptance-nobel-peace-prize, paragraph 17.

36. Ibid., paragraph 24.

37. Ibid., paragraphs 40, 47.

38. The text of Kennedy's American University speech is in *Public Papers of the Presidents:*

John F. Kennedy, 1963 (Washington: US Government Printing Office, 1964), 459–64. It also can be found in Lucas and Medhurst, 362–68.

39. Obama, "Remarks by the President at the Acceptance of the Nobel Peace Prize," paragraph 42.

40. Alter, *The Promise,* 225.

41. An editorial in the *New York Times* does note approvingly that the Obama defense budget rejects Cold War assumptions and acknowledges that "while the United States remains the world's leading military power, it is much more dependent on allies to help maintain international stability." See "The Defense Budget," *New York Times,* February 4, 2010, A26. Of course, one cannot assume that a *New York Times* editorial necessarily reflects American public opinion.

42. George W. Bush, Address before a Joint Session of Congress on the State of the Union, Washington, DC, January 20, 2004, in *The American Presidency Project* [online], eds. John Woolley and Gerhard Peters, http://www.presidency.ucsb.edu/ws/index. php?pid=29646&st=&st1=.

43. Paul Richter, "Obama's Nuke-Free Vision Drawing Fire," *Chicago Tribune,* December 27, 2009, 34.

44. See Garry Wills, *Bomb Power: The Modern Presidency and the National Security State* (New York: Penguin Press, 2010).

45. For example, see criticisms cited by Fareed Zakaria, "Obama's Big Gamble," *Newsweek,* October 5, 2009, 20.

46. John Quincy Adams, "Speech to the U.S. House of Representatives on Foreign Policy," July 4, 1821, *Miller Center, University of Virginia,* http://millercenter.org/president/speeches/detail/3484.

47. Chaim Perelman and L. Olbrechts-Tyteca, *The New Rhetoric: A Treatise on Argumentation,* translated by John Wilkinson and Purcell Weaver (Notre Dame, IN: University of Notre Dame Press, 1969), 411–59.

48. See, for example, Mitt Romney, *No Apology: The Case for American Greatness* (New York: St. Martin's, 2010).

CHAPTER 7

Resetting America's Role in the World

President Obama's Rhetoric of (Re)Conciliation and Partnership

JASON A. EDWARDS

In his inaugural address, President Barack Obama declared that "we are ready to lead once more."[1] The president's argument that the United States was ready to lead again implied that eight years of George W. Bush administration foreign policy had diminished America's global leadership and role in the world. Bush administration policies such as withdrawing from the Kyoto Accords, the International Criminal Court, and the Anti-Ballistic Missile treaty with Russia, the creation of the Guantanamo Bay prison, the Abu Ghraib prison scandal, the rumors of forced rendition and enhanced interrogation tactics on international terrorists, and the ongoing struggles with the wars in Iraq and Afghanistan directly harmed US foreign affairs.[2] Bush's foreign policy made the United States look like a lone cowboy who was out to tame the wild, wild west of international affairs.[3] In turn, this foreign policy agenda was viewed by many as hubristic, dictatorial, and dangerous for world peace.[4] For example, the Pew Global Attitudes Survey found only three countries—India, Tanzania, and Nigeria—out of twenty-four surveyed had confidence in the United States to lead on global issues.[5] President Bush left office with global public opinion of the United States at an all time low.[6] With America's reputation in tatters, President Obama faced an incredible burden as he attempted to reset America's role in the world.

In this chapter, I argue President Obama began to reset US foreign policy by enacting a rhetoric of "democratic exceptionalism."[7] Arguments over US global leadership and its basic role in the world are structured by the precepts of American exceptionalism.[8] American exceptionalism defines the United States as a unique, if not superior, nation when compared to other states.[9] In foreign policy matters, exceptionalism functions to give

Americans "order to their vision of the world and defining their place in it."[10] Unlike Bush, Obama's vision of America's foreign policy encompassed a "pragmatic version of a national mission and world leadership steeped in a democratic tradition that emphasizes global cooperation over global domination."[11] Obama's exceptionalism was dedicated much more to cooperation, diplomacy, and egalitarianism than his predecessor. Democratic exceptionalism, like traditional American exceptionalism, declares the United States is a unique nation and leader of the free world. Where it differs is how we enact this leadership. Democratic exceptionalism emphasizes the language of "cooperation, partnership, discussion, negotiation, openness, transparency, bridging differences, respecting diversity, and promoting civil society, the rule of law, freedom of the press, and human rights.[12] By pledging to listen, cooperate, and engage in more multilateral activities, the United States enhances its leadership and reinforces its exceptionalism because more countries will come to share America's vision of a global order.

President Obama's Democratic Exceptionalism

As noted above, during George W. Bush's presidency the United States' reputation within the world was severely damaged, hindering its ability to promote democracy, freedom, expansion of free trade, and other policies where it had been a leader since the end of World War II. For example, the US State Department issued a congressionally mandated report in which it advised that "America's image and reputation could hardly be worse" and that as a nation it was "viewed much less as a beacon of hope than as a dangerous force to be countered."[13] Although global opinion of the United States has never been as glowing as Americans have believed it to be, the invasion of Iraq and President Bush's unilateralist foreign policy agenda created even more hostility for the United States abroad.[14] For example, the 2006 Pew Global Attitudes Project found in practically every country America's favorable ratings had declined precipitously since the beginning of the Bush administration.[15] When asked the question "Has the Iraq War made the world safer or more dangerous?" the Pew survey found overwhelmingly in every country surveyed, except for the United States, that the invasion of Iraq was viewed as making the world more "dangerous."[16]

Steven Kull, the director of the Program of International Policy

Attitudes, concluded from these findings that "the common theme is hypocrisy" regarding the United States and its role in the world. The United States puts itself out as "a champion of a certain set of rules. Now you are breaking your own rules, so you are being hypocritical."[17] As a result, Bush administration policies diminished America's reputation and its influence as a powerful nation. As David S. Mason pointed out, "the United States [is viewed] as weakened and less influential and emboldened by public opinion polls that reflect that foreign leaders have fewer compunctions about criticizing the United States (or its leadership). Furthermore, a less appealing, less powerful, and less influential America leads other countries to look elsewhere for political, social, or military partners."[18] One can certainly conclude that by the end of the Bush administration, the influence of American ideals, leadership, and policies were certainly on the decline, imperiling America's status as a world power.

In view of that, former Deputy Secretary of State Strobe Talbott astutely observed:

> The President of the United States inaugurated on January 20, 2009 will inherit the most complex, difficult, and dangerous array of challenges ever facing a newcomer in the Oval Office…In dealing with these and other problems, the United States, under its next president, will need all the help it can get from other nations. Therefore, the incoming chief executive will have to move quickly to improve—and indeed repair—America's image in the world.[19]

The Obama administration faced a global environment where America's reputation, influence, and leadership had been diminished over the past eight years. Thus, a key component to combating Obama's burden was to counter these foreign policy decisions. The president did so primarily by carrying a different foreign policy message to the world. In that message, Obama emphasized:

> The world shares a common future. No longer do we have the luxury of indulging our differences to the point of exclusion of the work that we must do together. I have carried this message from London to Ankara, from the Port of Spain to Moscow, from Accra to Cairo…because the time has come for the world to move in a new direction. We must now embrace a new era of engage-

ment based on mutual interest and mutual respect, and our work must begin now.[20]

Moreover, President Obama argued that America "is a critical actor and leader on a world stage" that exercises its leadership best

> when we are listening; when we recognize that the world is a complicated place and that we are going to have to act in partnership with other countries; when we lead by example; when we show some element of humility and recognize that we may not always have the best answer, but we can always encourage the best answer and support the best answer.[21]

In these passages, President Obama embraced a new mission and signaled to the world that the Bush era of unilateralism and "coalition of the willing" alliances was over. Instead, the values of interdependence, cooperation, humility, listening, focusing on common interests, and embracing common respect of all nation-states were ascendant and part of his "new era of engagement." To that end, the Obama administration pursued three rhetorical strategies—using the language of contrition, using the language of partnership, and leading by example—to carry forward this democratic exceptionalist ethos.

The Language of Contrition

One of the Obama administration's strategies to reset America's relations with the international community has been an emphasis on demonstrating contrition for America's recent foreign policy sins. Confessing these foreign policy mistakes is a subset of discourse I have labeled in past research as collective apologies.[22] Collective apologies come about because of some chasm created by historical transgressions (e.g. Germany's apologies to Jews for the Holocaust). These apologies function to repair communal relationships hurt by this past wrongdoing. Additionally, these apologies are meditations on these past events. In effect, they help to rewrite the historical relationship between victim and victimizer so the past does not serve as an impediment to building, maintaining, and strengthening future relationships. Rhetors who issue a collective apology signal that they learned lessons from the past and those transgressions will not be repeated in the future.

An important, if not the most important, component of this discourse is the acknowledgment of wrongdoing. Acknowledgment of past offenses is, according to Aaron Lazare, the most important part of any apology or statement of contrition.[23] By not acknowledging a specific problem and the potential impacts from that problem, the rhetor's overall contrition might be viewed as suspect. Acknowledgment of past offenses can serve as a starting point down the larger path of reconciliation when attempting to rebuild, recalibrate, strengthen, and deepen relationships between communities, including nation-states. Although the Obama administration did not fully apologize for America's foreign policy mistakes, the administration did recognize and acknowledge past sins, implying it would not happen again during Obama's presidency. Acknowledging foreign policy offenses is a fairly recent rhetorical development in presidential rhetoric. President Clinton was the first president to confess the transgressions of America's foreign policy past.[24] President Bush and Secretary of State Condoleezza Rice also admitted that America had made mistakes in its policies toward Latvia, Hungary, and Egypt.

The Obama administration continued this trend by expressing regret for the creation of the Guantanamo Bay prison and American officials' use of enhanced interrogation techniques.[25] Notably, the Obama administration's most striking penitence came in its travels abroad. For example, President Obama's first apologetic gesture occurred on a trip to Europe where he spoke with G-20 leaders about coordinated efforts to deal with the global economic crisis, discussed NATO's strategy for Afghanistan, and began negotiations with Russia on a new nuclear arms reduction treaty. At the same time, Obama recognized and acknowledged severe cracks had developed in America's relationship with Europe, cracks that led the United States to take Europe's global importance for granted. As the president put it at a town hall meeting in Strasbourg, France:

> In recent years, we've allowed our alliance to drift. I know that there have been honest disagreements over policy, but we also know that there's something more that has crept into our relationship. In America, there's a failure to appreciate Europe's leading role in the world. Instead of celebrating your dynamic union and seeking to partner with you to meet common challenges, there have been times where America has shown arrogance and has been dismissive, even derisive.[26]

Two weeks later, the president published an op-ed in the *Washington Post* before he traveled to the Summit of the Americas in Trinidad and Tobago. Writing about relations with Latin America, President Obama admitted, "Too often, the United States has not pursued and sustained engagement with our neighbors. We have been too easily distracted by other priorities and have failed to see that our own progress is tied directly to progress throughout the Americas."[27] A day later, President Obama struck a similar tone at the opening ceremony of the Summit of the Americas, observing, "I know that promises of partnership have gone unfulfilled in the past, and that trust has to be earned over time. While the United States has done much to promote peace and prosperity in the hemisphere, we have at times been disengaged, and at times sought to dictate our terms."[28]

In Obama's contrition toward Europe and Latin America, the common thread was an acknowledgment that America had allowed its partnership with both regions to "drift." America had discounted the notion that its fate was "tied directly to progress" in Europe and Latin America. This led the United States to show "arrogance," as it had "been dismissive," "derisive," "distracted," "disengaged," and it often "sought to dictate our terms" instead of listening to other voices in these regions. By confessing America's foreign policy sins, the president implicitly rebuked previous administrations, particularly his predecessor, while pledging he would not make the same mistakes as past presidents. The US–European and US–Latin American relationships would not drift again. Rather, greater cooperation to meet "common challenges" would be the fundamental basis for a new global community.

Secretary of State Hillary Clinton, touring the globe on behalf of President Obama, also confessed a history of mistakes made in foreign relations. For example, in a July 17 interview with Anwar Iqbal of Pakistan's *Dawn Television*, Clinton articulated her understanding of America's historical relations with Pakistan, stating:

> If you go back and look at the history of the United States and Pakistan, we were not always as sensitive or understanding of the needs of the Pakistani people. We were not always constant in our support and our friendship for Pakistan. We encouraged Pakistan to create the forces that fought against the Soviet Union occupation in Afghanistan, and then left you to deal with the aftermath. So it's been, I would argue, a relationship that hasn't been as con-

stant and effective as we would want it to be. Now we will continue to make mistakes. I mean we are just human beings; we know
that. But we want to be as honest in admitting them as possible,
learning from them, and then trying to move forward. We weren't
as supportive of Pakistan's democracy as we could have been and
should have been in the past.[29]

A day later, Secretary Clinton traveled to India. After a morning meeting
with Indian business leaders, the Secretary of State addressed a group of
reporters and dignitaries at the Taj Palace Hotel, where she discussed a
variety of subjects, including climate change. Clinton emphasized that "our
point is very simple: that we acknowledge, now with President Obama,
that we have made mistakes—the United States—and we, along with other
developed countries, have contributed most significantly to the problems
that we face with climate change. We are hoping that a great country like
India will not make the same mistakes."[30]

These passages illustrate two key approaches. First, Clinton acknowledged that the United States had a history of making several mistakes in
its relationship with Pakistan and the world at large. However, her rhetoric pointed to larger lessons to be garnered from these mistakes. Clinton
recognized that the United States would continue to make mistakes, but
it was committed to "learning from them" and then "moving forward"
to build stronger relationships in South Asia. The past served as lessons
for great countries "like India" to avoid the same errors in the future.
The confessions of America's foreign policy sins became mechanisms to
engage in corrective action to counter the past and provide for greater
cooperation on regional and global issues.

Clinton's use of the phrase "now with President Obama" in conjunc-
tion with the acknowledgment of mistakes is illustrative. For Clinton, it
would not have been possible for the relationship between Pakistan and
India to move forward without the election of President Obama. It was
President Obama's leadership that provided the opportunity for better
associations between the United States and South Asian countries, as
well as other states throughout the world. By acknowledging America's
foreign policy mistakes, the Obama administration engendered a new
era of engagement that restored and reset America's standing in the
world.

Ultimately, the recognition of past mistakes was an important part of the Obama administration's goal of striking a new tone with its allies. As Obama noted earlier, acting with an "element of humility" was part of the administration's approach to foreign affairs. Admitting America's foreign policy sins was an act of humility. It functioned to rebuild and reset relationships with regions and countries of the world that had been taken for granted or slighted during the Bush administration and in past administrations. By admitting these transgressions, the Obama administration created a discursive space where old relationships can be restructured and strengthened, while new ones were created. In turn, America's image could be resuscitated within these regions and states, which laid the groundwork for states to have confidence in its global leadership role. Furthermore, it offered the Obama administration the ability to negotiate global issues and issues regarding its national security from a position of strength. Obama's use of contrition positioned the United States to extricate itself from the burdens left by the Bush administration, while setting the stage for the United States to restore its leadership role and meeting a primary presidential expectation.

Moreover, the Obama administration's acknowledgment of past mistakes functioned to restore a semblance of moral authority within its global leadership role, which President Obama called "America's strongest currency in the world."[31] As President Obama asserted, "If we are practicing what we preach and if we occasionally confess to having strayed from our values and our ideals, that *strengthens* our hand; that allows us to speak with *greater* moral force and clarity around these issues."[32] For President Obama, his administration's confessions allowed it to speak with authority on issues like human rights, international security, renewing alliances, and climate change. Acknowledgment of American foreign policy sins offered the president greater symbolic capital to employ on pressing global issues. By recognizing America's mistakes, the president symbolically began to wipe the slate clean and move the United States forward (as Secretary of State Clinton asserted) in its relations with the international community. In other words, Obama's contrition enhanced and strengthened America's role in the world.

Renewing and Restoring Partnerships

A second aspect of restoring America's role in the world was President Obama's consistent message: the United States would rebuild relationships with other nation-states and regions based on "mutual respect and mutual interests." The world, according to Obama, was a "complicated place" that shared a "common future."[33] To deal with the burdens of foreign policy, the president advocated that the world needed to act in concert to deal with a host of global problems such as the economic crisis, climate change, nuclear weapons, and terrorism. To that end, Obama argued, "It is very important for us to be able to forge partnerships as opposed to dictating solutions."[34] Partnership is a family metaphor.[35] The president's emphasis on "dictating solutions" is instructive. Obama called upon this idea to show he believed previous administrations, particularly the Bush administration, dictated solutions to the international community rather than seeking consensus. Accordingly, the president sought to change tactics and "forge partnerships" to move forward collaboratively. By creating and renewing different partnerships, President Obama enlarged the global family to fortify the United States' attempts to deal with global problems.

President Obama focused on reforging partnerships in three areas: Europe, Latin America, and the Middle East. In Europe, as noted in the last section, the president observed the United States allowed its relationship to drift. According to Obama, America was "derisive" and "dismissive" of European concerns for American actions. The president wanted to rebuild that relationship, doing so with contrition but also with an explicit promise to work in greater and more forthright collaboration with America's European allies. In an April 3, 2009, town hall meeting in Strasbourg, France, President Obama pledged to use his trip to Europe "to renew our partnership, one in which America listens and learns from our friends and allies, but where our friends and allies bear their share of the burden. Together, we must forge common solutions to our common problems."[36]

Two notable ideas inform this passage. First, the president's emphasis on "renewing our partnership" with Europe was a form of corrective action recognizing America's past foreign policy mistakes. For years, American administrations took the US–European partnership for granted, focusing instead on forging deeper relationships with other states and regions across the world. The United States did not take proper care to maintain and deepen America's familial relationship with Europe. In pledging to renew and enhance the US–European alliance, Obama suggested the familial community can move forward and work collaboratively to address "common problems."

Additionally, observe the principle of balance President Obama wanted to bring to US leadership on the world stage. The president pledged to "listen and learn" from America's friends and allies, but he implored those same friends and allies to "bear their share of the burden" for the globe's "common problems." The theme of balance and reciprocity has been a common one for the president since the 2008 campaign. For example, Obama maintained the American economy needed to be rebalanced toward greater emphasis on production and less on consumption. The president continued to modify America's relationship with China by arguing China and the United States needed to achieve greater parity in their import-export relations. Likewise, in America's renewed partnership with Europe, Obama argued for more balance between the two bodies in dealing with global challenges. He implied the United States shouldered much of the burden, perhaps too much, for solving the world's problems, particularly those related to NATO and security.

In Obama's vision, it was time for Europeans (as well as China, India, Japan, Brazil, Russia, and other developed nations) to make their alliances more equitable. According to the president's logic, sharing the burdens of leadership with other nation-states on issues like terrorism and climate change would create greater unity throughout the world because these nations would be investing and exchanging ideas on combating mutual concerns. More investment and exchange to combat these challenges meant more ideas and resources to solve those problems. More ideas and resources would lessen the amount of work the United States would have to do to deal with these issues, which would reduce the burden on America's domestic resources. Reducing the burden of our domestic resources would allow the United States to do its own nation-building, allowing the economy to recover and grow more quickly. A growing and recovering economy would give the United States more resources at its disposal to tackle global problems and make it a model for the world to emulate. Accordingly, the United States would be able to reassert its role as the exemplar of global commerce. Additionally, greater collaboration would give the United States the opportunity to demonstrate "the kind of leadership we need to show—one that helps guide the process of orderly integration."[37] By balancing its partnership with Europe, the United States would continue its global "leadership" role, not as dictator, but more as a "guide," providing the opportunity for more and (ideally) better solutions to the world's problems. In turn, this reconceptualized role would lay the groundwork for a more equitable US–European relationship in both the short and long term, reducing America's global familial discord.

President Obama also attempted to reset America's partnership with Latin America. For example, in one of his addresses at Summit of the Americas, Obama openly talked about the troubling historical relationship between the United States and Latin America, noting that "promises of partnership have gone unfulfilled." The president declared he would "launch a new chapter of engagement" that would be sustained throughout his administration. In this "new chapter of engagement" there would be no "senior partner and junior partner in our relations." Rather, his administration would do everything it could to create an "equal partnership" between the United States and Latin America, through "engagement based on mutual respect and common interests and shared values."[38]

Obama's pledge of equitability in US–Latin American relations was unusual, remarkable, and potentially groundbreaking. For over two hundred years, presidents and politicians have constructed the Western Hemisphere as America's backyard; a place for the United States to play and do what it wants with it. This backyard mentality has created a paternal tone in US–Latin American relations.[39] There have been presidents who tried to realign America's relationship with Latin America, attempts illustrated by Franklin Delano Roosevelt's Good Neighbor policy, John F. Kennedy's Alliance for Progress, and Bill Clinton's Partnership for Prosperity. However, these initiatives were not true partnerships. Rather, they left Latin America in a quasi-dependent status with the United States.[40] President Obama's argument that there would be no "senior partner" or "junior partner" in US–Latin American relations marked an important turning point. For Obama, the United States would continue to look out for its interests, but pledging an "equal partnership" with Latin America began a recasting and rebalancing of its relations with the region, creating greater potential opportunity for cooperation in addressing regional and global problems.

Perhaps President Obama's greatest effort and greatest challenge in resetting American partnerships focused on the Middle East. The president took great pains to rhetorically retune the tone of America' relationship with the region and argued for a new way forward. For example, in his inaugural address, President Obama sent a message "to the Muslim world" stating the United States sought "a new way forward based on mutual interest and mutual respect."[41] Likewise, the president signaled in his first interview with Al-Arabiya television that putting a different foreign policy message out to the Middle East was of paramount importance. During his first trip to Europe, President Obama addressed the Turkish Parliament and amplified the importance of the US–Turkish relationship but also shared messages with the wider Muslim world. The president proclaimed, "The United States is not, and will never be, at war with Islam. In fact, our partnership with the Muslim world is critical not just in rolling back the violent ideologies that people of all faiths reject, but also to strengthen opportunity for its people."[42] In a major address at Cairo University, Obama stressed that he came "to Cairo to seek a new beginning between the United States and Muslims around the world, one based on mutual interest and mutual respect and one based upon the truth that America and Islam are not exclusive and need not be in competition."[43] Throughout that speech, the president delineated what he believed were the sources of tension between the West, particularly the United States, and the Muslim world: extremism, the Israeli–Palestinian conflict, nuclear weapons, democracy, religious freedom, and economic development. He pledged to work in concert with Middle Eastern states to deal comprehensively with all of these challenges. In this way, Obama's discourse suggested he sought to undo damage done to America's relationship with the Middle East in prior years.

The above passages all displayed values the president brought in recasting its relationships with the Middle East region. The president affirmed that he wanted a new beginning with the Muslim world based on "mutual interest and mutual respect." This new beginning called for each state to do its part to deal with the common problems that the United States and the Middle East faced. Obama's rhetoric attempted to strike a new balance in America's foreign affairs with Muslims throughout the world. Democratic exceptionalist values of cooperation, partnership, respect for diversity, discussion, and serving the common good were all evident in Obama's Middle Eastern partnership discourse.

Many presidents have attempted to recast America's relationships with the Middle East. However, Obama's discourse was different because he took on the role of teacher rather than dictatorial father. For example, in his interview with Al-Arabiya TV, Obama declared his job was to "communicate to the American people that the Muslim world is filled with extraordinary people who want to live their lives and see their children live better lives. My job to the Muslim world is to communicate that the Americans are not your enemy."[44] In his Cairo University address, Obama continued this theme:

> I consider it part of my responsibility as President of the United States to fight against the negative stereotypes of Islam wherever they appear. But that same principle must apply to Muslim perceptions of America. Just as Muslims do not fit the crude stereotype, America is not the crude stereotype of a self-interested empire. The United States has been one of the greatest sources of progress that the world has ever known. We were born out of revolution against an empire. We were founded upon the idea that all are created equal, and we have shed blood and struggled for centuries to give meaning to those words, within our borders and around the world. We are shaped by every culture, drawn from every end of the Earth, and dedicated to a simple concept: *E pluribus unum*—"Out of many, one."[45]

In both passages, the president's rhetoric was didactic in nature. Presidential scholar Erwin Hargrove argued the first task of presidential leadership was to teach reality to various publics and politicians.[46] President Obama worked for a shared reality of common humanity valued by Americans and Muslims alike. Neither group fit the "negative stereotypes"[47] that extremists put forth. Rather, both groups were full of "extraordinary people who simply want to live their lives and see their children live better lives."[48] By actively trying to combat negative stereotypes ascribed to both sides, the president offered Americans and Middle Eastern Muslims a civics lesson and suggested a better way to approach relations between the United States and the Middle East. In turn, this new reality, new beginning, and new partnership expanded the family of nations and built momentum for greater cooperation on world issues.

Restoring the Force of Our Example?

Finally, President Obama attempted to restore America's standing in the world through the "force of our example."[49] The president's most eloquent statement on this domestic renewal came in his address to the United Nations General Assembly in September 2009. In that oration, President Obama welcomed the dawn of a "new era of engagement based on mutual interests and mutual respect." To demonstrate a tangible commitment to this "new era," the president ticked off a number of actions that he argued would restore America's image. He pointed out that "on my first day in office, I prohibited—without exception or equivocation—the use of torture by the United States of America; I ordered the prison at Guantanamo Bay closed." To deal with al-Qaeda, President Obama averred he wanted "to work with all members of this body to disrupt, dismantle, and defeat" the terrorist organization." This policy stance stood in stark contrast to prior instances of the United States working unilaterally and against the counsel of the international community. Moreover, President Obama assured international leaders attending the opening of the UN General Assembly that the Iraq issue would soon be a thing of the past because the United States was "responsibly ending a war" and would leave by 2011.[50]

Obama also outlined steps he stated would strengthen America's image. The president asserted that his administration began laying out a "comprehensive agenda to seek the goal of a world without nuclear weapons." This comprehensive agenda encapsulated a nuclear arms reduction treaty with Russia, redefining America's nuclear posture, and hosting a forty-seven nation nuclear summit where the attendees pledged to secure their nuclear stockpiles from ending up in the hands of terrorists. Furthermore, unlike his predecessors, "upon taking office" President Obama "appointed a Special Envoy for Middle East Peace," seeking to begin peace negotiations at the start of his administration rather than leaving it to the end. In dealing with climate change, the president explained that, through his advocacy, the United States invested over "$80 billion in clean energy,…substantially increased our fuel-efficiency standards…provided new incentives for conservation, launched an energy partnership across the Americas, and moved from a bystander to a leader in international climate negotiations." In dealing with the economic crisis, the president maintained he worked diligently "with the G-20 nations to forge a coordinated international response of over $2 trillion in stimulus to bring the global economy back from the brink." Finally, the president explained to the audience how his administration has "also reengaged the United Nations. We have paid our bills. We have joined the Human Rights Council. We have signed the Convention of the Rights and Persons with Disabilities. We have fully embraced the Millennium Development Goals." The sum total of these actions, as Obama viewed it, was to let "every nation know, America will live its values, and we will lead by example."[51] Former Bush administration official and Council on Foreign Relations President Richard Haass concluded, particularly regarding the nuclear weapons agenda, "These are not transformational developments, but in foreign policy it's important to keep the ball moving down the field in the right direction, and that's what's happening."[52]

Despite moving in the "right direction" President Obama's foreign policy agenda hit many rough patches, particularly in how the administration dealt with the Guantanamo Bay issue. In November 2009, Obama explained Gitmo would not be closed by the end of the year; by February 2010, the president asserted Guantanamo Bay would not be closed in his first term. Additionally, the president received a great deal of criticism for adjustments he made to the war in Iraq and for his delay of troop requests for Afghanistan.[53] Also, despite his soaring rhetoric on resetting relations with the Middle East, President Obama's special envoy for the Israeli–Palestinian peace process made no significant progress by the end of 2009, and his attempts to build new "partnerships" with the Middle East fell short.

Ultimately, Obama's discourse and actions were attempts to reset America's status as an exemplar nation. One of the ways American exceptionalism is enacted is through an emphasis on perfecting the United States at home, allowing the United States to be a model for other nations.[54] The actions of the Bush administration left that exemplar mission in peril. Rhetorically, Obama promised to prohibit torture, close Guantanamo Bay, increase America's commitment to combating climate change, and reduce the threat of nuclear weapons, all ways of demonstrating that the United States was once again going to "lead by example." However, the administration reneged on a key promise to close Guantanamo Bay and did not make significant progress on resetting US–Middle Eastern relations. Accordingly, the president's attempts to renew America's image as a "shining city upon a hill" were a mixed bag. Certainly, Obama tried to distance US foreign policy from eight years of the Bush administration, but his foreign policy record created its own burden. The president's rhetoric and actions suggested he kept the foreign policy ball "moving down the field" and "in the right direction," but full restoration of America's global leadership did not come to fruition.

Conclusions

Throughout this chapter, I have noted how President Obama's foreign policy rhetoric was laced with a democratic exceptionalist ethos carried forward through three rhetorical strategies: engaging in a language of contrition, recasting America's partnerships with individual nations and regions, and restoring the force of America's example as a model nation. When these three strategies are combined, they reveal two important ideas. First, President Obama altered the discourse of American exceptionalism. Traditionally, there are two dominant narratives of American foreign policy rhetoric: the mission of exemplar and the mission of intervention.[55] Typically, there is an inherent tension between exemplarism and interventionism because both narratives prescribe fundamentally different ideas to maintain and strengthen America's exceptionalism.[56] In his foreign policy rhetoric, President Obama removed the rhetorical tension embedded in American exceptionalism. By pledging to prohibit torture and lessen the danger of nuclear weapons, and by advocating for health care, financial, and energy reform, as well as other policy decisions, the president positioned the United States to lead by example, which may have helped to restore its exemplar status. In doing so, Obama's rhetoric acted as argument for even greater American engagement. During Obama's first year in office, he positioned the United States to get its domestic house in order while becoming a more cooperative actor on the international stage. This may have signaled to the world that the United States was changing its foreign policy posture. Accordingly, Obama could gain more cooperation from other states to fulfill his foreign policy agenda. In other words, exemplarism and interventionism worked hand in hand with each other. The president enhanced himself politically, while the United States maintained and advanced its leadership abroad, further cementing its claims as an exceptional nation.

Second, President Obama's foreign policy rhetoric suggested a growth in its global identity. The president's emphasis on contrition and enhancing its partnerships with other regions implied the United States did not always have the right answers to global solutions. One of Obama's assertions was that his presidency marked a new era in American engagement with the world. The president argued that engagement included listening more, not dictating, to the concerns and needs of other nations. Obama's rhetoric suggested he took a much more global approach, instead of a singularly

American one, to solving the world's most pressing issues. Thus, America's identity became more cosmopolitan and globalized, which may have helped to reshape its interests at a national, regional, and international level.

In turn, both conclusions served as means for Obama to meet the rhetorical expectations Americans have for its president. We expect the president to maintain a proper role for the United States in world affairs. We expect the president to lead and articulate a vision for the changing global environment as the United States attempts to navigate the rocky shoals of globalization. We expect the president to articulate our exceptional values.[57] President Obama attempted to do both in the early months of his presidency by rhetorically fusing the missions of exemplar and intervention together and articulating a growth in America's global identity to deal with political, cultural, and economic realities of the world. The president believed the United States is an exceptional nation, but the United States faced new global realities where the unilateralist, hegemonic, and hubristic foreign policy of the Bush administration would not do if the twenty-first century were to be an American century. This rhetoric led President Obama's opponents to accuse him of "leading from behind,"[58] which entailed the United States taking a back seat to other powers and/or organizations as they attempt to grapple with other global issues. For critics like Charles Krauthammer, this policy of leading from behind diminished American power and standing in the world.[59] Yet, according to Krauthammer, Obama was meeting the American public's expectations. President Obama's rhetorical focus on virtues of cooperation, diplomacy, egalitarianism, and listening, rather than the projection of raw American hard power, was exactly the foreign policy tone and foreign policy agenda Americans favor.[60] To that end, Obama carved a discursive space where the United States eschewed the role of unilateral dictator, instead engaging in multilateral, collaborative activities to deal with the multitude of challenges the international community faced. Obama's democratic exceptionalism turned a burden into an opportunity to reset America's standing in the world and resume the mantle of global leadership it held for the past sixty years. Perhaps President Obama's foreign policy rhetoric will create new expectations as the United States attempts to manage the forces of globalization for its own interests, yet navigates forces beyond its own control.

Notes

1. Barack Obama, "Inaugural Address," January 20, 2009, http://www.presidency .ucsb. edu/ws/print.php?pid=44, paragraph 15.

2. Andrew Bacevich, *The Limits of Power: The End of American Exceptionalism* (New York: Macmillan Books, 2009); and Geoffrey Hodgson, *The Myth of American Exceptionalism* (New Haven, CT: Yale University Press, 2009).

3. Karen S. Hoffman, "Visual Persuasion in George W. Bush's Presidency: Cowboy Imagery in Public Discourse," *Congress and the Presidency* 38 (2011), 322–43; and Mark West and Chris Carey, "(Re)Enacting Frontier Justice: The Bush Administration's Tactical Narration of the Old West Fantasy after September 11," *Quarterly Journal of Speech* 92 (2006): 379–412.

4. For an excellent critique of Bush's foreign policy, see Bacevich, *Limits of Power*; and Tony Smith, *A Pact with the Devil: Washington's Bid for World Supremacy and the Betrayal of the American Promise* (New York: Routledge, 2007).

5. "Global Public Opinion in the Bush Years (2001–2008)," Pew Research Global Attitudes Project, December 18, 2008, http://www.pewglobal.org/2008/12/18/global-public-opinion-in-the-bush-years-2001–2008/.

6. David S. Mason, *The End of the American Century* (Lanham: Rowman and Littlefield, 2009), 155–76.

7. Robert L. Ivie and Oscar Giner, "American Exceptionalism in a Democratic Idiom: Transacting the Mythos of Change in the 2008 Presidential Election," *Communication Studies* 60 (2009): 359–75.

8. See Jason A. Edwards, *Navigating the Post-Cold War World: President Clinton's Foreign Policy Rhetoric* (Lanham: Rowman and Littlefield, 2008); G. John Ikenberry, *Liberal Leviathan: The Origins, Crisis, and Transformation of American World Order* (Princeton: Princeton University Press, 2010); Trevor McCrisken, *American Exceptionalism and the Legacy of Vietnam: US Foreign Policy Since 1974* (New York: Palgrave, 2003); Walter A. McDougall, *Promised Land, Crusader State: America's Encounter with the World Since 1776* (New York: Houghton Mifflin); Siobahn McEvoy-Levy, *American Exceptionalism and US Foreign Policy: Public Diplomacy at the End of the Cold War* (New York: Palgrave, 2001); Walter Russell Mead, *Special Providence: American Foreign Policy and How It Changed the World* (New York: Knopf, 2001); and Tony Smith, *America's Mission: The United States and the Worldwide Struggle for Democracy in the Twentieth Century* (Princeton: Princeton University Press, 1994).

9. Jason A. Edwards and David Weiss, *The Rhetoric of American Exceptionalism: Critical Essays* (Jefferson City: McFarland Press, 2011).

10. Michael H. Hunt, *Ideology and U.S. Foreign Policy* (New Haven: Yale University Press, 1988), 15.

11. Ivie and Giner, "American Exceptionalism in a Democratic Idiom," 361–62.

12. Ibid.

13. *Cultural Diplomacy: The Linchpin of Public Diplomacy,* Report of the Advisory Committee on Cultural Diplomacy (Washington, DC: US State Department, 2005), http://www.state.gov/documents/organization/54374.pdf.

14. Kevin Sullivan, "Views on U.S. Drop Sharply in Worldwide Opinion Poll," *Washington Post,* January 23, 2007, A14.

15. Mason, *The End of the American Century,* 158.

16. Andrew Kohut and Bruce Stokes, *America Against the World: How We Are Different and Why We Are Disliked* (New York: Times Books, 2006), 25.

17. Sullivan, "Views on U.S. Drop Sharply," A14.

18. Mason, *The End of the American Century,* 167.

19. Strobe Talbott, "America's New Agenda: How the US Can Fix Its Damaged Reputation Abroad," Spiegel Online International, October 13, 2008, http://www.spiegel.de/international/america-s-new-agenda-how-the-us-can-fix-its-damaged-reputation-abroad-a-583723.html.

20. Barack Obama, "Address to the United Nations General Assembly in New York City," September 23, 2009, http://www.presidency.ucsb.edu/ws/index.php?pid=86659&st=&st1=, paragraph 5.

21. Barack Obama, "News Conference by President Obama in London, United Kingdom," April 2, 2009, http://www.whitehouse.gov/the-press-office/news-conference-president-obama-40209, paragraph 45.

22. Jason A. Edwards, "Apologizing for the Past for a Better Future: Collective Apologies in the United States, Australia, and Canada," *Southern Journal of Communication* 75 (2010): 57–75; see also Jason A. Edwards, "Community-Focused Apologia in International Affairs: Japanese Prime Minister Tomiichi Murayama's Apology," *The Howard Journal of Communications* 16 (2005): 317–36; and Jason A. Edwards and Lindsay R. Calhoun, "Redress for Old Wounds: Canadian Prime Minister Stephen Harper's Apology for the Chinese Head Tax," *Chinese Journal of Communication* 4 (2011): 73–89.

23. Aaron Lazare, *On Apology* (New York: Oxford University Press, 2004), 75–82.

24. President Clinton acknowledged US foreign policy mistakes in Africa, Guatemala, and Greece. See Edwards, *Navigating the Post-Cold War World,* 115–22.

25. See Barack Obama, "Remarks at a Town Hall Meeting and a Question-and-Answer Session in Strasbourg, France," April 3, 2009, http://www.presidency.ucsb.edu/ws/print. php?pid=85946; Barack Obama, "Remarks by President Obama to the Turkish Parliament," April 6, 2009, http://www.whitehouse.gov/the_press_office/Remarks-By-President-Obama-To-The-Turkish-Parliament; Barack Obama, "Remarks by the President at the Summit of the Americas Opening Ceremony," April 17, 2009, http://www.whitehouse.gov/the_press_office/Remarks-by-the-President-at-the-Summit-of-the-Americas-Opening-Ceremony; Barack Obama, "Remarks in Cairo," address at Cairo University in Cairo, Egypt, June 4, 2009, http://www.presidency.ucsb.edu/ws/print.php?pid=86221; and Obama, "Address to the United Nations."

26. Barack Obama, "Remarks at a Town Hall Meeting," paragraph 17.

27. Barack Obama, "Op-Ed by President Obama: 'Choosing a Better Future in the

Americas," April 16, 2009, http://www.whitehouse.gov/the_press_office/Op-ed-by-President-Barack-Obama-Choosing-a-Better-Future-in-the-Americas, paragraph 2.

28. Obama, "Remarks by the President at the Summit of the Americas," paragraph 4.

29. Hillary Clinton, "Interview with Anwar Iqbal of Dawn Television," July 17, 2009, http://www.state.gov/secretary/rm/2009a/july/126198.htm, paragraphs 24 and 25.

30. Hillary Clinton, "Remarks at the Taj Palace Hotel," July 18, 2009, Mumbai, India, http://www.state.gov/secretary/rm/2009a/july/126199.htm, paragraph 24.

31. Barack Obama, "Remarks by the President on National Security," May 21, 2009, National Archives, Washington, DC, *The White House,* http://www.whitehouse.gov/the_press_office/Remarks-by-the-President-On-National-Security-5-21-09/, paragraph 27.

32. Barack Obama, "The President's News Conference in Port of Spain," in *The American Presidency Project* [online], eds. John Woolley and Gerhard Peters, http://www.presidency. ucsb.edu/ws/index.php?pid=86033&st=&st1=, paragraph 34 (emphasis mine).

33. Obama, "News Conference by President Obama in London," paragraph 45.

34. Ibid., paragraph 88.

35. Francis A. Beer and Christ'l De Landtscheer, "Metaphors, Politics, and World Politics," in *Metaphorical World Politics,* eds. F. A. Beer and C. De Landtscheer (East Lansing: Michigan State University Press, 2004), 17.

36. Obama, "Remarks at a Town Hall Meeting," paragraph 20.

37. Obama, "News Conference by President Obama in London," paragraph 90.

38. Obama, "Remarks by the President at the Summit of the Americas," paragraph 4.

39. Martha Cottam, *Images and Intervention* (Philadelphia: University of Pennsylvania Press, 1994).

40. Edwards, *Navigating the Post Cold War World,* 138–39; and Smith, *America's Mission.*

41. Obama, "Inaugural Address," paragraph 18.

42. Obama, "Remarks by the President to the Turkish Parliament," paragraph 38.

43. Obama, "Remarks in Cairo," paragraph 5.

44. Barack Obama, "Obama's Al Arabiya Interview: Full Text," Huffington Post, February 27, 2009, http://www.huffingtonpost.com/2009/01/26/obama-al-arabiya-intervie_n_161127.html, paragraph 40.

45. Obama, "Remarks in Cairo," paragraphs 11–12.

46. Erwin C. Hargrove, *The President as Leader: Appealing to the Better Nature of Ourselves* (Lawrence: University of Kansas Press, 2000), viii.

47. Obama, "Remarks in Cairo," paragraph 10.

48. Obama, "Obama's Interview with Al Arabiya."

49. Obama, "Inaugural Address," paragraph 16.

50. Obama, "Address to the United Nations General Assembly," paragraphs 5, 7, 8, 9.

51. Ibid., paragraphs 10, 11, 12, 13, 14, 7.

52. Peter Baker, "Obama Puts His Own Mark on Foreign Policy Issues," *New York Times,* April 13, 2010, http://www.nytimes.com/2010/04/14/world/14prexy.html? _r=0, paragraph 21.

53. Stephen Clark, "Obama's Delay on Troop Request for Afghanistan Stirs Criticism

of War Strategy," *Fox News,* September 29, 2009, http://www.foxnews.com/poli tics/2009/09/29/obamas-delay-troop-request-afghanistan-stirs-criticism-war-strategy/; and "Obama Rejecting Afghanistan Criticism," *CNN*.com, December 14, 2009, http:// politicalticker.blogs.cnn.com/2009/12/14/obama-rejecting-afghanistan-criticism/.

54. McDougall, *Promised Land, Crusader State;* McEvoy-Levy, *American Exceptionalism and US Foreign Policy;* and McCrisken, *American Exceptionalism and the Legacy of Vietnam.*

55. Exemplarists, as we noted earlier, emphasize that America best demonstrates its leadership by perfecting its institutions at home to serve as a model for other states to emu-late. However, it does not involve itself in the political and social affairs of others because it would endanger and potentially infect the American body politic. Interventionists, on the other hand, advocate that American leadership is best demonstrated by engagement and ultimate leadership within the international community. Interventionists argue that exemplarists are naïve to believe that the United States can merely close itself off to the world and not be involved with it.

56. H. W. Brands, "Exemplary America Versus Interventionist America," in *At the End of the American Century,* ed. Robert Hutchings (Baltimore: Johns Hopkins University Press, 1998), viii.

57. Dan Gilgoff, "Despite Fights about Its Merits, Idea of American Exceptionalism a Powerful Force through History," *CNN.com,* June 30, 2012, http://religion.blogs.cnn. com/2012/06/30/despite-fights-about-its-merits-idea-of-american-exceptionalism-a-powerful-force-through-history/.

58. Charles Krauthammer, "The Obama Doctrine: Leading from Behind," *Washington Post,* April 28, 2011, http://www.washingtonpost.com/opinions/the-obama-doctrine-lead-ing-from-behind/2011/04/28/AFBCy18E_story.html; and Ryan Lizza, "The Consequential-ist: How the Arab Spring Remade Obama's Foreign Policy," *The New Yorker,* May 2, 2011, http://www.newyorker.com/reporting/2011/05/02/110502fa_fact_lizza?currentPage=all.

59. Krauthammer, "The Obama Doctrine: Leading from Behind."

60. Chicago Council on Global Affairs, "Foreign Policy in the New Millennium," September 10, 2012, http://www.thechicagocouncil.org/files/Surveys/2012/files/Stud-ies_Publications/POS/Survey2012/2012.aspx.

CHAPTER 8

Obama's Two Bodies

A Study in American Economic Theology

JAMES ARNT AUNE

Grounded perhaps in our collective unconscious and in dim institutional memory, the American president was created out of the ashes of the medieval mythos of the *King's Two Bodies,* first brought to light by the medievalist Ernst Kantorowicz.[1] He describes the transformation in the concept of political authority over the course of the Middle Ages. The change began when the concept of the body of Christ evolved into a notion of two bodies—one, the *corpus naturale,* the consecrated host on the altar; and the other, the *corpus mysticum,* the social body of the church. As Christ's "body" was taken at Communion, the social body of Christians as a people was nourished. Likewise, while the king's natural, mortal body would pass away upon his death, his *corpus mysticum* could not be destroyed, even by assassination. As the early modern concept of "sovereignty" developed, the mystical body of the king was transferred to the "state," a territorially bounded unity with a specific set of interests and legitimacy, yet retaining the monarchic aura of mystery and authority. The mystical attribute of authority gradually came to apply to the rule of the people themselves, whether through a constitution or an institution such as the Communist Party. We continue to refer to Presidents or Prime Ministers as "heads of state," retaining a vestige of the original physical metaphor for the body politic.

Although most recent discussions of sovereignty have centered on issues of national security and international relations, specifically the "state of exception" described by Carl Schmitt and, later, Giorgio Agamben, the analysis proposed in this chapter takes the "body" metaphor much more literally.[2] Bodies need to be fed, clothed, and housed. Their property needs to be protected by the state. The periodic cycles of boom and bust characteristic of a modern capitalist economy have created a political burden for heads of state. The "Economy" has taken on the mystical attributes of the King's Body. The oft-quoted slogan from the Clinton era—It's the Economy, stupid"—illustrates our human tendency to turn complex social and political forces into a single figure. In the public realm, we speak less of "economics" than of The Economy itself, which seems to behave as mysteriously as the weather or the gods do to primitive minds.

If we turn from the long-term symbolism of political power and sovereignty to the present-day American presidency, we see similar patterns of mystery and, perhaps, mystification. It is a truth universally acknowledged that the state of the US economy at the time of a presidential election helps predict the outcome. Precisely how the state of the economy *does* so remains uncertain, largely because political scientists and economists seem to have difficulty establishing which particular economic variable(s) are decisive and why. Nate Silver's popular blog *FiveThirtyEight* identified forty-three separate economic indicators and measured how well they have predicted presidential election results since 1948. Yet Silver, who has done such effective scholarly and journalistic work to explain the mysteries of polling to the average educated reader, continues to criticize mainstream political science for "physics envy," the assumption that one can reduce complex human behavior to a few simple variables.[3]

A recent article in *Election Studies* summarizes well the state of the scholarly consensus, but proposes the relationship between the economy and voter behavior should not be viewed solely in terms of the "valence" of the economy but also on two other measures, position (existing economic ideology) and patrimony (extent of property-holding). However, it concludes, humbly enough, that these measures taken together only explain short-term forces acting on voting.[4] The study's innovative use of the concepts of "position" and "patrimony," however, illustrates the need to interrogate the symbolic dimensions of the economic narratives that make up existing economic ideology and the physical anxieties connected to the holding of property.

Without rejecting the enterprise of quantitative social science studies of the presidency, what additional insights might more than twenty years of books and articles on presidential rhetoric bring to the issue of the presidency and the economy? The bibliography remains fairly slim, perhaps partially because economics remains the most isolated discipline in the human sciences and partially because topics such as foreign policy or civil rights seem to lend themselves more immediately to rhetorical studies. There are still only a handful of studies of presidential economic rhetoric in rhetorical studies.[5] Perhaps the most important related work in political science is B. Dan Wood's *The Politics of Economic Leadership: The Causes and Consequences of Presidential Rhetoric*.[6] Through a statistical analysis of presidential discourse on the economy, Wood demonstrates how such presidential talk matters by influencing both public opinion and policy outcomes. If we add Stephen Skowronek's work on presidential leadership to the mix, specifically his work on "reconstructive" presidents who are able to be both order affirming and order shattering, we can find ways to integrate the more sweeping historical concerns with which I have begun this essay to a more fine-grained analysis of President Barack Obama's peculiar economic burdens after he assumed office in 2009.[7]

The purpose of this essay is to analyze the rhetorical strategies of President Obama's first few months in office, as he dealt with the aftermath of the Great Recession of 2008. My primary thesis is that Obama's strategic response, whether appropriate or not in strict policy terms at the time, illustrates a signature rhetorical style of his presidency. He relies upon soaring, even religious, appeals to universal values combined with a careful—one might say "wonkish"—devotion to policy details. What he fails to do, however, is to provide simple narratives about complex economic issues for a public ill equipped—by history or education—to follow them. Obama's burden, in Skowronek's terms, was reconstructive—to define precisely why the previous administration's economic order was shattered and to propose a new one. In addition to the specific contextual burdens of 2008, however, Obama has also remained haunted by the ghost of FDR, to whom Obama has inevitably been compared by left-wing critics, whose arguments I take up later in this chapter. I believe that the disjunction between the heroic expectations of the 2008 campaign and the messy realities of governance have thus far hampered Obama's ability to become a reconstructive leader. I begin by identifying the narrative context of economic argument in the 2000s, proceed to an analysis of Obama's major economic policy speech at Georgetown, and conclude with some more speculative inquiries into the long-term problems of economic leadership faced by any American president.

Four and a Half Narratives in Search of a Leader

The central focus of what we consider the best part of the rhetorical tradition has been on invention—the sizing up of a rhetorical situation. Much—probably too much—of the main trajectory of the rhetorical tradition has overemphasized the strategic and tactical power of the orator over situations and audiences. Twentieth-century rhetorical theory increased the scope of rhetorical studies but in many respects attenuated the power of the individual orator, identifying the role of language and ideology in prefiguring the terrain on which rhetorical actions occur. We have developed better ways of reading how texts and their performances enact what we might call "Deep Invention"—the only partially conscious way that advocates respond to and at times create new metaphors, narratives, and other ways of framing the ever-elusive Real. The most productive recent work in rhetorical history or public address studies analyzes the interaction between traditional rhetorical invention in key texts and the deep inventional frames that constitute the meanings that speakers and audiences inhabit. Thus, for example, John Murphy's study of JFK's Yale speech in 1962 illustrates, by examining surface strategies of ethos and dissociation, how JFK participated in the deeper reconstruction of the language of political liberalism—a language that now may be exhausted in Obama's economic rhetoric.[8]

By fall 2008, it had become painfully clear that something had gone wrong with the cognitive maps most economists and policy makers had been using since at least 1975, the year of the Great U-Turn in the Western economies away from Keynes. People who had been warning about free market fundamentalism for years could be forgiven a little schadenfreude when Allan Greenspan, disciple of Ayn Rand and hero of "the Markets," participated in a degradation ritual on Capitol Hill on October 22, 2008: "Those of us who have looked to the self-interest of lending institutions to protect shareholders' equity, myself included, are in a state of shocked disbelief," he told the House Committee on Oversight and Government Reform.[9]

Following the study of Lewis-Beck and Nadeau on the valence of economic factors in voting as based on position (economic ideology) and patrimony (extent of property ownership), I would argue that we need more work on the core rhetorical narratives that underlie both economic policy argument and the discourse of property. (I note in passing that one explanation for the Great Recession of 2008 was the overzealous expansion of property ownership, in the form of speculation on sub-prime mortgages.) By the start of the Obama administration, four main economic "positions" were in contention. For purposes of comparison, I propose that each consists of a core concept, a narrative, and an internal contradiction.

First, there is the Marxist tradition, with its core concepts of class struggle and of the mode of production as divided into productive forces and productive relations. Although Marxists historically have differed about the relative primacy accorded to productive forces or productive relations as the motor of history, the core narrative about capitalism remains the same: capitalism is simultaneously the best and the worst thing that could have happened to human beings; capitalism is driven to commodify everything, from labor to sex, to the divine; the constant drive of mature capitalism is to replace living labor with dead labor—the squeeze of technology on employment—and to replace exhausted domestic markets with foreign markets. "Accumulate! Accumulate! That is Moses and the Prophets," writes Marx.[10]

And yet this restless productive drive is prone to crises, crises solved each time by technology or imperialism or, in their most recent form, by reckless expansion of credit to solve the chronic problem of overproduction. Consume! Consume! has been Moses and the Prophets since the 1970s. The cultural requirements for efficient production and those for ever-expanding consumption completely contradict each other, as Daniel Bell presciently diagnosed in 1976.[11] The most persuasive narrative of the Great Recession as the culmination of decades of over-competition and overproduction is probably that of UCLA economic historian Robert Brenner, in his recently updated book *The Economics of Global Turbulence*.[12] And yet the internal contradiction of the Marxist narrative remains its inability to mediate its ever more persuasive diagnosis of global economic structures with the possibility of local, national, and global struggles.

A second economic ideology, which developed as an effort to mediate between the extremes of nineteenth-century liberalism and Soviet-style Communism, is that of social democracy. Social democracy emerged, preeminently in Scandinavia, as an effort to save capitalism through regulation (its key term, I would argue)—not through state ownership, but through highly progressive tax policy, a strong welfare state, and the encouragement of management–labor cooperation rather than conflict.

Christian Democrats in Germany, Red Tories in Canada, and their Social Democratic adversaries came, after 1948, to achieve a remarkable consensus on economic issues.[13] Yet social democracy was in many ways the victim of its own success, as Habermas has argued, for it enacted a contradiction between communicative reason and technical reason. It displaced economic conflict into the technocratic realm of expertise, with its success eventually undercutting the political passions that once made structural change possible. A crisis of legitimation resulted.[14]

The third position is what Europeans refer to as the "liberal" one, or what the world has come to call "neoliberalism," or, perhaps better, the "Washington consensus." I have discussed in my 2001 book, *Selling the Free Market*, the history and rhetorical dynamics of the way market fundamentalism emerged out of the 1970s economic crisis, although I stopped short of extending my analysis to the issue of globalization.[15] I redress this omission briefly here. The term *Washington Consensus* was initially coined in 1989 by John Williamson to describe a set of ten specific economic policy prescriptions that he considered should constitute the "standard" reform package promoted for developing countries by Washington, D.C.–based institutions such as the International Monetary Fund (IMF), World Bank, and the United States Department of the Treasury. The consensus included ten broad sets of recommendations, including "fiscal policy discipline," tax reform, market-determined interest rates, trade liberalization, privatization of state enterprises, and deregulation.[16] As Dani Rodrik of Harvard summarized, "Stabilize, privatize, and liberalize" became the mantra of a generation of technocrats who cut their teeth in the developing world and of the political leaders they counseled. Rodrik pointed out a paradox: although China and India increased their economies' reliance on free market forces to a limited extent, their general economic policies remained the exact opposite to the Washington Consensus' main recommendations. Both had high levels of protectionism, no privatization, extensive industrial policies planning, and lax fiscal and financial policies through the 1990s. Had they been dismal failures, they would have presented strong evidence in support of the recommended Washington Consensus policies. However they turned out to be successes. Rodrik concludes that no one really believes in the Washington Consensus any more.[17] Not only did facts tend to have a left-wing bias, but market fundamentalists had the same internal contradiction as Marxists: they could not generate an effective set of rhetorical and political strategies to implement their radical program with real life audiences who had gotten used to social security, Medicare, and farm price supports.

The fourth position is the hard-core market fundamentalism of Ron Paul and Glenn Beck, grounded in Austrian economics. It is sharply distinguished by its rejection of mathematical models in economics, a rigidly syllogistic method, a rejection of nearly all government intervention in the economy—including and especially regulation of money by the Federal Reserve—and a return to the gold standard. Austrian economists have been given little respect in mainstream economics, existing only on the fringe of the profession, notably at the Mises Institute at Auburn University, but their analysis has become the dominant economic view of the hard-core Christian Right.[18] The angry fulminations against Keynes in Congress stem directly from talking points distributed by savvy Austrian economists. The apparent takeover of the Conservative Political Action Committee meeting in Washington, D.C., in February 2010 by disciples of Ron Paul and the intense popularity of Glenn Beck suggests the return of a narrative in which "Progressives," going back to Theodore Roosevelt, are the cancer that must be eliminated from the body politic. The current realignment of economic narratives suggests that we need a better understanding of what I might call "folk economics." There is a deeply ingrained distrust in the United States of finance capital, grounded in a "producerist" ideology that we can trace back to the civic republican assertion of the incompatibility of virtue and commerce. By focusing on "work" as a central value, it becomes possible to attack the poor, educated elites—Obama the "law professor," as Sarah Palin says—and bankers simultaneously. It remains unlikely, however, that the Austrian fringe can persuade more diverse groups, especially ruling elites, but they are poised to make considerable political mischief for years to come, unless some sort of economic stabilization occurs.

The "four and a half" in the heading of this section refers to the unstable position of "liberalism" in the American tradition, from Franklin Delano Roosevelt through Jimmy Carter. Although Harry S. Truman and Lyndon Baines Johnson may have been the closest we have had to social democracy in the European sense, what has passed for "liberalism" has been closer to the standard free market narrative, with Carter and Bill Clinton as zealous advocates for deregulation.

The financial crisis of 2008 was both caused by the instability of the "four and a half" previously dominant economic narratives and an effect of the instability of those narratives—quite simply the explanatory power of each of the narratives had become exhausted by the end of 2008. It may be profitable therefore to think of the financial crisis of 2008 as conjuncture or as a "Thucydian crisis" of economic narratives.[19] Such crisis and instability meant that we had a chance to reconstitute our public economic rhetoric in a way that comes only once every 50 years or so. Yet, Obama may have already failed, both institutionally and rhetorically. As Joseph Stiglitz, whose position most closely resembles my own, points out in his book *Freefall,* the stimulus plan was inadequate for the following reasons: (1) It was not large enough; (2) It did not provide long-term assistance to the states, who are now functioning as fifty little Hoovers with drastic cutbacks on spending; (3) It did not fill holes in the safety net, including help with mortgage payments; (4) It cut taxes too much—a third of the stimulus was tax cuts, but as Stiglitz points out, the tax cuts failed because they were used for short-term debt relief. Whereas $800 billion seemed like a lot of money—although when compared with the Iraq War, the Bush tax cuts for the top 1 percent, and the Medicare prescription bill, it was quite small—it was not enough. Just offsetting the states' revenue shortfall would require federal stimulus spending greater than 1 percent of GDP per year.[20]

Now, this explanation of stimulus policy does not seem terribly complicated to me, and if I can pinpoint one core rhetorical failure of Obama's presidency, it was his failure to explain and sell even the stimulus that he got. His speech at Georgetown University on April 14, 2009,[21] illustrates the failure.

The Georgetown Speech

A full discussion of Obama's economic rhetoric during this period would need to include all of his speeches related to economic questions from the 2008 campaign to his first year in office, perhaps using a method similar to that of B. Dan Wood's work noted previously. It would also need to include the coordinated responses of his economic team—notably Christina Romer, Austan Goolsbee, and Cecilia Rouse of the Council of Economic Advisors; Larry Summers, Assistant to the President for Economic Policy; Peter Orzsag, Director of the Office of Management and Budget; and Timothy Geithner, Secretary of the Treasury.[22] Federal Reserve Chair Ben Bernanke played an obviously important public voice as well, although his putatively independent status complicates the situation. Perhaps the most interesting document created thus far by the administration is the February 26, 2010, "Annual Report of the White House Task Force on the Middle Class," which strikes a markedly more "populist" tone than previous administration economic rhetoric.[23]

Based on a systematic reading of the president's economic messages during his first few months in office, the Georgetown Speech, however, sums up the key themes and tone of his attempt to reconstruct the body politico-economic. It is representative of Obama's economic rhetoric for these reasons: (1) It integrates economic policy into all of his other policy initiatives, including and especially health care reform; (2) it consistently uses the notion of building a foundation as an organizing image; (3) it avoids divisive or potentially alarming rhetoric; and (4) it builds on an assertion of macroeconomic policy consensus among experts, especially on the idea of the stimulus.

Here are brief examples of each:

(1) In the introduction, Obama immediately responds to critics, summarized in one tidy paragraph:

I know that some have accused of us taking on too much at once. Others believe we haven't done enough. And many Americans are simply wondering how all of our different programs and policies fit together in a single, overarching strategy that will move this economy from recession to recovery and, ultimately, to prosperity.[24]

He goes on:

I want every American to know that each action we take and each policy we pursue is driven by a larger vision of America's future— a future in which sustained economic growth creates good jobs and rising incomes; a future where prosperity is fueled not by excessive debt, reckless speculation, and fleeting profit, but is instead built by skilled, productive workers; by sound investments that will spread opportunity at home and allow this nation to lead the world in the technologies, innovations, and discoveries that will shape the 21st century. That is the America I see. That is the future I know we can have.[25]

A more specifically religious, even mystical, dimension of the argument appears with Obama's citation of the following passage from Matthew 7. Here is the full passage, in the King James Version:

> 7:24 Therefore whosoever heareth these sayings of mine, and doeth them, I will liken him unto a wise man, which built his house upon a rock:
> 7:25 And the rain descended, and the floods came, and the winds blew, and beat upon that house; and it fell not: for it was founded upon a rock.
> 7:26 And every one that heareth these sayings of mine, and doeth them not, shall be likened unto a foolish man, which built his house upon the sand:
> 7:27 And the rain descended, and the floods came, and the winds blew, and beat upon that house; and it fell: and great was the fall of it.

Biblical references are certainly a staple of presidential rhetoric—FDR's money changers in the Temple being the most famous example—but the entailments of the parable as applied to the modern political economy are particularly interesting. Note the appropriation of sacred language—even using the direct words of the Son of God in the Sermon on the Mount—to describe the economic body politic. Note also the comparison of economic crisis to bad weather, which implies a certain degree of inevitability in Obama's subtle rewriting of the neoliberal narrative discussed earlier.

(2) At the *peripeteia* of the speech, after quoting the Sermon on the Mount passage, he previews future policy with this statement:

> It's a foundation built upon five pillars that will grow our economy and make this new century another American century: new rules for Wall Street that will reward drive and innovation; new investments in education that will make our workforce more skilled and competitive; new investments in renewable energy and technology that will create new jobs and industries; new investments in health care that will cut costs for families and businesses; and new savings in our federal budget that will bring down the debt for future generations. That is the new foundation we must

build. That must be our future—and my administration's policies are designed to build that future.[26]

The rest of the speech expands each "pillar" and then ties them back to the house built on rock parable.

(3) The body of the speech begins with a narrative of the crisis—a very short narrative for, I believe, strategic purposes:

Recessions are not uncommon. Markets and economies naturally ebb and flow, as we have seen many times in our history. But this recession is different. This recession was not caused by a normal downturn in the business cycle. It was caused by a perfect storm of irresponsibility and poor decision-making that stretched from Wall Street to Washington to Main Street.[27]

He then rather abstractly lays blame in this order, Americans who ceased to save their pennies to buy their dream house, deceptive mortgage lenders, and Wall Street, which bought and packaged questionable mortgages into securities, even though "no one really knew what the actual value of these securities were."[28] He lays the blame rather equally and briefly, and then spends a bit more time listing actions taken thus far: "the Recovery Act, the bank capitalization program, the housing plan, the strengthening of the non-bank credit market, the auto plan, and our work at the G-20."[29]

(4) To describe the administration's actions, he uses rather technical language—by the standards of the American public and most politicians: "They have been designed to increase aggregate demand, get credit flowing again to businesses, and help them ride out the storm."[30] The use of the rather technical Keynesian term "aggregate demand," offered without a clear definition, illustrates what I believe to be the main rhetorical feeling of the speech. He tackles objections to the stimulus in this way:

Economists on both the left and right agree that the last thing a government should do in the middle of a recession is to cut back on spending.…If every family in America…cuts back…then no one is spending any money, which means…there are more layoffs, which means the economy gets even worse. That's why the government has to step in and temporarily boost spending in order to stimulate demand. That's exactly what we're doing right now.[31]

To return to my previous mapping of the four and a half narratives about political economy, note that Obama's arguments are squarely in the "half" category—he proposes modest reregulation, a modest stimulus, and modest hope. There is no sweeping call to create jobs through government spending or to extend the welfare safety net. Obama's rhetoric stays safely within the bounds of the neoliberal consensus, with a modestly Keynesian twist. Rather than take advantage of the Thucydian crisis of 2008 to offer a new economic narrative, Obama retreated to previously exhausted narratives. It is safe to conclude, on several levels, that the Georgetown speech reveals that Obama is no FDR, for good or bad. He has consistently failed to express macroeconomic theory in terms accessible to the American people or to offer new economic narratives by which we can understand the role of government in the economy. The fact that so many people want Obama to "unleash his inner FDR," as rhetorical scholar John Murphy put it, leads me to my next main topic.[32]

Contextual Burdens within Obama's Rhetorical Invention

Any discussion of presidential economic rhetoric inevitably leads back to FDR's First Inaugural Address, with its biblical reference to driving the money changers from the temple or of his Madison Square Garden speech in 1936:[33]

> For twelve years this Nation was afflicted with hear-nothing, see-nothing, do-nothing Government. The Nation looked to Government but the Government looked away. Nine mocking years with the golden calf and three long years of the scourge! Nine crazy years at the ticker and three long years in the breadlines! Nine mad years of mirage and three long years of despair! Powerful influences strive today to restore that kind of government with its doctrine that that Government is best which is most indifferent....We had to struggle with the old enemies of peace—business and financial monopoly, speculation, reckless banking, class antagonism, sectionalism, war profiteering....We know now that

Government by organized money is just as dangerous as Government by organized mob. Never before in all our history have these forces been so united against one candidate as they stand today. They are unanimous in their hate for me—and I welcome their hatred.[34]

FDR entered office in similar, albeit even more dire, circumstances as Obama—his was also an era of economic narrative crisis and collapse. Part of FDR's political and rhetorical genius was his ability to connect his New Deal policies to a new narrative that explained the relationship between the government and the economy in such a way that his controversial policies appeared to be reasonable responses to existing economic conditions. Obama appears to lack FDR's ability to connect his policies to new economic narratives. There are, however, three main contextual reasons why, even assuming he wished to, Obama could not "unleash his inner FDR."

1. *Major structural economic reforms require super-super-majorities.* As Nate Silver pointed out, when FDR took over the presidency in 1933, the Democrats controlled 64 percent of the Senate seats and 73 percent of the House seats. Those numbers only increased over the next couple of midterms—during their peak during 1937–38, the Democrats actually controlled about 80 percent of the seats in both chambers. Obama, by contrast, came into his term with 59 percent majorities in both chambers. Of recent "liberal" presidents only FDR's first term and LBJ's 1965–66 period provided a sufficient congressional majority for sweeping reforms.[35]

2. *The structure of the securities market has changed.* It hardly mattered much in 1932 when FDR went after the small number of major investors in the stock market or Keynes rather intemperately proposed "the euthanasia of the rentiers." Now, millions of Americans directly or indirectly invest in the stock and bond market, as my readers on TIAA-CREF or other academic pension plans will attest. "Restoring confidence" in the markets means something rather different now, as a result. A story about the early days of the Clinton administration, told by Bob Woodward, illustrates the problem:

Bentsen and Greenspan quickly persuaded Clinton that attacking the federal deficit was essential, and silenced more populist advisers such as James Carville and Paul Begala. Clinton famously blew up at Rubin and at Alan Blinder, also on the council of economic advisers, 'You mean to tell me that the success of the program and my reelection hinges on the Federal Reserve and a bunch of fucking bond traders?' But Clinton got the message.[36]

Obama thus had to negotiate between the need to lay blame for the meltdown of 2008 in order to construct his firm foundations and the need to "reassure the markets."

   3. *He was constrained by his own centrist ideology and his choice of economic advisors.* Neither Romer nor Summers were particularly sympathetic to the strong Keynesian position, and Summers himself once boasted that legalizing the sale of derivatives (those questionable financial instruments to which Obama alludes in the Georgetown speech) at the end of the Clinton presidency was one of his major achievements. Perhaps the single greatest cause of the collapse—the repeal of the New Deal Glass-Steagall banking laws separating commercial and investment banks—was orchestrated as much by the deregulatory impulses of Clinton as much as by Phil Gramm, the author of the bill repealing those laws. It is significant that Obama steers away from any indictment of deregulation in the Georgetown speech, although at the end of January 2010 Obama finally announced that a restoration of Glass-Steagall was now a major goal of the administration—an announcement that occurred only the day after Scott Brown was elected to replace Ted Kennedy.[37]

If the key to Obama's economic reconstruction of the body politic was the stimulus, two questions remain. The first, certainly beyond the scope of the present essay, concerns the actual impact of the stimulus. Michael Grunwald, for example, has recently published an exhaustive, detailed account of the internal deliberations in the Obama White House during the first months of 2009.[38] In contrast to Stiglitz, Grunwald makes a persuasive case that the economic recovery program did avert greater economic catastrophe. Given the fact that economists continue to argue about the relative success of the Keynesian policies of the first four years of the New Deal, it is uncertain when a clear consensus will emerge. The second question, however, is a specifically rhetorical one. The subtitle of Grunwald's book, *The New New Deal: The Hidden Story of Change in the Obama Era,* illustrates the point. Based on my reading of the Georgetown speech and of all the economic policy messages of the first half of 2009, it is clear that Obama never developed a clear, repeated set of narratives or talking points on the importance of the stimulus package. What might an alternative narrative or image have been?

Consider the following passage from Genesis 41: Joseph has been imprisoned by Pharaoh, but Pharaoh has a disturbing dream that only Joseph can interpret. The King James Version reads:

> And Joseph said unto Pharaoh, The dream of Pharaoh is one: God hath shewed Pharaoh what he is about to do. [26] The seven good kine are seven years; and the seven good ears are seven years: the dream is one. [27] And the seven thin and ill favoured kine that came up after them are seven years; and the seven empty ears blasted with the east wind shall be seven years of famine. [28] This is the thing which I have spoken unto Pharaoh: What God is about to do he sheweth unto Pharaoh. [29] Behold, there come seven years of great plenty throughout all the land of Egypt: [30] And there shall arise after them seven years of famine; and all the plenty shall be forgotten in the land of Egypt; and the famine shall consume the land; [31] And the plenty shall not be known in the land by reason of that famine following; for it shall be very grievous. [32] And for that the dream was doubled unto Pharaoh twice; it is because the thing is established by God, and God will shortly bring it to pass. [33] Now therefore let Pharaoh look out a man discreet and wise, and set him over the land of Egypt. [34] Let Pharaoh do this, and let him appoint officers over the land, and take up the fifth part of the land of Egypt in the seven plenteous years. [35] And let them gather all the food of those good years that come, and lay up corn under the hand of Pharaoh, and let them keep food in the cities. [36] And that food shall be for store to the land against the seven years of famine, which shall be in the land of Egypt; that the land perish not through the famine. [37] And the thing was good in the eyes of Pharaoh, and in the eyes of all his servants.

Could Obama have reinvented the stimulus and economic recovery act as an instance of wise stewardship by the state, whose responsibility it is to spend during times of famine while remaining careful during years of plenty? Given the ongoing dispute about federal government power since at least the Reagan administration, perhaps more attention to biblical political economy is in order.[39]

Conclusion

I have made two main arguments in this chapter: first, even though President Obama was burdened by his particular political and economic context in the first year of his administration, he failed to develop a sufficiently clear narrative to explain or sell it to the public. A Pew Research Poll conducted in April 2010, for example, found that two-thirds of the public believed that the stimulus had failed to create jobs.[40] The second argument is far more speculative and requires further development, but I believe I have a made a *prima facie* case for the persistence of sacred and monarchical images in current economic discourse.

The American experience since the 1970s, and the experience of the world under capitalist globalization, manifests itself as a crisis of sovereignty. Beginning with Kantorowicz's insight, the development of the concept of sovereignty in the late medieval/early modern period joined the corporal body of the King to the mystical body of Christ. After the breakdown of absolute monarchy, the same image, however, continued below the surface of discussions of state sovereignty and popular will. What I have tried to do by developing the concept of the President's Two Bodies is to illustrate how the notion of the sovereign becomes unstable over time, given the pressures of the modern capitalist economy and, increasingly, globalization, which in the neoliberal imaginary, at least, behaves much like the weather. Everyone talks about it, but nobody is doing anything about it.

To bring the body analogy full circle, let me briefly raise a topic normally unconnected to economic discourse: the particular materiality of President Obama's body as a black man of mixed race. It is not surprising that in times of anxiety about a shrinking white population the most salient and polarizing public issues involve the body: abortion, homosexuality, torture, the president's race. The ghost of King Charles I has come to inhabit the executive office. The only president since Coolidge who has not left the

White House in death or disgrace was Dwight D. Eisenhower. I need not name the anxiety over the fate of President Obama that hit me, watching him speak in Grant Park on Election Night 2008. If the health of the body politic is figured in the body of the American president, our ongoing economic and political crisis points only toward a now symbolically violent but soon literally violent cure. I can only hope it is not already too late.

Notes

1. Ernst Kantorowicz, *The King's Two Bodies: A Study in Medieval Political Theology* (Princeton, NJ: Princeton University Press, 1957). For an application of Kantorowicz's thesis to the American presidency, see Michael Rogin, "The President's Two Bodies," in *Ronald Reagan, the Movie, and Other Episodes in Political Demonology* (Berkeley: University of California Press, 1987).

2. See Carl Schmitt, *The Concept of the Political,* translated by George D. Schwab (Chicago: University of Chicago Press, 1996); and Giorgio Agamben, *State of Exception* (Chicago: University of Chicago Press, 2005).

3. Silver points specifically to the ISM manufacturing index (averaged from January to September and conducted by the Institute of Supply Management, based on a survey of three hundred manufacturing firms), which explains 46 percent of the popular vote margin for the incumbent president, followed by change in nonfarm payrolls (44 percent) and changes in the unemployment rate (September less January, at 40 percent). Nate Silver, "Which Economic Indicators Best Predict Presidential Elections," *New York Times,* November 18, 2011, http://fivethirtyeight.blogs.nytimes.com/2011/11/18/which-economic-indicators-best-predict-presidential-elections/.

4. Michael Steven Lewis-Beck and Richard Nadeau, "Economic Voting Theory: Testing New Dimensions," *Electoral Studies* 30 (2011): 288–94.

5. See Amos Kiewe and Davis Houck, *A Shining City on a Hill: Ronald Reagan's Economic Rhetoric, 1951–1989* (NY: Praeger, 1991); and Davis Houck, *Rhetoric as Currency* (College Station: Texas A&M University Press, 2001). See also James Arnt Aune, "The Econo-Rhetorical Presidency," in James Arnt Aune and Martin J. Medhurst, eds., *The Prospect of Presidential Rhetoric* (College Station: Texas A&M University Press, 2008), 46–68.

6. B. Dan Wood, *The Politics of Economic Leadership: The Causes and Consequences of Presidential Economic Rhetoric* (Princeton, NJ: Princeton University Press, 2007).

7. Stephen Skowronek, *The Politics Presidents Make: Leadership from John Adams to Bill Clinton* (Cambridge, MA: Harvard University Press, 1997).

8. John M. Murphy, "The Language of the Liberal Consensus: John F. Kennedy, Technical Reason, and the 'New Economics" at Yale University," *Quarterly Journal of Speech* 90 (2004): 133–62.

9. Edmund L. Andrews, Greenspan Concedes Error on Regulation, *New York Times,* October 23, 2008, http://www.nytimes.com/2008/10/24/business/economy/24panel.html).

10. Karl Marx, *Capital I,* chapter 24, section 3.

11. Daniel Bell, *The Cultural Contradictions of Capitalism* (NY: Basic Books, 1976).

12. Robert Brenner, *The Economics of Global Turbulence* (London: Verso, 2006).

13. Sheri Berman, *The Primacy of Politics: Social Democracy and the Making of Europe's Twentieth Century* (Cambridge: Cambridge University Press, 2006).

14. Jürgen Habermas, *Legitimation Crisis,* translated by Thomas McCarthy (Boston: Beacon Press, 1975).

15. James Arnt Aune, *Selling the Free Market: The Rhetoric of Economic Correctness* (NY: Guilford, 2001).

16. John Williamson, "What Washington Means by Policy Reform," in *Latin American Readjustment: How Much has Happened,* ed. John Williamson (Washington: Institute for International Economics," 1989.

17. Dani Rodrik, "Goodbye Washington Consensus, Hello Washington Confusion?" *Journal of Economic Literature* 44 (December 2006): 969–83.

18. A prominent figure in both Austrian economics and the Christian Right is Gary North, who runs the "Institute for Christian Economics" in Tyler, Texas (see http://www. garynorth.com/).

19. Thomas Gustafson, *Representative Words: Politics, Literature, and the American Language, 1776–1865* (Cambridge: Cambridge University Press, 1992); Louis Althusser, "Ideology and Ideological State Apparatuses," in *Contemporary Critical Theory,* ed. Dan Latimer (San Diego: Harcourt Publishing, 1989); Antonio Gramsci, *Selections from the Prison Note Books,* "Past and Present," 148–49; Louis Althusser, *Machiavelli and Us,* ed. Francois Matheron, translated by Gregory Elliot (London: Verso, 1999), 18; Stuart Hall, "Gramsci and Us," *Marxism Today,* June 1987, 16–21; Lawrence Grossberg, *Caribbean Reasonings: Culture, Politics, Race, and Diaspora in the Thought of Stuart Hall,* ed. Brian Meeks (Kingston, Jamaica: Ian Randle: 2007); David Scott, "The Permanence of Pluralism," in *Without Guarantees: In Honour of Stuart Hall* (Verso, 2000); and Raymond Williams, "Base and Superstructure in Marxist Cultural Theory," *New Left Review* (1973): 3–16.

20. Joseph E. Stiglitz, *Freefall* (NY: W.W. Norton 2010), 58–76.

21. Barack Obama, "Remarks on the National Economy," Georgetown University, Washington, DC, April 14, 2009, in *The American Presidency Project* [online], eds. John Woolley and Gerhard Peters, http://www.presidency.ucsb.edu/ws/index.php?pid=86000&st=&st1=.

22. For useful background on the "team," see Ryan Lizza, "Inside the Crisis: Larry Summers and the White House Economic Team," *New Yorker,* October 12, 2009, http://www.newyorker.com/reporting/2009/10/12/091012fa_fact_lizza.

23. "Annual Report of the White House Task Force on the Middle Class," http://www. whitehouse.gov/sites/default/files/microsites/100226-annual-report-middle-class. pdf).

24. Obama, "Remarks on the National Economy," paragraph 6.

25. Ibid., paragraph 8.

26. Ibid., paragraph 46.

27. Ibid., paragraph 10.

28. Ibid., paragraph 12.

29. Ibid., paragraph 37.

30. Ibid.

31. Ibid., paragraph 19.

32. "Liberal Eye on the Republican Guy," *Oratorical Animal,* http://oratoricalanimal .typepad.com/oratorical_animal/.

33. For an in-depth analysis, see Davis Houck, *FDR and Fear Itself: The First Inaugural Address* (College Station: Texas A&M University Press, 2002).

34. Franklin Delano Roosevelt, "Speech at Madison Square Garden," October 31, 1936, http://millercenter.org/scripps/archive/speeches/detail/3307).

35. Nate Silver, *538* blog, Obama's No F.D.R.—Nor Does He Have F.D.R.'s Majority," March 1, 2010, http://www.fivethirtyeight.com/2010/03/obamas-no-fdr-nor-does-he-have-fdrs.html).

36. Bob Woodward, *Maestro: Greenspan's Fed and the American Boom* (NY: Simon and Schuster, 2000), 125–126.

37. Andrew Leonard, "Obama Finally Listens to Paul Volcker," *Salon,* January 20, 2010, http://www.salon.com/2010/01/21/a_new_glass_steagal.

38. Michael Grunwald, *The New New Deal: The Hidden Story of Change in the Obama Era* (New York: Simon and Schuster, 2012).

39. Shortly after I wrote this paragraph, I discovered that the liberal economist Brad DeLong uses the same biblical passage as a justification for Keynesian aggregate demand policies: http://delong.typepad.com/sdj/2012/10/bls-employment-release-talking-points-october-5–2012.html.

40. Cited in Andy Barr, "Poll: Most Americans Think the Stimulus Didn't Help," *Politico,* http://www.politico.com/news/stories/0410/36544.html.

CHAPTER 9

The Secular Messianic Style in Barack Obama's "Call to Renewal" Speech

CATHERINE L. LANGFORD

In 2004, Barack Obama catapulted into the national political scene when, as a candidate for the United States Senate, he gave the keynote address at the Democratic National Convention. His speech confirmed public speculation that Obama was the new face of the Democratic Party. *Chicago Magazine*'s David Bernstein reports that the speech "changed Obama's profile overnight and made him a household name."[1] Communication scholars Robert Rowland and John Jones locate the significance of Obama's message in his ability to construct "a narrative that balanced personal and societal values and in so doing made the American Dream more accessible to liberals, thereby laying the groundwork for reclaiming the narrative center of American politics for the Democratic party."[2] The success of his speech led to the reissuing of his biography, *Dreams from My Father*[3] and to talk by journalists and political pundits that he might be a possible future presidential candidate and the first African American President of the United States.[4] However, although a party hopeful, Barack Obama had many personal burdens—ranging from preexisting identity issues to political slander—that meant that he was not the presumptive nominee for the Democratic Party in the 2008 presidential election.

Obama's preexisting personal burdens are a collection of fixed and irreversible facts about the person and his history. He faced many such challenges to his candidacy: he was the first candidate of mixed race to receive a major party nomination for president; he had no military experience, little national political experience, and no executive experience; he admitted to drug use in his youth; he spent his childhood outside of the United States mainland—four years of which were lived in Indonesia; and he cannot be located within the white protestant tradition of most presidential office holders who preceded him.[5] Obama could not alter these personal burdens; they related to his identity, his childhood, his up-bringing, and his professional career. He would draw upon them, however, during campaign speeches to create rapport with potential voters.

Obama's fixed personal burdens were heightened by rumors that he was Muslim and that his policy positions were anti-Christian. Only two weeks after he gave his keynote address at the DNC, *Out2.com* columnist Andy Martin held a press conference during which he stated, "Obama is a Muslim who has concealed his religion."[6] In what could be character-ized as a post-9/11 Islamophobic society, such an accusation could have been damning. Less than one month later, Alan Keyes, his Republican opponent for the Illinois senatorial seat, augmented fear about Obama's faith tradition by claiming that Jesus Christ would not support Obama as a political candidate. Keyes asserted, "Jesus Christ would not vote for Barack Obama. Christ would not vote for Barack Obama because Barack Obama has behaved in a way that it is inconceivable for Christ to have behaved."[7] According to Keyes, Obama voted against legislation for new-born survivors of abortion, thus supporting the practice of infanticide.[8]

Although Obama could not change his personal history, the reports that he was Muslim and that his policies were against biblical principles presented him with a rhetorical exigence to which he could respond. Obama's remarks immediately following Keyes's accusation drew upon the ideals of secular humanism and therefore did not alter the rhetorical exigence that Martin's and Keyes's discourse created. He needed a different strategy. Two years later, Obama strengthened his public profile by framing his personal experiences as similar to the experiences of other citizens. Within the rhetorical audience of freestyle evangelicals and Catholics, he found persons who could be mediators of change. He addressed the per-ceived constraint about his viability as a candidate and lessened the force of the personal burdens created by political slander. He did so by merging traditional religious discourse with the ideals of secular humanism.

On June 26, 2006, Barack Obama addressed the Sojourners—a progres-sive Christian organization. Delivered the summer before he announced his presidential candidacy, his "Call to Renewal" speech can be consid-ered as the most important piece of public discourse about faith made by a Democrat since John F. Kennedy addressed the Houston Ministerial Society in 1960.[9] Steven Waldman—senior advisor to the Chairman of the Federal Communications Commission and confounder of Beliefnet, a multifaith Web site—characterized Obama's speech as "historic."[10] In an editorial in the *Washington Post,* Pulitzer Prize–winning author Jim Hoagland praised Obama's remarks for "an unusual combination of clarity and civility."[11] Obama used this speech deliberately to woo freestyle evangelicals—persons who have a clearly defined religious orthodoxy but who adapt their traditions to the changing sociopolitical landscape—and the Catholic vote. His campaign mailed copies of his "Call to Renewal" speech to thousands of ministers around the nation, met with them in person or spoke with them on the phone, visited almost a dozen Christian colleges in swing states, and organized house meetings.[12] Doing so enabled Obama to appeal to persons outside of the traditional Democratic voter base, thus expanding the base.

In this speech, Obama authoritatively reinterpreted the role of faith in a secular democratic society by reframing social ills as the burden of the body politic. He appealed to a universal audience, cognizant of the importance of the present in the social reality of the public. Obama seemed to heed John Lucaites's call "to develop an argumentative rationale for human action which is carefully consistent with the shared principles of a consensually constituted society, but simultaneously is flexible enough to allow *both* the leaders and the members of a society to adapt actively to the exigencies of the social and political world."[13] Obama offered a prudent consideration of his auditors' material welfare. Prudence, according to Robert Hariman, enables a person to balance the needs of the individual against the needs of the community, and to evaluate possible ways to achieve the ends that would be best given the situational constraints.[14] Obama acknowledged the failures and limitations of humanity and organized government with "[a] hope that we can live with one another in a way that reconciles the beliefs of each with the good of all."[15] Obama combined religious discourse and secular humanism, producing a distinctive style of rhetorical discourse that I call the secular messianic style.

This essay begins with a summary of secular humanism and the "God gap" that led progressive Christians to call for a new understanding of the relationship between religion and the public sphere. I then summarize the rhetorical markers of the secular messianic style, before providing a close textual analysis of Obama's use of it in his "Call to Renewal" speech. My analysis allows me to explain how Obama's "Call to Renewal" message strategically appealed to religious voters.

Secular Humanism and the God Gap

When questioned by the media about Keyes's remark that Jesus Christ would not vote for him, Obama recounts, "I answered with what has come to be the typically liberal response in such debates—namely, I said that we live in a pluralistic society, that I can't impose my own religious views on another, that I was running to be the U.S. Senator of Illinois and not the Minister of Illinois." Obama's response implied that individuals should be regulated by their conscience, rather than by religious doctrine. Obama later expressed regret for his comment, contending that "my answer did not adequately address the role my faith has in guiding my own values and my own beliefs."[16]

Obama's response to Keyes was consistent with secular humanism, which does not allow for the use of religious beliefs and principles to guide public policy decisions. When writing about secularism in the 1800s, George Jacob Holyoake explained, "Secularism is the study of promoting human welfare by material means; measuring human welfare by the utilitarian rule, and making the service of others a duty of life."[17] Holyoake's explanation demands that secularism be bound by the temporal concerns of material reality, without any consideration of the eternal. Secular humanism is guided by the concept of natural law—the belief that rights are inherent and unalienable to human beings. Public policy regarding the common good can be determined through a person's use of reason.

Secular humanism, however, is problematic in a nation-state whose populace overwhelmingly avows the existence of a God.[18] Although the Democratic Party advanced the ideals of secular humanism throughout the latter part of the twentieth century, their stance was questioned when exit polls in 2004 revealed that white evangelical born-again Christians who are frequently churchgoers represent a significant base of support who vote largely as a block for Republicans.[19] Amy Sullivan, contributing editor to *Time* magazine, refers to religious Americans voting Republican and secular Americans voting Democratic as the "God gap."[20] Sullivan explains that, as the Religious Right grew in prominence, Democrats "chose to beat a retreat in the competition for religious voters and the discussion of morality, effectively ceding the ground to conservatives. The emergence of the God gap represents a failure of the left as much as it does an achievement of the right."[21] It was not until Bush's reelection that progressive Christians began to counter the Republican claim that Christians only vote Republican. Pew Forum on Religion and Public Life Senior Fellow John C. Green reports that 22 million voters in the United States are "freestyle evangelicals."[22] They do not identify strongly with the Republican Party, but they lean toward the GOP because it projects an image of itself as the political party for persons of faith. The 2004 election revealed that Democrats could increase their voter base if they could articulate a message appealing to such voters.

As progressive evangelicals began discussing the God gap publicly, their commentary provided examples of discourse that did not project the idea that the speaker's policy positions represented the infallible will of God. Religious leader Jim Wallis summarized how the Religious Right ignored social justice issues, whereas the secular left did not know how to talk about moral values.[23] First Amendment scholar Noah Feldman concluded that the tension between unity and diversity could only be lessened if secular Americans recognize that religious values shape political ideologies and if evangelical Americans accept that their faith cannot be public policy.[24] Politician Kathleen Kennedy Townsend criticized evangelicals for their tendency to focus on personal salvation at the expense of social justice.[25] Religious leader Tony Campolo argued that Jesus Christ transcends partisan affiliation, and voters need to do their best to determine, on an issue-by-issue basis, the will of God as consistent with scripture.[26] *Washington Post* columnist E. J. Dionne advocated using religion to encourage discussion through "reflection, self-criticism, and doubt."[27] All agree that neither party can claim to be the mouthpiece of God and that religion should work to improve local communities and to further social justice. Most importantly, however, their writings reveal that both parties need to engage issues of faith.

The Secular Messianic Style

The secular messianic style fuses secular humanism and religious discourse in a rhetor's communications. It uses the language of religion to secular, not sacred, ends. Religion does not propel an auditor to act, call a lost people into repentance, or seek transformation or transcendence. The secular messianic style uses a prudential approach to policy making, seeking measurable alterations to citizens' material realities. Not concerned with the ultimate issue of the sacred—damnation or redemption—but with the substance of reality in the present, it allows for the possibility that those interests will be guided by a person's faith.

The secular messianic style can be distinguished from other forms of religious discourse. It does not employ the jeremiad as characterized by Sacvan Bercovitch; orators do not call the people back from their sins to avoid the wrath of God.[28] Nor do they employ the secular jeremiad as explained by Kurt Ritter and Richard Johannesen, which purports that the promises of the American Dream are the fulfillment of the covenant.[29] Rather, the secular messianic style unites a fractured public in order to give citizens a sense of belonging. This style is not based on the prophetic tradition as explained by James Darsey.[30] Orators do not assume the prophet ethos; they speak for no one except themselves. Neither does this style espouse the rhetoric of civil religion, which Robert Bellah explains is belief in "the existence of God, the life to come, the reward of virtue and the punishment of vice, and the exclusion of religious intolerance."[31] Concerned with community, the secular messianic style calls the body politic not to communion with a higher power, but with itself. Although it does not seek sacred ends, it exhibits qualities similar to the messianic style used by the biblical Jesus Christ. Four rhetorical markers identify the style: the rhetor speaks as one who has authority, reinterprets the law, includes all persons within the action of the American faith, and is concerned with present time. These elements work together, directing the people to put aside their differences and help one another.

The first characteristic is to speak as one who has authority. Repeatedly, the gospels portray Christ as one who taught with authority. Matthew 7:28–29 recounts, "He was teaching them as one having authority, and not as their scribes."[32] Mark 1:27 declares, "They were all amazed, so that they debated among themselves, saying, 'What is this? A new teaching with authority!'" Luke 4:32 asserts that the people "were amazed at his teaching, for His message was with authority." Although most scholarly work regarding authority considers external authorizing agents such as law, government, God, or political or cultural processes, scholars also regard authority as a performative enactment. For anthropologist Bruce Lincoln, "[D]iscursive authority is not so much an entity as it is (1) an effect; (2) the capacity for producing that effect; and (3) the commonly shared opinion that a given actor has the capacity for producing that effect."[33] Legal scholar James Boyd White concludes, "[T]he object of authority is not an 'object' at all but a way of talking and thinking, an activity of mind and imagination and art;

it receives its fullest definition not descriptively, but performatively, as the writer finds a way of using language that transforms it, a way of defining himself and others in order to create a new community, a community of discourse, in the world."[34]

Unlike the messiah of the scriptures, the secular messianic rhetor who speaks with authority makes no grandiose claims regarding origin. Regarding the role of agency in the humanistic tradition, Michael Leff states, "[T]he humanistic approach entails a productively ambiguous notion of agency that positions the orator both as an individual who leads an audience and as a community member shaped and constrained by the demands of the audience."[35] The secular messianic orator simultaneously is consubstantial with, and distinct from, his audience. His shared faith (in)experience combined with his privileged position in civil society act together to authorize his capacity to speak. His message is one of concern for the welfare of the public writ large. The orator privileges the deeds of the auditors rather than his speech; he does not base his authority upon rituals and customs, nor the strength of the message presented, as the traditional and rational forms of legitimization require.[36] One with his audience, he knows their loneliness and understands their need for belonging.

The second characteristic is one who reinterprets the law. Most of Christ's ministry reinterprets the manner in which the Jewish people observe the law. In the Sermon on the Mount, Christ repeatedly asserts, "You have heard" to describe teachings from Mosaic Law before altering auditors' understandings of the commands. Anger becomes synonymous with murder.[37] Adultery,[38] oaths,[39] retribution,[40] personal relationships,[41] giving,[42] prayer,[43] fasting,[44] and earthly possessions similarly are reenvisioned.[45] Reinterpreting the law serves epistemic and constitutive functions. Rhetorical critic Jean Goodwin surmises, "When exercising authority, the speaker does not *give* reasons so much as *create* them. That is, she directly modifies the world in such a way that she changes the courses available to her auditor" (emphasis in original).[46] Regarding the constitutive function of authority in discursive practices, Lincoln asserts that authority can produce "consequential speech,"[47] whereas White contends that a person with authority "finds a way of using language that transforms it, a way of defining himself and others in order to create a new…community of discourse."[48] For these scholars, language has transformative powers. Discourse produces knowledge about what is permissible for community members. Using the tradition of teaching, Christ reinterprets the scriptures through the authority of his divinity. The secular messianic style uses the tradition of public address to reinterpret the problems in civil society. Problems are diminished as community members bear one another's burdens.

The third characteristic includes all persons in the action of the American faith. In the gospels, Christ opens the doors of heaven to "everyone," "all," "whoever," "anyone," and "everyone" who would seek and obey him. "For everyone who asks receives" (Matthew 7:8); "Everyone therefore who shall confess Me before men, I will also confess him before My Father" (Matthew 10:32); and "Come to Me, all who are weary and heavy-laden" (Matthew 11:28). Regardless of religious affiliation, the promises of scripture are accessible to all. Similarly, the secular messianic style invites all persons to participate in the promises of the democratic republic. The American faith is the belief in the transcendent values of American democracy (justice, equality, liberty, pluralism, and fairness), accessible only by acting together. According to Chaim Perelman and Lucie Olbrechts-Tyteca, discourse "addressed to a universal audience must convince the reader that the reasons adduced are of a compelling character, that they are self-evident, and possess an absolute and timeless validity, independent of local or historical contingencies."[49] Regardless of particular problems facing civic society, the telic ends of the nation persist and serve as aspiration for all persons. Within this style, the orator challenges his rhetorical audience to join with others, to realize the promises of the nation.

The fourth characteristic is a concern with the present time. According to Michael Leff, two forms of oratorical time exist: "secular" and "sacred." Secular time corresponds to chronological time and "proceeds in a similar direction; it is homogeneous, continuous, and irreversible."[50] Sacred time, however, "calls us to a moment of origins…It manifests itself recurrently as an interruption in our normal sense of temporality; and thus sacred time is cyclical and discontinuous; it is something always there that we occasionally recover."[51] The gospels are concerned with sacred time—the eternal-made-present, whereas the secular messianic tradition is concerned with secular time—the present-absent-the-eternal. In the book of Matthew, John the Baptist proclaims, "[T]he kingdom of heaven is at hand."[52] Jesus is the manifestation of the eternal made now; the timeless became corporal to experience ephemeral materiality.

The secular messianic style is constrained by time as it uses lessons of the past to inform action within the present. The past is a site of struggle as well as a chronicle of exemplary persons and deeds; the present provides an opportunity to enact the morals and values derived from the past. Time is processed through the physical body, the communal body, and the body politic. As people unite in larger associations (e.g., churches and service organizations), the good deeds of the communal body positively alter the body politic. The secular messianic style does not concern itself with issues of the eternal. Citizens should focus on living life in the community, which has tangible consequences, rather than attaining admittance to the afterlife.

Obama's Authority to Speak

Obama uses public discourse to reinterpret our understanding of the role of religion in the public sphere through his authority as a citizen of the community and as an elected official representing that community. Modeling the Aristotelian artistic proof of *ethos,* Obama asserts his authority by speaking from experience, and by his knowledge of—and goodwill toward—his audience. He constructs his authority within the textual parameters of his speech; he does not lay claim to any inartistic forms of evidence common to the American experience, such as the Constitution or a deity.

Obama's participation in his audience's faith system authorizes him to speak. He, like his audience, was transformed by his conversion. "I heard God's spirit beckoning to me. I submitted myself to His will, and dedicated myself to discovering His truth." Yet, Obama's faith experience transcends religious or denominational affiliation: "That's a path that has been shared by millions upon millions of Americans—evangelicals, Catholics, Protestants, Jews and Muslims alike,"[53] he explains. His faith makes him consubstantial with his immediate audience—members of a progressive faith—and an extended audience—persons of any faith.

His knowledge of his audience also frames Obama as a credible leader. John Murphy explains, "To identify with someone is to transform identity; we become different as a result of sharing our substance, sharing identity, with another."[54] Obama knows his audience's desires, struggles, and inconsistencies because they are his own. His authority is rooted in a similar history, a related want.[55] He claims that Americans seek "a sense of purpose" in their lives. His personal struggles coming to faith empower him to speak about the challenges of the faith experience. He asserts, "Faith doesn't mean that you don't have doubts,"[56] thus validating his audience's struggle with uncertainty as his own.

Obama's goodwill toward his audience also reifies his ability to speak. He chastises ideological extremes and encourages his audience to labor for their neighbor's benefit. He declares that if he opposes abortion, "I cannot simply point to the teachings of my church or evoke God's will. I have to explain why abortion violates some principle that is accessible to people of all faiths, including those with no faith at all."[57] The common good, not religious orthodoxy, should dictate public policy choices.

The people are the authorizing agent in a pluralistic democracy. Humanity itself is the standard by which the good is determined, yet the people are not monolithic. The will of individuals needs to be tempered to attain the communal good. Obama contends that religious denominations cannot direct the governance of secular society. In his discourse, the values and morals of faith are catalysts to action, but they are not the standard against which outcomes are judged. In fact, Obama mocks the application of Biblical principles in contemporary society, claiming that if our system of government enacted Hebrew or Christian directives, the Department of Children and Family Services would remove Isaac from Abraham's custody and the Department of Defense would be disbanded. Biblical edicts have efficacy only to the extent that they encourage persons of faith to act to join together to better the secular realm. Secular political leadership must allow for difference, but difference does not have to be divisive.

In his speech, God calls Obama to faith, but not to act as a religious leader of His people. Neither priest nor prophet, Obama situates himself as a temporal guide who can recommend, but not mandate, courses of action. His rhetorical construction imbues him with qualities similar to those of an omniscient narrator: he has full knowledge of the nation's history, and he understands the thoughts, motives, and needs of individual citizens. Empowered to step outside of his material reality and give voice to different people's perspectives, Obama's citizenship, his faith, and his elected status enable him to move rhetorically between the perspective of the people and that of a temporal guide. Obama is *of* the people while simultaneously being *beyond* them. He becomes consubstantial with his audience when he shares his testimony, and he reminds his audience of his connection with them through his conjoining of himself with his audience, using the personal pronouns "we" and "our."[58] The people, the authorizing agent in our constitutional democracy, designate him a representative of their collective political will. Narratives about his previous election remind his audience that Obama maintains special status within the body politic. As a citizen, Obama hopes for the telic promises of democratic governance; as a temporal guide, he recognizes the need to discuss the nexus of religion and politics. As a person of faith, he admits to having questions and doubts; as a temporal guide, he warns against implementing religious faith in deliberative democracy. As an elected official, he is subject to the criticisms of citizens; as a temporal guide, he criticizes both liberals and conservatives for the mistakes they have made in creating national division. Obama's personal experience and his knowledge of, and goodwill for, his audience empower him to reinterpret the law.

Re-Envisioning the Relationship between Religion and Government

Obama clarifies and reinterprets left-leaning persons and people of faith, the ends of religion and politics, and the problems of society. His reinterpretations function rhetorically to reenvision his audience's understandings of the intersections and functions of religion and government in secular society. Obama differentiates between liberals and progressives and between religion and faith. Liberals, characterized by hackneyed responses and inaction, are intolerant of religion in the public sphere. Progressives are persons of action who assume leadership for resolving national social problems. Religion is an organized entity that has leaders, rituals, and traditions. Faith is a belief. Religion is an external manifestation of an internal faith. When talking about religion Obama references Keyes's 2004 criticism of him, political parties and politics, church attendance, and organized religion. When talking about faith he alludes to personal conviction as an impetus for action. Political parties should not employ religion as a political tool, as faith and religion have a rich tradition of influencing the public sphere. Democrats abdicating faith and Republicans assuming the mantle of the religious threaten this tradition. Obama confronts the "God gap" and rejects the conventional wisdom that faith is a marker of political party identification. Rather than segregate the nation into churchgoers and non-churchgoers, faith imbues citizens with values about how to live one's life and care for others.

Obama's distinction between faith and religion recognizes a difference between constructive and destructive religion. Destructive religion directs religious practice and focuses on the religious practitioner. Constructive religion, an extension of a person's faith, compels the religious person to influence his or her community in a positive fashion. Destructive religion is limiting; constructive religion is liberating. Constructive religion united persons of different faith (or no faith at all), whereas destructive religion rends the body politic.

Religion and politics have opposing ends, according to Obama. He asserts, "Politics depends on our ability to persuade each other of common aims based upon a common reality. It involves the compromise, the art of what's possible. At some fundamental level, religion does not allow for compromise. It's the art of the impossible."[59] Obama's construction of politics creates a rhetorical space for him to propose possible avenues through which persons of faith can enact positive social change. Organized religions do not have a role in the public sphere—but faith does. Obama charges progressives with understanding "universal, rather than religion-specific, values."[60] The underlying value that Obama points to is caring for others, manifesting itself in different venues: ending poverty and racism; decreasing the number of people uninsured and unemployed; curbing gun violence; enhancing education; eliminating AIDS, debt in developing nations, and genocide; and investing in infrastructure and urban renewal. The people are not called to glorify a higher power or to adhere to a list of oughts, but to care for one another.[61]

For Obama, systemic failure does not cause problems as traditionally identified by progressives; these problems are the consequence of original sin. Social problems "are rooted in both societal indifference and individual callousness—in the imperfections of man,"[62] he claims. Locating culpability in the community as well as the person, for Obama individuals acting in community should bear the burden of solving social ills. If neighbors love others as themselves, then offenders, whom Obama characterizes as having holes in their hearts, will be healed. In the secular messianic style, the betterment of society is not dependent upon participation within a particular political party or faith tradition, or the fulfillment of a covenantal promise, but through all denizens of society aiding one another regardless of faith tradition.

Obama celebrates Frederick Douglass, Abraham Lincoln, William Jennings Bryant, Dorothy Day, and Martin Luther King Jr. as "great reformers…motivated by faith." He also identifies Rick Warren, T.D. Jakes, Jim Wallis, and Tony Campolo—ministers within different faith traditions—as examples of religious figures guided by progressive beliefs. Persons concerned with the enactment of religious rules, rather than the transformation of the soul or society, should be condemned. Obama associates Jerry Falwell, Pat Robertson, and Alan Keyes as paradigms of negative religion. These persons can be characterized as "inherently irrational or intolerant" and "fanatical,"[63] the modern-day Pharisees of American society.

The personal narratives Obama uses exemplify the difference between religion and faith. At the beginning of the speech, Obama recounts Keyes's criticism of him—an example of destructive religion that divides people and focuses on a politics of religion rather than a transforming faith. Obama characterizes Keyes as "religious," a member of the Religious Right, and a person "well-versed in the Jerry Falwell-Pat Robertson style of rhetoric that often labels progressives as both immoral and godless." Keyes's declaration that "Jesus Christ would not vote for Barack Obama" authorizes Obama to use his own life as a catalyst to reenvision the realm of religion beyond the purview of the Religious Right. "I had to take Mr. Keyes seriously," Obama contends, "for he claimed to speak for my religion, and my God. He claimed knowledge of certain truths."[64] After thoughtful consideration, Obama rejects Keyes's use of the prophetic voice. Keyes functions as a synecdoche for other Religious Right leaders, persons who divide the nation rather than unify it.

At the end of his speech, Obama shared how a person of faith criticized Obama's pro-choice statement on his campaign Web site. With faith as the motivating factor undergirding the criticism, Obama accepted the reprimand and repented. He wrote a thank you to his critic, clarified his altered policy to his staff, and prayed that he would "extend the same presumption of good faith to others"[65] that the critic had extended to him. The criticism invoked a renewed commitment for his approach to faith and the public sphere; faith promotes a constructive approach to life in the material world. The individual and the community intersect, and beliefs are tempered by encouraging denizens of the United States to act together to obtain a larger communal good.

Obama's representation of dichotomous terms—faith and religion—enables him to critique the enactment of both in democratic society. Obama reinterprets the praxis of faith to encourage the individual to use faith as the justification for actions that liberate themselves and others, while holding the community responsible for social problems. Reinterpreting faith serves the epistemic function of teaching the audience the appropriate ways their faith should manifest itself corporately to constitute the society our founding documents promise. Within Obama's reinterpreted vision of American society, all persons are invited to participate in the American faith.

All Persons Should Participate in Governing Change

The secular messianic style invites all persons to participate in their system of government. Everyone, regardless of religious affiliation, is guided by moral values. In a system such as ours that allows for the freedom of (and from) religious practice, "Politics depends on our ability to persuade each other of common aims based upon a common reality. It involves the compromise, the art of what's possible."[66] Although Obama self-identifies as a person of faith, participation in the public sphere is not restricted to Christians.

Obama celebrated the two concepts of liberty best explained by Isaiah Berlin in his essay, "Two Concepts of Liberty."[67] According to Berlin, people have the freedom to engage in certain activities and the freedom from participating in other activities. For Obama, all persons have the liberty to enter into, or refrain from, the public sphere. Citizens have the right to practice their faith while questioning particular tenants of their religious tradition. Progressives have the liberty to define their religious practice as they wish without having the Religious Right define it for them. Secularists have the liberty to access the public sphere, as do persons of faith. All persons, regardless of faith tradition, have the right to have the principles that justify our secular laws be based upon universal principles rather than religious codes.

Obama discloses his consubstantiality both with persons without faith (as he was one), and the persons of faith (of which he is now). He also can relate to non-sect "spiritual" individuals (such as his mother) and Muslims (such as his father). His consubstantiality with his audience extends to the United States' governmental system, history, geography, processes, and resources; the faith, or lack thereof, of her citizens; and community associations. He uses the personal pronoun "our" twenty-seven times and "your" or "you" five times each. He refers to "our personal beliefs," "our opponent," "our hopes and values," "our obligations towards one another," "our failure," "our fear," "our most urgent social problems," "our inner cities," "our leaders," "our non-discrimination laws," "our resources," "our laws," "our country," "our political debate," and "our democracy."[68] All auditors of his discourse are consubstantial with one another; therefore, all have the same governmental traditions, the same limitations, and the same burden to help one another.

Within the secular messianic style, all persons are brought into the action of the American faith—the belief in the telic values of our nation—to fulfill "our obligations towards one another."[69] All persons are responsible for enacting change; no one is free from the burden of helping to create a better social system. The time for change resides in the present.

The Past as Uncertainty, the Present as a Place of Action

Constrained by the materiality of a secular society, Obama does not attempt to make the eternal time present, but allows his understanding of the past to influence his projection of the future. His use of time is consistent with scholars' understanding of "public" time, which Roger Stahl explains "might be said to function as a kind of operating system for public deliberation, circumscribing boundaries and openings for discursive action."[70] For Obama, time is taken into the person, enacting change now, thus enabling people to perform time in such a manner that improves others' lives in a material fashion.

For Obama, the past is a place of uncertainty and struggle, whereas the present is a place of action. This pattern holds true for him, the black church, and persons of varying faiths. Obama's past struggles (he "was not raised in a particularly religious household"; he experienced a "spiritual dilemma"; he remained "apart, and alone"; and he realized that "something was missing" from his life) led him to Christianity. The "historical struggles for freedom and the rights of man"[71] experienced by the black church led them to become an agent of change for social justice issues. Churches across the country engage in similar activities as they care for children, the elderly, the ex-offender, and the needy.

Obama explained that his speech was motivated by a problem that has existed for thirty years. By locating the exigence thirty years ago, Obama positioned the problem as related to the issue of abortion and not as the faith practices of someone running for political office. The exigence, therefore, does not involve one person, but the entire nation. By framing the attack upon him as one repeated throughout three decades, Obama creates a rhetorical space for the role of religion in politics. It should not be viewed as one person seeking an office, but as a practice of the people every day of their lives.

Within the present people live their lives and seek their purpose. The present is the time to engage a national debate about the role of religion and politics. Obama affirmed, "[I]t's time that we join a serious debate about how to reconcile faith with our modern, pluralistic democracy"[72] to advance our telic purpose. Faith and action can be united as faith communities provide a vehicle through which to respond to national needs. And as people act together to resolve material needs, their need for belonging will be met.

Obama's speech does not invoke the eternal. His secular messianic style instead relies upon secularism's focus on the materiality of the present. The past acts to inform the present cause for action. The focus of the temporal action resides in the toggling back and forth between past and present; the future is gestured toward only as a site where change will occur and social problems will be solved. The future does not pass into the promised hereafter; the future is immediately and materially before us.

Conclusion and Implications

Obama's "Call to Renewal" speech achieved four rhetorical ends: first, it reclaimed religion and faith as talking points for Democrats; second, it addressed problems with conservative and progressive civic practices; third, it responded to critics in the Christian Right; and fourth, it provided progressive evangelicals with a public servant able to articulate their message. His speech captured the attention of persons of faith across the nation by offering them a nuanced critique of current political practices. His speech ended the strict separation of faith and politics encouraged by John F. Kennedy by reintroducing the topic within the Democratic presidential contest. The speech thus enabled him to access progressive evangelicals, securing a larger percentage of the voting population.

The Pew Research Center found that Obama's efforts to appeal to persons of faith paid off in a 5 percent increase in votes among white evangelicals and a 7 percent increase among Catholics in 2008 (compared to John Kerry's percentages in 2004)—a noteworthy increase as these voters constitute more than half of the voting population.[73] The *New York Times* reported that Obama increased his support among evangelicals most significantly in the targeted swing states. In Colorado, for example, evangelicals favored Obama 10 percent points more than they did Kerry in 2004.[74]

Perhaps even more importantly is the percentage of the religious vote that favored Obama over his 2008 Republican opponent John McCain. The Republican stronghold on religious voters ended in the 2008 election as the Republicans lost part of their evangelical base and the Democrats gained the support of persons with strong religious affiliations. According to the Pew Reach Center, in 2004 Kerry garnered 48 percent of voters who identified a religious affiliation (consistent with Al Gore's 48 percent in 2000), while George W. Bush attracted 51 percent of the vote (up 3 percent points from the 2000 election). In 2008, Obama attracted 53 percent of voters with a religious affiliation to McCain's 46 percent. When viewed from the perspective of persons who attend worship services more than weekly, Obama attracted 43 percent of the vote compared to McCain's 55 percent. Obama's share of the vote was up 8 percent over Kerry's 2004 numbers and 7 percent over Gore's 2000 numbers. Obama's effort to court religious voters was successful, although he attracted the nonreligious as well (67 percent voted for him as opposed to 30 percent who voted for McCain—an increase of 5 percent over Kerry's percentages and 6 percent over Gore's).[75]

Rather than reify the policy positions of the Sojourners organization, Obama challenged them to enact their faith in partnership with persons of differing political orientations and faiths. His consubstantiality with his audience and his privileged position as an elected official authorized him to address his audience and to reinterpret how his audience enacts their faith in the public sphere. Obama's speech vacillated between his personal narrative and the larger American story. He alluded to a difference between liberals and progressives and between the religious and persons of faith, considering how both sets of people have attempted to resolve social problems in the past, rejecting both and proposing another option. The audience is brought into Obama's life and thrown out into the midst of the American public. They address liberals and turn to confront conservatives. They hold onto their religious values and strive toward a collective solution to a communal problem. He distinguished different national actors and reinterpreted the goal to which they strive.

Obama used the biblical text and the religious experience to instruct his listeners about the difference between the sacred and the secular so they would not attempt to manifest the sacred within the secular, but labor with persons of other faiths (or no faith at all) to actualize a better democratic society. This better democratic society means a united body politic. The problem, as Obama sees it, is the separation people feel from other persons. Overcoming the religious divide does not require persons of differing faiths to negate differences, but to join together to work for the common good. Using past experiences to direct present action, Obama does not fulfill the telic ends of the nation at a distant point in time, but through joining together in the present.

Previous characterizations of religious discourse used in the United States have little explanatory force when applied to Obama's "Call to Renewal" address. In this speech, he did not claim that the United States has strayed from the chosen path and attempt to call the nation back from its secular sins. Nor did he use religious language as a form of civic ritual. He used the secular messianic style to explicate the role of faith in a democratic society. By framing the speech through the burden of belonging, Obama crafted a message that speaks to a fundamental need in every human being. Consequently, the solution he suggested—activism—enhances the material wellbeing of the community as well as the psychological need of the individual.

Notes

1. David Bernstein, "The Speech," *Chicago Magazine* (June 2007), http://www.chicagomag.com/Chicago-Magazine/June-2007/The-Speech/.

2. Robert C. Rowland and John M. Jones, "Recasting the American Dream and American Politics: Barack Obama's Keynote Address to the 2004 Democratic National Convention," *Quarterly Journal of Speech* 93 (2007): 434.

3. Barack Obama, *Dreams from My Father: A Story of Race and Inheritance* (New York: Crown Publishers, 1995).

4. E. J. Dionne Jr., "In Illinois, a Star Prepares," *Washington Post*, June 25, 2004, A29.

5. Since Kennedy, both the presidential and vice presidential candidates have been white protestant males until Joseph Lieberman in 2000. See Elizabeth Flock, "No More WASPs in Presidential Races," *US News and World Report*, September 4, 2012, http://www.usnews.com/news/blogs/washington-whispers/2012/09/04/chart-no-more-wasps-in-presidential-races.

6. Press release, "Columnist Says Barack Obama 'Lied to the American People;' Asks Publisher to Withdraw Obama's Book," *FreeRepublic.com*, August 10, 2004, http://www.freerepublic.com/focus/f-news/1189687/posts.

7. Joel Roberts, "Here's What Jesus Wouldn't Do," *CBSNews,* September 8, 2004, http://www.cbsnews.com/stories/2004/09/08/politics/main641858.shtml.

8. Annenberg Public Policy Center, "Obama and 'Infanticide': The Facts About Obama's Votes Against 'Born Alive' Bills in Illinois," *FactCheck.org,* August 25, 2008, http://www.factcheck.org/2008/08/obama-and-infanticide/.

9. E. J. Dionne Jr., "Obama's Eloquent Faith," *Washington Post,* June 30, 2006, A27.

10. Steven Waldman, "Obama's Historic 'Call to Renewal' Speech," *Beliefnet.com,* http://blog.beliefnet.com/stevenwaldman/2008/11/obamas-historic-call-to-renewa.html.

11. Jim Hoagland, "Melding Faith and Tolerance," *Washington Post,* July 2, 2006, B07.

12. Laurie Goodstein, "Obama Made Gains Among Younger Evangelical Voters, Data Show," *New York Times,* November 6, 2008, A24.

13. John Louis Lucaites, "Rhetoric and the Problem of Legitimacy," in *Dimensions of Argument* (Annandale, VA: Speech Communication Association, 1981), 807.

14. Robert Hariman, "Theory without Modernity," in *Prudence: Classical Virtue, Postmodern Practice,* ed. Robert Hariman (University Park, PA: The Pennsylvania State University Press, 2003).

15. Waldman, "Obama's Historic 'Call to Renewal' Speech."

16. Ibid.

17. George Jacob Holyoake, *The Principles of Secularism Illustrated* (London: Austin, 1871), 11.

18. Frank Newport, "More than 9 in 10 Americans Continue to Believe in God," *Gallup.org,* June 3, 2011, http://www.gallup.com/poll/147887/americans-continue-believe-god.aspx.

19. See "Election Results: U.S. President/National/Exit Polls," *CNN.com,* http://www.cnn.com/ELECTION/2004/pages/results/states/US/P/00/epolls.0.html.

20. Amy Sullivan, *The Party Faithful: How and Why Democrats Are Closing the God Gap* (New York: Scribner, 2008).

21. Ibid., 7.

22. As reported in Nancy Gibbs, "How the Democrats Got Religion," *Time* Magazine, July 12, 2007, http://www.time.com/time/magazine/article/0,9171,1642890–1,00.html.

23. Jim Wallis, *God's Politics: Why the Right Gets It Wrong and the Left Doesn't Get It* (New York: HarperCollins, 2006).

24. Noah Feldman, *Divided by God: America's Church-State Problem—and What We Should Do About It* (New York: Farrar, Straus and Giroux, 2005).

25. Kathleen Kennedy Townsend, *Failing America's Faithful: How Today's Churches Are Mixing God with Politics and Losing Their Way* (New York: Warner Books, 2007).

26. Tony Campolo, *Red Letter Christians: A Citizen's Guide to Faith & Politics* (Ventura, Cal.: Regal Books, 2008).

27. E. J. Dionne Jr., *Souled Out: Reclaiming Faith and Politics After the Religious Right* (Princeton: Princeton University Press, 2008), 184.

28. Sacvan Bercovitch, *The Puritan Origins of the American Self* (New Haven, CT: Yale University Press, 1975) and *The American Jeremiad* (Madison: University of Wisconsin Press, 1978).

29. Kurt Ritter, "American Political Rhetoric and the Jeremiad Tradition: Presidential Nomination Acceptance Addresses, 1960–76," *Central States Speech Journal* 31 (1980): 153–71; and Richard L. Johannesen, "The Jeremiad and Jenkin Lloyd Jones," *Communication Monographs 52* (1985): 156–72.

30. James Darsey, *The Prophetic Tradition and Radical Rhetoric in America* (New York: New York University Press, 1997).

31. Robert N. Bellah, "Civil Religion in America," in *A Reader in the Anthropology of Religion,* ed. Michael Lambek, (Malden, MA: Blackwell Publishing, 2002), 516.

32. All biblical references use the New American Standard Version translation.

33. Bruce Lincoln, *Authority: Construction and Corrosion* (Chicago: The University of Chicago Press, 1994), 10–11.

34. James Boyd White, *Acts of Hope: Creating Authority in Literature, Law, and Politics* (Chicago, The University of Chicago Press, 1994): 306.

35. Michael Leff, "Tradition and Agency in Humanistic Rhetoric," *Philosophy and Rhetoric* 36 (2003): 135.

36. Max Weber, *From Max Weber: Essays in Sociology,* translated by C. Wright Mills. (New York: Oxford University Press, 1958): 78–79.

37. Matthew 5:21–22 (NASV).

38. Matthew 5:27–32 (NASV).

39. Matthew 5:33–37 (NASV).

40. Matthew 5:38–42 (NASV).

41. Matthew 5:43–47 (NASV).

42. Matthew 6:2–4 (NASV).

43. Matthew 6:5–13 (NASV).

44. Matthew 6:16–18 (NASV).

45. Matthew 6:19–21 (NASV).

46. Jean Goodwin, "Cicero's Authority," *Philosophy and Rhetoric* 34 (2001): 50.

47. Lincoln, *Authority,* 2.

48. White, *Acts of Hope,* 306.

49. Chaim Perelman and Lucie Olbrechts-Tyteca, *The New Rhetoric: A Treatise on Argumentation* (Notre Dame, IN: University of Notre Dame Press, 1969), 32.

50. Michael Leff, "Dimensions of Temporality in Lincoln's Second Inaugural," *Communication Reports* 1 (1988): 29.

51. Leff, "Dimensions of Temporality," 29.

52. Matthew 3:2 (NASV).

53. Waldman, "Obama's Historic 'Call to Renewal' Speech."

54. John Murphy, "'Our Mission and Our Moment': George W. Bush and September 11th," *Rhetoric & Public Affairs* 6 (2003): 620.

55. Maurice Charland, "Constitutive Rhetoric: The Case of the *Peuple Quebecois,*" *Quarterly Journal of Speech* 73 (1987): 133–50.

56. Waldman, "Obama's Historic 'Call to Renewal' Speech."

57. Ibid.

58. Kenneth Burke, *A Rhetoric of Motives* (Berkeley: University of California Press, 1969).

59. Waldman, "Obama's Historic 'Call to Renewal' Speech."

60. Ibid.

61. Matthew 22:39 (NASV).

62. Waldman, "Obama's Historic 'Call to Renewal' Speech."

63. Ibid.

64. Ibid.

65. Ibid.

66. Ibid.

67. Isaiah Berlin, "Two Concepts of Liberty" in Berlin's *Four Essays on Liberty* (Oxford: Oxford University Press, 1969): 3–57.

68. Waldman, "Obama's Historic 'Call to Renewal' Speech."

69. Ibid.

70. Roger Stahl, "A Clockwork War: Rhetorics of Time in a Time of Terror," *Quarterly Journal of Speech* 94 (2008): 74.

71. Waldman, "Obama's Historic 'Call to Renewal' Speech."

72. Ibid.

73. The Pew Forum on Religion & Public Life, "How the Faithful Voted," *Pewforum. org,* November 5, 2008, http://www.pewforum.org/Politics-and-Elections/How-the-Faithful-Voted.aspx.

74. Goodstein, "Obama Made Gains."

75. The Pew Forum on Religion & Public Life, "How the Faithful Voted."

CHAPTER 10

The Exodus as Burden

Obama, Agency, and the Containment Thesis

DAVE TELL

In a much-quoted passage of *Dreams from My Father,* Barack Obama described, as a sort of conversion experience, his pathos-packed realization that the story of the Exodus could impart transcendent meaning to the daily struggles of "ordinary black people." Sitting "at the foot of the cross" in Chicago's now-infamous Trinity United Church of Christ, Obama

> imagined the stories of ordinary black people merging with the stories of David and Goliath, Moses and Pharaoh, the Christians in the lion's den, Ezekiel's field of dry bones. Those stories—of survival and freedom, and hope—became our story, my story… Our trials and triumphs became at once unique and universal, black and more than black.[1]

This realization had a decisive impact on Obama's 2007–08 campaign rhetoric. One of the most pronounced features of that rhetoric was Obama's penchant for "merging" the sacred story of the Exodus and the mundane history of American politics.

This merger was nowhere more evident than in a speech given at the March 4, 2007, Voting Rights Commemoration in Selma, Alabama. There, to an audience of civil rights veterans convened in the iconic Brown Chapel, Obama invoked the Biblical characters of Moses, Aaron, and Joshua to explain why he was running for president. He explained that the civil rights leaders in his audience were like Moses; they had made important gains and thereby made it possible for the people they led to envision a new form of life. But like Moses before them, they had fallen short of their final goal; they had reached only the mountaintop. They could, as it were, see the Promised Land from a distance, but the possession of that land they left for Joshua and his generation. Leaving nothing to chance, Obama made it explicit that his was the "Joshua Generation" and that he was running for president to pursue the unfinished work of the civil rights generation. Indeed, from Obama's perspective, the unachieved goals of the civil rights movement, read through the lens of the Biblical Exodus, provided a powerful spur to action: "That's what the Moses generation teaches us. Take off your bedroom slippers. Put on your marching shoes. Go do some politics. Change this country."[2] And that, Obama explained, was precisely what he was about to do.

In the language of this volume, Obama's speech at Selma suggests that the Exodus tradition did far more for Barack Obama than simply provide him with a rationale for his presidency. The Exodus *burdened him:* it goaded him to action and it instructed him to "go do some politics." The Joshua Generation might not face challenges of the same magnitude faced by the civil rights generation, and they might not deserve the responsibility they have been given, Obama explained, but "that doesn't mean that they don't still have a *burden to shoulder.*"[3] Thus was a burden written into Obama's own rationale for his candidacy: by claiming that he was running for president to fulfill the unfinished work of his storied forefathers, he understood himself to be taking on a burden that could not be discharged easily. The Exodus tradition might have helped him to explain his candidacy, but—and this is what I wish to stress—it did so at a cost: by his own accounts, this narrative drove him into the streets, it refused him rest, and it foisted upon him a nearly impossible standard against which his own efforts would be measured. In short, if we can trust Obama's own rhetoric, *the Exodus was his personal burden.* To be sure, Obama faced many contextual burdens—a flagging economy, the recalcitrance of public opinion, and the legacies of American exceptionalism, to name only those addressed in this volume—but from his perspective all of these were burdensome only because he was spurred to engage them by a past which, when filtered through Biblical history, drove him into public life.

The Exodus was a *personal* burden in the sense that it derived from Obama's particular choice of religious affiliation. Had he chosen another religion—or even a different tradition of Christianity—the burden of the Exodus could have been easily discharged. Yet, decades of scholarship teach us that the Exodus is not *merely* personal. In fact, on virtually every account—including Obama's—the burden of the Exodus is handed down by tradition rather than shouldered by choice. From Obama's perspective, he inherited his burden; he could no sooner shake it than he could his race or the much-rehearsed fact that his father was from Kenya and his mother from Kansas. He made this much explicit. He told the civil rights veterans gathered in Selma that were it not for their agitation, his own story would not have been possible. "I'm here because somebody marched. I'm here because you all sacrificed for me. I stand on the shoulders of giants."[4]

In their introduction to this volume, Jennifer Mercieca and Justin Vaughn suggest that the burdens on the United States presidency are a result of the heroic expectations of the office. In short, American expectations that the president wields an agency sufficient to "control world history" "sets up" the burdens of the presidency: institutional, contextual, and personal. They are surely correct. Obama's Exodus narrative dramatically confirms their articulation of burdens and agency: "Go do some politics. Change this country." In the remainder of this essay, then, I want to explore the nuances of this articulation, asking what the case of Obama teaches us about the intersection of heroic expectations, personal burdens, and presidential agency. I conclude that the Exodus narrative provides an important counterstatement to the rhetoric of presidential expectations. Whereas the latter celebrates an agency sufficient to "control the world," the former provides a much more chastened view of rhetorical agency.

The Exodus in Two Traditions

The speech in Selma was not exceptional. The "merging" of the sacred and profane may have been most explicit there, but it was by all accounts standard Obama fare. Even as a community organizer in Chicago's Altgeld Gardens, David Frank tells us, Obama drank deeply of historian Taylor Branch, for whom the Exodus functioned as the conceit *par excellence* of the civil rights movement.[5] Furthermore, John Murphy has recently argued that Obama's appropriation of the Exodus plays a decisive role in four of his most publicized campaign speeches. In addition to the Selma speech, Murphy argues that the January 8, 2008, concession speech in Nashua, New Hampshire; the January 20, 2008, speech in Atlanta's Ebenezer Baptist Church; and "A More Perfect Union," Obama's much-publicized response to Jeremiah Wright, were also deeply inflected with the rhetoric of the Promise Land.[6] Further, in his 2008 Philadelphia speech on race, Obama lifted the passage about Moses, the lion's dens, and dry bones verbatim from *Dreams from My Father*.[7] Despite differences in audience and occasion, the Exodus functioned similarly in each of these speeches. It stood behind Obama, burdening him: driving him into politics, energizing his campaign, goading him into the streets.

As the above passage from *Dreams from My Father* makes plain, Obama knew full well that his invocations of the Exodus were deeply traditional: he learned the importance of the Exodus from listening to Jeremiah Wright and perhaps also from reading Taylor Branch. Indeed, if he read his Branch as closely as Frank suggests, he certainly would have known just how appropriate were his March 4, 2007, invocations of the Exodus.[8] Selma, Branch suggested, was located "at Canaan's edge." It was the spot where, forty-two years earlier, Martin Luther King Jr. deployed civil rights activists James Bevel and Andrew Young "like Caleb and Joshua, to survey the land and look for the giants."[9] Moreover, it was the spot where C. T. Vivian, Joseph Lowery, and John Lewis—all now in Obama's audience— worked with King (and against the Student Nonviolent Coordinating Committee [SNCC]) to organize a six-hundred-person march from Brown Chapel over the Edmund Pettus Bridge enroute to Montgomery, Governor Wallace, and the franchise. Although 150 state troopers, tear gas, and— for Lewis at least—a skull fractured by a policeman's nightstick kept the marchers from reaching Montgomery on their first try, when they finally reached Alabama's State Capital it was, in Lewis's judgment, "almost like crossing our own Red Sea, our own river of Jordan."[10] King agreed, suggesting in 1965 that the march from Selma was reminiscent of Joshua's march on Jericho.[11] Since 1993, the march has been commemorated with the annual Bridge Crossing Jubilee—the very title of which reminds participants of the Biblical importance of both Selma and civil rights. Thus Obama's 2007 invocations of the Exodus would have resonated deeply with his Brown Chapel audience, not simply because the Exodus forms, as Frank has suggested, a "keystone of Africentric expression," but because Selma itself had been identified with the Promised Land since 1965.[12]

Selma's providential, Exodus-saturated history emphasizes just how deep the roots of Obama's chosen idiom reach. David Remnick writes, "From the early black church through the civil-rights movement, preachers used the trope of Moses and Joshua as a parable of struggle and liberation, making the explicit comparison between the Jewish slaves in Pharaoh's Egypt and black American slaves on Southern plantations."[13] And this is only the tip of the iceberg. As scholars such as Wilson Jeremiah Moses, David Howard-Pitney, and—most recently—Eddie Glaude Jr. have emphasized, the roots of the Exodus trope stretch back beyond the "early black church" to the American Puritans. And, as Sacvan Bercovitch has argued, when the Puritans bequeathed the Exodus trope to American activists of all stripes, they provided one of the most flexible, potent, and enduring rhetorical forms, a form that could be enlisted in the service of virtually any type of cultural politics. From Moses to Howard-Pitney, to Glaude Jr., to Bercovitch, the Exodus narrative may be America's most studied, its most overdetermined rhetorical form.

Given the long, well-documented history of the Exodus trope, it is no surprise that critics have explained Obama's Selma address by placing him in various prophetic traditions. As C. T. Vivian put it, "Barack was putting matters into the context of church history."[14] In his tellingly entitled account of Obama's rise, *The Bridge,* David Remnick argued that the Selma speech is wholly traditional: Obama "adopted the gestures, rhythms, and symbols of the prophetic voice for the purposes of electoral politics."[15] If we look beyond the Selma speech, the impulse to explain Obama's penchant for the Exodus with recourse to prophetic traditions remains. David Frank places Obama's rhetoric in an African American faith tradition; John Murphy adds a layer of complexity by considering the symbiosis of African American and Puritan traditions in Obama's campaign rhetoric.

In this essay I situate the speech at Selma—and Obama's Exodus rhetoric more generally—at the nexus of African American and Puritan traditions of Exodus tropology. The scholarship on both of these traditions emphasizes that the Exodus narrative is inextricably intertwined with issues of agency. Accordingly, I engage Obama on these terms, asking after the place and scope of rhetorical agency in Obama's rhetoric. I argue that Obama provides us with a deeply chastened view of rhetorical agency. Understanding the nuance of this agency, however, requires attending to *both* Exodus traditions. On the one hand, if we situate Obama's Selma address vis-à-vis the Puritan tradition only, we risk an inflated, over-empowered view of Obama's sense of agency—as if "Yes, We Can" was his final statement on the matter. On the other hand, if we explain Obama's Exodus-quoting penchant with recourse only to the black church, then we risk ascribing to Obama a disempowered view of rhetorical agency. When Obama is placed within both traditions, however, a compelling but qualified view of rhetorical agency emerges.

To explain this vision of agency—and its distinctiveness vis-à-vis the competing traditions from which it springs—I stress the uniqueness of Obama's rhetoric and its distance from the traditions that inform it. Proceeding chronologically, I consider first the Puritan tradition and then the African American faith tradition, emphasizing in both sections Obama's commitment to social change.

Obama and the Puritan Tradition

Is Barack Obama a Puritan? This question, posed by the *Independent* in November of 2008, is more difficult to answer than it might seem.[16] On the one hand, Obama's storied 2009 "beer summit" is only the most visible of the manifold ways in which he might be distinguished from the austere founders of the Massachusetts Bay Colony. On the other hand, his Exodus-filled rhetoric unquestionably registers in a Puritan tradition. John Murphy makes this explicit, situating Obama in a line descending from Oliver Cromwell and the American Puritans.[17] More common, of course, is the approach shared by pundit David Remnick and critic David Frank. Both of these situate Obama in an African American prophetic tradition. Yet, it is important to note that the leading scholars of African American prophetic rhetoric root that rhetoric in a distinctively Puritan tradition. As Eddie Glaude Jr. put it in his recent *Exodus!,* the African American prophetic tradition was "inherited, in large measure, from colonial New England, Puritans who imagined their migration from the Old World as an exodus to a New Canaan and an errand into the wilderness."[18] Wilson Jeremiah Moses and David Howard-Pitney make similar claims.[19] Thus, Frank's and Remnick's contextualization of Obama is just a roundabout manner of agreeing with John Murphy: Obama's rhetoric does indeed register in a Puritan tradition. Perhaps it was for this reason that the *Independent* left its provocative question unanswered.

I too will leave the question unanswered. My goal in this section is only to plot Obama's invocations of the Exodus and the Puritan tradition on a common map in order to understand better questions of rhetorical agency. To do so, I will focus on the path-breaking work of Sacvan Bercovitch: *The American Jeremiad.* Published in 1976, *The American Jeremiad* provided a close reading of the American Puritans and argued that the Biblical stories of an Exodus, a Covenant, and a Promised Land have provided both an enduring resource for contemporary dissent and ensured that such dissent never challenged fundamental conceptions of American identity. It is difficult to overstate the influence of this argument. Beyond meriting its own shorthand slogan—the "containment thesis"—it has also dominated nearly every attempt to explain the political work of the *jeremiad,* Bercovitch's broad, generic term for any rhetorical practice that merges divine history and mundane politics.[20] Because of Bercovitch, those in rhetorical studies have, for thirty-plus years and counting, understood invocations of the Exodus tradition less as a goad to social change than as an instrument of societal stability. To cite a representative example, John Murphy argued in 1990 that the Exodus tradition "acts as a rhetoric of social control" and "limits the scope of reform and the depth of social criticism."[21] Despite Bercovitch's influence inside the academy, Barack Obama does not appear to view Exodus as constraining, but as enabling. Far from "limiting the depth of social criticism," when Obama's Exodus-laden rhetoric is contextualized vis-à-vis the Puritan tradition, it seems to invest his auditors with a nearly unqualified sense of political agency.

At the heart of Bercovitch's thesis is his insistence that the jeremiad is *figural.* In his telling, a rhetoric is figural if it is capable of resonating in two registers at once. For example, in the Puritan lexicon, the word "errand" was figural: it at once denoted their historical journey across the Atlantic and their providential journey toward the promised land.[22] As such, the primary function of the jeremiad is, as Bercovitch put it in various places, to "obviate the distinction" between allegory and chronicle, fact and ideal, sacred and historical, moral and spiritual.[23] In this sense, Bercovitch's *figure* is Obama's *merger*—both are defined by collapsing the temporal and eternal. For Bercovitch, everything hinges on the double meaning of a figure. When confronted with terms like *errand, pilgrimage,* and *wilderness,* Bercovitch insists that we hold on to both sets of meaning at once: the historical and the providential. This both/and hermeneutic lies at the heart of his containment thesis. Because Jeremiahs cast their dissent from the "figural vantage point," the providential register functioned to constrain the historical.[24] For example, to denounce by accusing the audience of abandoning an errand or faltering in a pilgrimage was to suggest that reform—no matter how radical—would always be invested in continuing the errand or resuming the pilgrimage. The Puritans needed to control agency without obliterating it, and thus they insisted on the double meaning of *errand* in which the metaphor encouraged individual agency *and* channeled it in a predetermined direction.

This much seems plausible. But as Bercovitch's argument proceeds, so too does the list of figures capable of containing dissent. To the Puritan tropes of *errand, wilderness,* and *pilgrimage,* Bercovitch adds—to name only a few—*New England, Puritanism, the Revolution, Liberty, Property, translatio studii,* and, eventually, *America* itself.[25] As the list of figures proliferates, it begins to seem as if the containment thesis depends not so much on the particular figures deployed but on the very fact of figuration. As if *any* term that mediated between two registers could contain dissent in the same fashion as *errand* and *pilgrimage.* Bercovitch thus refers to the Jeremiad as, simply, a "mode of ambiguity," and a product of the "American figural imagination."[26]

This is too much. Let me illustrate the problems of Bercovitch's extension from Puritan tropes to tropology writ large with recourse to Obama's speech in Selma. Bercovitch would certainly read this speech as yet another example of the "American figural imagination," for it is chock full of figures which "obviate the distinctions" between sacred and historical. One such figure is Obama's much-repeated phrase "because they marched," a phrase that he used to refer both to the crossing of the Red Sea on a miraculously dry path and the crossing of the Alabama River on the Edmund Pettus Bridge. Another figure is Obama's exhortation that the Joshua generation "be strong and have courage." For Obama, "strength" and "courage" referred both to the qualities Joshua needed to enter the Promised Land and the qualities required of the Little Rock Nine to enter Central High School.[27]

Thus: *errand, pilgrimage, marching, strength,* and *courage*—figures all. And yet there is a qualitative difference between the Puritan figures and Obama's. The Puritan figures impose a teleology on social action. The Puritan *errand,* Bercovitch writes, was not simply a spur to action, but a means of directing that action toward a particular end: "*Together,* these *two* elements define the ritual import of the jeremiad: to sustain process by imposing control, and to justify control by presenting a *certain form of process* as the only road to the future kingdom."[28] Obama, we might say, retains the emphasis on process while dropping the emphasis on control. For it seems clear that the figure of the *errand* and the figure of *marching* function rather differently. To be sure, they both obviate the distinction between the sacred and mundane, and they both function as a goad to social action, but only the *errand* contains within it a means of directing that action or, in Bercovitch's terms, of imposing control on the process it unleashes. Otherwise put: the Puritan "errand" contains within it a particular Christian, social ideal, and when the puritan Jeremiahs figured dissent in its terms, such dissent could do nothing but channel "revolution into the service of society."[29]

"Marching," however, is another figure entirely. Whereas Bercovitch's Jeremiahs used a partisan social ideal to spur social protest, Obama uses a protest from the past to spur a protest in the present. *Marching, strength,* and *courage*—these figures certainly do, as Murphy put it, imply that the civil rights movement is "more than historical fact," but they do not, of themselves, impose a particular direction on that movement. Eddie Glaude Jr. argues that the Exodus narrative, extracted from Puritan ideology, is far more about the journey toward something new and unexpected than it is about the affirmation of something previously known.[30] Obama, as we have seen, made this explicit: "That's what the Moses generation teaches us. Take off your bedroom slippers. Put on your marching shoes. Go do some politics. Change this country." Here the Exodus tradition is nothing more than a motivation to get involved in politics. To be sure, Obama had his partisan causes, but these causes were not inscribed in the *figures* that turned his campaign speeches into covenantal rhetoric. Because Obama's standard figures—and here I take *marching* and *strength* as typical—contained no such intrinsic vision of the good; they aligned themselves in the service of his unbounded theory of change.

Consider the New Hampshire speech made popular by will.i.am. Here, *"Yes, we can"* replaces *marching*. It connects Moses on the mountaintop with westbound pioneers and northbound slaves. But like the earlier figure of *marching, "Yes, we can"* is a figure that inspires progress without the possibility of directing it. Exemplary here is will.i.am's musical rendering of the speech. The song brought together celebrities dedicated to a wide variety of political causes: the rights of Asian Americans, animal rights, antipoverty legislation, and the national awareness of both Narcolepsy and seafood poisoning.[31] Celebrities Kelly Hu, Scarlett Johansson, Kate Walsh, and Amber Valleta were each spurred on by Obama's figure, but the distance separating their respective causes testifies that although Obama's figure inspires progress, it does not channel it in a predetermined direction. Indeed, the sheer diversity of political causes is telling, functioning as a reminder that Obama's prophetic rhetoric could not, or rather did not, control the processes it unleashed. Thanks to Obama's New Hampshire speech and will.i.am's adaptation of it, "Yes, we can" became nearly synonymous with political agency during the 2008 Obama campaign—an agency that was rather conspicuously uncontained. Even more exemplary is freeform, Jesse Dylan's media company, which turned will.i.am's song into a YouTube sensation. Here is the mission statement of freeform:

> Our clients are the change-agents across industry, society and culture. They are helping to make the world a better place through new ideas and innovations. We help focus and find voice for their ideas through film, design and new media.[32]

There could hardly be a better description of Obama's figural rhetoric. *Marching, strength, courage, "Yes, we can"*—all are figures that add force to political commitments generated elsewhere. As Obama put it in New Hampshire, "[T]he reason our campaign has always been different is because it's not just about what I will do as President, it's also about what you, the people who love this country, can do to change it." And as it turns out, these relatively conscious, country-achieving people can do almost anything. Powered by the covenantal figure of "Yes, we can," Obama concluded that "nothing can withstand the power of millions of voices calling for change." This, in microcosm, is a perfect picture of Obama's prophetic rhetoric as contextualized by the Puritan tradition: it emerges as a rhetoric that draws on the Exodus to inspire process without controlling it. It paints a picture of unqualified rhetorical agency. To be sure, the Selma address, the New Hampshire address, and the will.i.am video are all parts of a campaign, and as such it is safe to assume that Obama had a vested interest in controlling the direction of the energies he unleashed (he wanted votes). This makes the diversity of the causes in the video all the more remarkable, for the diversity itself proves that, at least for some, Obama's covenantal rhetoric was received in the terms it was delivered: as a goad to social change.[33]

Obama and the African American Jeremiad

This, however, is only half the story. It is not enough simply to say that Obama inspired in some of his auditors a powerful sense of agency. If Obama's Exodus tropes are to constitute a unique contribution to a long tradition of prophetic rhetoric, we must say something about the nature of this agency. To do so, I return to the same speeches, and read them—as

David Frank and David Remnick have suggested—in light of the African American Jeremiad. Unlike the Puritan Jeremiad described by Bercovitch, the African American variant has long been understood as a powerful mode of investing rhetorical agency in ambivalent audiences. In Wilson Moses' classic formulation, "jeremiad" describes "the constant warnings issued by blacks to whites, concerning the judgment that was to come for the sin of slavery."[34] Building on Moses' work, Howard-Pitney argues that the black jeremiad is a "pervasive idiom for expressing sharp social criticism." In language virtually identical to Obama's at Selma, he emphasizes that the criticism expressed by the jeremiad is intended as a goad to action:

> A more frequent feature of the cultural landscape has been incessant jeremiads castigating the present sons for infidelity to the fathers' missionary purpose and lamenting America's decline from its sacred beginnings. The Founding Fathers cast a gigantic shadow over future generations, *laying on them the burden of measuring up to the fathers' awesome achievements.*[35]

For Howard-Pitney, then, as for Obama: history is a burden. For both of them, it was as much a burden foisted upon them by tradition as one taken up by choice. And for both of them, this burden inspired action. Whether it is the divine history of the Exodus or the divinized history of the Founders, the memory of the past functions as a goad to social action, a profound investment of political agency.

African American traditions of prophecy are often understood as promoting rhetorical agency of a particular type: a constrained, qualified, and—to use the language of the civil rights era—chastened type of rhetorical agency. No one has made this point with more force than historian David Chappell. In his award-winning 2004 *A Stone of Hope,* Chappell accounts for the fact that although liberalism was at the height of its powers in mid-twentieth-century America, it contributed virtually nothing to the most important social movement of the time: the civil rights movement. Indeed, in Chappell's telling, the civil rights movement succeeded in spite of liberalism, not because of it. The problem with liberals? Their unmerited faith in the power of human reason to overcome injustices. In sum, Chappell suggests, liberals placed too much hope in rhetoric: in the willingness of smart people to respond reasonably to arguments thoughtfully made. As evidence, Chappell cites the longings of liberal stalwarts such as Dewey, Mill, Lippmann, and Schlesinger for something more powerful than reason, more trenchant than intellectual conviction, more stirring than persuasion, more vivid than education, and, ultimately, more effective in cultural politics than the marketplace of ideas. As Dewey well knew: "The source had to lie in faith."[36] Specifically, Chappell argues, the wellspring of the civil rights movement lay in the political insights of the Hebrew prophets.

To understand these insights, Chappell turned to the writings of Reinhold Niebuhr—not because Niebuhr "invented the prophetic tradition but rather [because] he codified its teachings and expressed them for his contemporaries in vivid, arresting language that King understood."[37] At the heart of Niebuhr's social theory was the conviction that social change required coercion and force rather than reason and persuasion. As he put it in his 1932 *Moral Man and Immoral Society,* individuals may respond to reason, but "collective behavior" "can never be brought completely under the dominion of reason or conscience." Given this, social change can never be enacted without coercion, without physical force, without "power raised against" the status quo.[38] It was, Chappell argues, precisely this substitution of coercion and force for reason and persuasion that drove the supposedly "nonviolent" movement. Even John Lewis—that icon of nonviolence whose capacity to "get up after repeated jailings and beatings and go back for more" was "legendary"—recognized the importance of force:

> I think that somewhere in the history of the Judeo-Christian tradition is the idea that there can be no salvation without the shedding of blood and there may be some truth in that. Personally, though, I now accept the philosophy of non-violence ... but I think that when we accept non-violence, we don't say it is the absence of violence. We say it is the present assumption—much more positive—that there might be the shedding of blood.[39]

Here, Lewis challenges the memory of civil rights as a form of nonviolent resistance. Nonviolence may have been the reputation of the movement, but this should not suggest that violence was not ingredient at every turn. In sum, the key thinkers and activists of the civil rights movement, Chappell concluded, "resembled the Hebrew Prophets" and "clearly disagreed with the coherent philosophy of liberalism expressed by Schlesinger and his followers."[40] In practical terms, this meant that their faith in rhetorical agency was limited by the perceived necessity of violence.

Obama's debts to the tradition are obvious. One month after his Selma speech, Obama told David Brooks that Reinhold Niebuhr was one of his "favorite philosophers." When Brooks pushed him to explain, Obama sounded the limits of liberalism. From Niebuhr, Obama explained, "I take away...the compelling idea that there's serious evil in the world, and hardship and pain." For this reason, Brooks rightly concluded Obama "dislikes liberal muddle-headedness on power politics."[41] Two and a half years later, upon the reception of his Nobel Prize, Obama sounded the Niebuhrian refrain once again, this time sounding like no one so much as the chastened John Lewis. As Lewis put it before him, Obama emphasized the necessity of force complementing rhetorical action:

> As someone who stands here as a direct consequence of Dr. King's life work, I am living testimony to the moral force of non-violence. I know there's nothing weak—nothing passive—nothing naïve—in the creed and lives of Ghandi and King. But as a head of state sworn to protect and defend my nation, I cannot be guided by their examples alone. I face the world as it is, and cannot stand idle in the face of threats to the American people. For make no mistake: Evil does exist in the world....To say that force may sometimes be necessary is not a call to cynicism—it is a recognition of history; the imperfections of man and the limits of reason."[42]

In this quotation, Obama sounds the limits of rhetorical agency. He argues that the twenty-first century requires physical force as much as rhetorical eloquence. He recognizes that he cannot talk his way out of evil. Words, Obama explained, could never redress slavery: "words on parchment would not be enough to deliver slaves from bondage....What would be needed were Americans in successive generations who were willing to do their part—through protests and struggle, on the streets and in the courts, through a civil war and civil disobedience and always at great risk."[43] With these words, spoken in 2008 in Philadelphia, Obama rearticulated an old Niebuhrian creed. In fact, *Slate's* Fred Kaplan wrote that it is a "faithful reflection" of Niebuhr's political theology. It emphasizes the "limits of reason" and the necessity of force. Near the end of the speech, Obama explained that although he cherished the liberal ideals of John F. Kennedy—human rights, progress, strong institutions—these commitments could not alone provide for social change: "And yet, I do not believe that we will have the will, the determination, the staying power, to complete this work without something more—and that's the continued expansion of our moral imagination; an insistence that there's something irreducible that we all share."[44]

Staying power requires "something more" than liberal ideals. In Selma he explained that this "something more" could be found in the Exodus. Obama reminded his audience, "Joshua said, you know, 'I'm scared.' The Lord, however, assuaged Joshua's fears with a promise: 'Be strong and have courage, for I am with you wherever you go.'" It was this strength and courage, Obama explained, that took Joshua to Jericho, the Selma marchers to Montgomery, Elizabeth Eckford to Central High School, John Lewis to "Bloody Sunday," and, now, Americans to the Promise Land.[45] In sum, the will, determination, and staying power to change America for the better is located in the burden of a divine history: the Exodus. The Exodus should, Obama suggested, burden all Americans as it did John Lewis: goading them into a public life, even if the most conspicuous features of that life are state troopers, nightsticks, and violence. For as both Lewis and Obama knew: the Exodus provided a chastened vision of rhetorical agency, a vision that conjoined "millions of voices calling for change" with the "shedding of blood."

This chastened view of rhetorical agency found perfect expression in Obama's recollection of Martin Luther King. Speaking in Atlanta in January 2008, Obama explained how Dr. King brought about change. "He did it with words—words that he spoke not just to the children of slaves, but the children of slave owners. Words that inspired not just black but also white...." Yet, Obama does not for a moment let us think that words alone are sufficient, for Dr. King "also led with deeds....He led by taking a stand against a war...[and] challenging our economic structures."[46] For Obama, the lesson is as consistent as it is clear: rhetorical agency will never amount to an unalloyed ability to control the world.

Conclusion

It is an often overlooked fact that Barack Obama spoke at Brown Chapel on August 4, 2007, because Congressman John Lewis invited him. This invitation marks a perfect, synecdochal way to remember Obama's address. For the speech he gave was not only in memory of the Bloody Sunday Lewis helped to orchestrate, the speech itself was a perfect reflection of John Lewis's philosophy of social change. A member of Congress representing Georgia's Fifth District for over twenty-five years, Lewis knew well the importance of rhetorical deliberation. As a cofounder and later chairman of SNCC, however, Lewis knew also the importance of coercion. In this sense, Lewis is the living embodiment of Niebuhr's claim that political action will always be a "compound" of reasoned address and coercive force.[47] More to the point, he is also the perfect example of Obama's Exodus-inspired agency: a view of agency that balances the power of "millions of voices" against the ever-present need of extra-rhetorical force.

With this background, it is clear that Obama will never be a so-called "great president." Not, that is, if we accept the Schlesinger family's definition of a great president. As Mercieca and Vaughn put it in the introduction to this volume, the Schlesingers defined the "great president" as a "hero who protects human freedom and democracy by changing the course of history." Obama never believed one person could change the course of history. In New Hampshire, he called for millions of voices; in Philadelphia, he called for the "next generation"; in Atlanta, he argued that unity was the only path forward; and, of course, in Selma, he traced the origins of the civil rights movement to a "bunch of women." Obama's insistence on cooperation likely has many origins. One of them is the Exodus tradition. As we have seen, the Exodus tradition is a powerful spur to "go do some politics," but it is also sounds the limits of politics. In so far as it does the latter, it provides a powerful rational for cooperation.

Notes

1. Barack Obama, *Dreams from My Father: A Story of Race and Inheritance* (New York: Times Books, 1995), 294.

2. Barack Obama, "Selma Voting Rights March Commemoration," March 4, 2007, in *The American Presidency Project* [online], eds. John Woolley and Gerhard Peters, http://www.presidency.ucsb.edu/ws/index.php?pid=77042.

3. Ibid. (emphasis mine).

4. Ibid.

5. David Frank, "The Prophetic Voice and the Face of the Other in Barack Obama's 'A More Perfect Union' Address, March 18, 2008," *Rhetoric and Public Affairs* 12 (2009), 172.

6. John M. Murphy, "Barack Obama, the Exodus Tradition, and the Joshua Generation," *Quarterly Journal of Speech* 97 (November 2011): 387–410.

7. Barack Obama, "Remarks of Senator Barack Obama: 'A More Perfect Union,'" March 18, 2008, Philadelphia, PA, https://my.barackobama.com/page/content/hisownwords.

8. There is reason to believe that perhaps Obama didn't read his Branch as closely as Frank suggests: his evidence for this claim is of uncertain status. Frank cites a particular article in the *Toronto Star*. Although the article does mention that Obama was "assigned" Taylor Branch, it provides no evidence that he was "deeply influenced," as Frank claims. See Tim Harper, "The Making of a President; Chicago Helped Shape Obama's Outlook as He Connected with Mentors and Honed His Political Elbows," *Toronto Star,* August 16, 2008, http://academic.lexisnexis.com/. On Obama and Branch, see also David Remnick, *The Bridge: The Life and Rise of Barack Obama* (New York: Alfred A. Knopf, 2010), 13.

9. Taylor Branch, *At Canaan's Edge: America in the King Years, 1965–68* (New York: Simon and Schuster, 2006), 10.

10. John Lewis, "Introduction," in *A Call to Conscience: The Landmark Speeches of Dr. Martin Luther King, Jr.,* eds. Clayborne Carson and Kris Shepard (New York: Grand Central Publishing, 2002), 114.

11. Martin Luther King, Jr., "Address at the Conclusion of the Selma to Montgomery March," in *A Call to Conscience: The Landmark Speeches of Dr. Martin Luther King, Jr.,* ed. Clayborne Carson and Kris Shepard (New York: Grand Central Publishing, 2002), 111.

12. Frank, "The Prophetic Voice and the Face of the Other," 171.

13. Remnick, *The Bridge,* 19.

14. Quoted in Remnick, *The Bridge,* 24.

15. Remnick, *The Bridge,* 24.

16. Howard Jacobsen, "Obama's Cool Can Translate into Political Substance," *Independent,* November 8, 2008, http://www.independent.co.uk/opinion/commentators/howard-jacob-son/howard-jacobson-obamas-cool-can-translate-into-political-substance-1001091.html.

17. Murphy, "Barack Obama, the Exodus Tradition."

18. Eddie S. Glaude Jr., *Exodus! Religion, Race, and Nation in Early Nineteenth-Century Black America* (Chicago: The University of Chicago Press, 2000), 46.

19. Wilson Jeremiah Moses, *Black Messiahs and Uncle Toms: Social and Literary Manipulations of a Religious Myth* (University Park: The Pennsylvania State University Press, 1993), 31; and David Howard-Pitney, *The African American Jeremiad: Appeals for Justice in America* (Philadelphia: Temple University Press, 2005), 6.

20. On the influence of Bercovitch, see Ernest G. Bormann, "Fetching Good Out of Evil: A Rhetorical Use of Calamity," *Quarterly Journal of Speech* 63 (1977): 130–39; Kurt W. Ritter, "American Political Rhetoric and the Jeremiad Tradition: Presidential Nomination Acceptance Addresses, 1960–1976," *Central States Speech Journal* 31 (1980): 153–71; Murphy, "'A Time of Shame and Sorrow;'" James Jasinski, "Rearticulating History in Epideictic Discourse: Frederick Douglass's 'The Meaning of the Fourth of July to the Negro,'" in *Rhetoric and Political Culture in Nineteenth-Century America,* ed. Thomas W. Benson (East Lansing: Michigan State University Press, 1997): 71–89; A. Susan Owen, "Memory, War and American Identity: *Saving Private Ryan* as Cinematic Jeremiad," *Critical Studies in Media Communication* 19 (2002): 249–82; and James Jasinski and John M. Murphy,

"Time, Space, and Generic Reconstruction: Martin Luther King's 'A Time to Break Silence' as Radical Jeremiad," in *Public Address and Moral Judgment,* ed. Shawn Parry-Giles and Trevor Parry-Giles (East Lansing: Michigan State University Press, 97–125).

21. John M. Murphy, "'A Time of Shame and Sorrow': Robert F. Kennedy and the American Jeremiad," *Quarterly Journal of Speech* 76 (1990): 402.

22. On the multiple meanings of the Puritan "errand," see Perry Miller, *Errand into the Wilderness* (Cambridge: Harvard University Press, 1956).

23. Sacvan Bercovitch, *The American Jeremiad* (Madison: University of Wisconsin Press, 1978), 33, 14, 16, 123, 46.

24. Ibid., 15.

25. On the expansion of Bercovitch's argument, see Glaude, *Exodus!,* 47.

26. Bercovitch, *The American Jeremiad,* 17, 143.

27. Barack Obama, "Selma Voting Rights March Commemoration."

28. Bercovitch, *The American Jeremiad,* 24 (emphasis mine).

29. Ibid., 150.

30. Glaude, *Exodus!,* 5.

31. The song includes Kelly Hu (CAUSE USA, which encourages Asian Americans to participate in the political process), Scarlett Johansson (antipoverty campaigns with Bono), Kate Walsh (national awareness of Narcolepsy), Amber Valletta (seafood poisoning), and Common (PETA; HIV Awareness).

32. www.free-form.tv, http://free-form.tv/add/ford.html.

33. For this reason, Obama's rhetoric stands as an important reminder that Bercovitch's containment thesis—as smart as it is and enduring as it has been—is nonetheless the product of a particular time and a particular place. The Puritans unquestionably bequeathed to us a great deal of our cultural forms, but just because we still invoke the Exodus does not mean that such invocations function for us as they did for the Puritans. Indeed, the lesson of Obama's campaign rhetoric is that the jeremiad need not restrict the depth of social criticism as it did for the Puritans. Obama has thus done us a tremendous favor: by foregrounding the Exodus, and by interpreting it as a burden and putting in the service of his "Yes, We Can" theory of change, he has, as it were, reclaimed the Jeremiad from its thirty-years service to the containment thesis.

34. Moses, *Black Messiahs and Uncle Toms,* 30–31.

35. Howard-Pitney, *The African American Jeremiad,* 10, 9 (emphasis mine).

36. David L. Chappell, *A Stone of Hope: Prophetic Religion and the Death of Jim Crow* (Chapel Hill: The University of North Carolina Press, 2004), 17. The arguments I summarized are made in pages 1–43.

37. Ibid., 47.

38. Reinhold Niebuhr, *Moral Man and Immoral Society: A Study in Ethics and Politics* (1932; New York: Charles Scribner's Sons, 1960), xii. See also Chappell, *A Stone of Hope,* xvi, xx, 4, 6.

39. Chappell, *A Stone of Hope,* 76.

40. Ibid., 85–86.

41. David Brooks, "Obama, Gospel and Verse," *New York Times,* April, 26, 2007, http://select.nytimes.com/2007/04/26/opinion/26brooks.html?_r=1&scp=1&sq=%2522David%20Brooks%2522%200bama%20Niebuhr&st=cse.

42. "Obama's Novel Remarks," *New York Times,* December 11, 2009, http://www.nytimes.com/2009/12/11/world/europe/11prexy.text.html

43. Obama, "Remarks of Senator Barack Obama.

44. "Obama's Novel Remarks."

45. Barack Obama, "Selma Voting Rights March Commemoration."

46. Barack Obama, "Remarks of Senator Barack Obama: The Great Need of the Hour," Atlanta, GA, January 20, 2008, http://www.dailykos.com/story/2008/01/20/440020/-Barack-Obama-The-Great-Need-of-the-Hour.

47. Niebuhr, *Moral Man and Immoral Society,* 4, 13.

CHAPTER 11

Picturing the Presidents

Obama and the Visual Politics of White House Art

CARA FINNEGAN

In November of 2009, Rachel Maddow asked her MSNBC viewers, "Is there a message in White House paintings?"[1] Picking up on a Politico.com piece, Maddow explained that the work of art hung prominently in the President's private dining room had been switched more than once since Barack Obama took office that January. Using White House photographs, Maddow showed that a large portrait of John Quincy Adams had hung there during the last months of George W. Bush's presidency. Some time after President Obama took office, that portrait was replaced first by a landscape and then, more recently, by George P. A. Healy's 1868 history painting, *The Peacemakers*. That work seemed to appear around the time Israel's Benjamin Netanyahu lunched with President Obama. Its appearance prompted Politico to wonder if the Obama administration sought to use *The Peacemakers* to make a rhetorical point to the Israeli visitor.[2] Maddow pressed her guest, presidential historian Michael Beschloss, on the significance of the apparent switcheroo. But Beschloss did not take the bait; he dismissed the suggestion of a connection, calling it all just a "coincidence." He then offered an analogy: to say that *The Peacemakers* was hung in Obama's private dining room to send some sort of policy message "would be sort of like if Bill Clinton were meeting with Boris Yeltsin and somehow an anti-drinking poster materialized behind his head." For Beschloss, to read the placement of *The Peacemakers* as purposeful would require one to read it as blatantly propagandistic. Because that was obviously ridiculous, the only conclusion was not to read anything into it at all. Undeterred, Maddow concluded the interview by asking a broader, more serious question: "Have spaces like the Oval Office and those private, small spaces around where the president works, have they always had things in them tweaked for symbolic value or for symbolic public appearances?" The short answer to this question is yes. The longer answer is one that I explore in this essay on how, during its first eighteen months, the Obama administration employed White House art as a rhetorical resource.

We owe much of our cultural imaginary of the White House to Jacqueline Kennedy. When her husband took office in 1961, Kennedy took on the task of remaking the White House into a space that commemorated national history.[3] Working with academics and archivists, Mrs. Kennedy argued the White House "must be restored—and that has nothing to do with decoration. That is a question of scholarship."[4] Historians of the White House point out that Kennedy's goal was not to turn the White House into a museum frozen in time in one historical period, but rather to employ "a more artistic interpretation of the past."[5] This ecumenical view of history is embodied in the White House art collection. According to William Kloss, the White House art collection is "unified by three basic concerns: art—chiefly American art—as historical document, as decoration, and as vehicle for celebrating American values and achievements."[6] White House art visualizes an American past, offering images of who and what we should value as Americans. And it does so in ways that connect the current occupant of the Executive Mansion with the whole history of the presidency. Indeed, as Forrest McDonald has noted, "The president lives in a museum of the history of the presidency."[7] White House art thus constitutes an epideictic rhetoric that, as Jeffrey Walker puts it, "shapes the ideologies and imageries with which, and by which, the individual members of a community identify themselves."[8]

Despite its symbolic capacity as a rhetoric of display, White House art has been ignored as a site for rhetorical analysis.[9] Yet there is ample evidence that presidents care very much about the art objects with which they surround themselves. First Lady Hillary Clinton hinted as much in an interview with *ARTnews* in 1994, which produced a cover story on the Clintons' favorite White House art:

> When we first got here my husband and I looked through the
> book on the collection and tried to find everything in it....What
> we couldn't find on the walls, we brought in...to study. I think
> we've pulled out every painting that's been in storage.[10]

The article highlighted the art the Clintons chose for the family residence and their offices. One of the Clintons' favorite portraits, Mrs. Clinton noted, was a portrait of John Tyler by George P.A. Healy (the same artist who painted *The Peacemakers*).[11] Clinton stated, "I like it because of the composition and emotion," adding, "my husband likes it because Tyler is crumpling up the newspapers!"[12]

Presidents may decorate any of their private work spaces as well as the private residence with any art works of their choice. These typically are a mix of pieces from the White House's permanent collection and pieces borrowed from other museums or collections.[13] Since the Kennedy Administration, however, any changes the first family wishes to make to the public staterooms of the White House must be approved by the White House Historical Association.[14] Presidential choices regarding White House art are not merely reflections of personal taste but also a way that presidents make visible certain ideological or affective commitments. For example, much ink was spilled by magazine writers and bloggers on George W. Bush's favorite painting, *A Charge to Keep,* which hung both in his Texas governor's office and in the Oval Office.[15] Bush was known to show this painting to Oval Office visitors and explain to them its significance to his faith and leadership; he even appeared in a video tour of the Oval Office to describe how the painting and other art objects in the Oval Office illustrated what he called his "nature." The painting is now featured prominently in the background of his official White House portrait.[16]

Evidence for President Obama's early attention to White House art may be found in a White House photograph of the president made in the Oval Office just ten days after his inauguration.[17] Captioned "President Barack Obama tries out different desk chairs in the Oval Office," the photograph depicts the new president sitting in one office chair while several other candidates await their audition nearby. The tone of the photo is teasing, with Obama-as-Goldilocks clearly seeking the chair that's "just right." But I am interested in the image for another reason entirely: a book on the President's desk. Studying the high-resolution version of the image, I was able to identify the book as William Kloss's *Art in the White House: A Nation's Pride.*[18] A catalogue of every object in the White House art collection, this is the book that the Clintons consulted as they made decisions about the art they wanted to display; the photograph reveals that Obama clearly is gearing up for the same task. Coincidentally, the book is open to page 345, the page on which George P. A. Healy's *The Peacemakers* appears. Maddow's tongue-in-cheek questions of an art conspiracy aside, the photo offers good evidence that just ten days into office, the new president had already set about selecting the works of art with which he would surround himself.

Scholars writing on the visual politics of the presidency tend to focus on the politics of the "photo op," unmasking the instrumentality of images of presidential power by encouraging us to look behind or past images rather than at them.[19] I seek to model a way of looking at presidential photographs that points instead to their value as foci of sustained critical attention. This chapter participates in scholarly conversations about the visual politics of the presidency by examining one recurring motif in the visual archive of the early Obama presidency: photographic depictions of him with White House art, especially portraits or busts of past presidents.[20] In *The Exemplary Presidency,* Philip Abbott observes that "it is common for presidents to cite other presidents," in effect constituting them as exemplars for imitation.[21] Presidents do so for reasons both instrumental and constitutive. They may wish to associate their policy choices with similar tough choices faced by iconic leaders. They might also seek to highlight "an ideal behavior to be imitated" by citizens and leaders of the present. Relatedly, they may wish to signal the kind of leadership they seek to provide in their own presidencies.[22] Finally, they may use presidential exemplars to signal a broader "way of reading American political culture." That is, when presidents cite other presidents, they perform their own "hermeneutic" act of interpretation that offers up their own readings of the American story.[23] Overall, Jason Edwards explains, such appropriation "is a form of collective memory that performs important political and symbolic work in American politics."[24]

This essay builds on these ideas in two ways. First, it illustrates that such citation is not only verbal; it may also be visual. Second, it advances the argument that, although all presidents recognize the value of citing presidential exemplars, as the nation's first African American president Barack Obama may have recognized that value even more keenly in the early months of his presidency. Despite careful control of candidate Obama's visual image during the campaign, the visual culture at large offered its own mediated, vernacular, and often problematic images of Barack Obama. Ralina Joseph observes that "the production, consumption, and circulation of [Obama's] image" in the 2008 campaign involved "conflicting emotions of race, identity, Blackness, belonging" and included both implicit and explicit moments of racism.[25] In his response to a previous conference version of this essay, Michael Shaw curated a masterful, disheartening visual catalog of the ways that Obama's opponents as well as white mainstream media negatively depicted the candidate.[26] As Joseph,

Shaw, art historian Dora Apel, and others have shown, throughout his campaign Obama was depicted using disturbing racial stereotypes; the repeated circulation of images of Obama as a terrorist, thug, or monkey, among other visual topoi, proved a complex personal burden for the candidate to overcome.[27]

Although some might argue that Obama did overcome that burden because he was elected, images of Obama with White House art need to be read in light of the imagery examined by these scholars. While all presidents are invested in controlling their own visual image, the visual evidence from 2009–10 suggests that the Obama administration made it a key priority. If some rhetorical scholars are interested in how President Obama took advantage of the bully pulpit during his first months in office, I want to ask how President Obama sought to authorize his presidency, and therefore address the rhetoric of presidential expectations, by working and reworking the rich canvas of White House art. In this chapter, I argue that White House photographs of President Obama visually cited presidential exemplars in order to perform rhetorical tasks that involved both association and dissociation. By putting the president into the visual frame with paintings and busts of George Washington, Abraham Lincoln, the two Roosevelts and others, the Obama administration used White House art as an inventional resource for associating the president with American values and achievements. Such images aligned him with the history of the presidency and encouraged the viewer to see ideological and affective links between President Obama and past presidents. Although the majority of the early photographs of Obama with the presidents in White House art were grounded in a visual rhetoric of association, a few photographs invited the viewer to consider how Obama's presidency challenged our mythologized history of the presidency. What I call "dissociative images" are those composed in ways that visually separated President Obama from presidential exemplars, marking him as distinct from his predecessors even as he continued to appear "presidential." Such images challenged viewers to reconsider the nature and mythic status of the presidency itself. Some of these dissociative photographs even featured Obama in the act of viewing White House art, suggesting that Obama recognized, and indeed may even have welcomed the rhetorical possibilities of dissociation. The visual ghosts of presidents past lurk on the walls of the White House and haunt every president. My analysis illustrates how the nation's first African American president took visual advantage of those ghosts to authorize

his leadership and thus address presidential expectations during his first
eighteen months in office.

Flickr and White House Photography

My corpus of photographs is drawn from a new and unprecedented
real-time visual archive of the presidency: Flickr.[28] A popular online
photo-sharing site, Flickr was a key part of the early Obama administration's communications strategy.[29] Flickr embraces the ethos of vernacular
photography: anyone can create an account, upload images, organize them,
tag them, share them, and comment on them.[30] Yet although the White
House used new media to tell its story with pictures, those pictures were
orchestrated by an old hand at visual politics: Pete Souza, who served in
the same position during the second Reagan Administration.[31] The White
House debuted its Flickr photostream in April 2009, just in time for the
inevitable "First 100 Days" retrospectives, and quickly backfilled it with
photographs from Inauguration Day on. In choosing to use Flickr, the
White House did something unprecedented: it made the photos it produced on a regular basis publicly accessible in a living archive that grew
over time. As a result, Flickr offered the Obama administration precisely
what social media promise: direct access to audiences without the institutional filters of traditional news media. The White House photographs
uploaded to Flickr regularly offered viewers a "behind-the-scenes," though
by no means transparent or unfiltered, view of the president.[32] And one
did not have to wait for the presidential library to be built in order to
view the pictures.

Eighteen months into Obama's presidency, the White House Flickr
photostream contained just over 2,300 photographs made by Souza and
other White House photographers. Using Flickr as my image database,
I searched the names of all public and key private rooms in the White
House, separating out for study those images that fit my criteria. To be
relevant for the purposes of this analysis, photographs had to include the
president in the frame and they had to be ones in which White House
art objects were integral to the photograph's composition. An art object
was considered integral to the composition when it appeared in relation
to the figure of Obama via the photographer's compositional choices of
spatial arrangement, color, focus, light, or some combination of these.
There are numerous images in which White House art objects appear

more incidentally; I did not include these for study. At the end of this selection process, I had identified 114 photographs of President Obama pictured with White House art. I focused specifically on the 82 images of President Obama that featured him with portraits and busts of presidents. The photographs I discuss here are representative of broader patterns of visual representation I identified in the corpus, but were also selected to provide the most vivid and rhetorically interesting examples of those patterns.

Association: Hailing Mythic Presidents as Authorizing Figures

It is to be expected that presidents will use the mise-en-scène of the White House to their rhetorical advantage. Although all images made in the White House work to some extent to authorize the sitting president's authority as the nation's leader, my focus here is on the way portraits and busts of past presidents functioned as authorizing figures during the eighteen months of Obama's first term. Donald Rice defines authorizing figures as "past figures of authority" that rhetors use "to boost their own authority."[33] Jason Edwards elaborates that an authorizing figure is "a person of historical importance that rhetors invoke and interpret in justifying their own policies and principles."[34] Authorizing figures function as rhetorical resources in both the epideictic and deliberative modes to make "history do work in the present."[35] Not all former presidents are up to the rhetorical job. The artwork most frequently included in photographs of President Obama was that which represented the so-called "mythic presidents." Patricia Misciagno defines the mythic presidency as "a set of expectations and perceptions that are grounded in American political ideology and folklore, by which a president is viewed as larger than life and, above all else, is seen as a strong leader."[36] Such expectations, Janis Edwards and Stacey Smith contend, encourage citizens to see the president as "the embodiment of the 'essence and legacy of the American spirit.'"[37] The mythic presidency is thus grounded in the nation's affective expectation that the president be "the living symbol of America's 'past and future greatness,' the heir to Washington, Jefferson, Lincoln, and the Roosevelts."[38] In photographs of President Obama with White House art, the cast of characters shifted but was a relatively limited group: Washington, Jefferson, Madison, Lincoln, Theodore Roosevelt, and Franklin Roosevelt appeared most frequently.

Chaim Perelman and Lucie Olbrechts-Tyteca write that association brings "separate elements together and allow[s] us to establish a unity among them."[39] In Souza's photographs, Obama was put into visual association with past presidents via modes of composition that produce a hailing effect. In the Althuserrian sense, hailing photographs literally "call on" the subject of the work of art, effectively making the subject of a work of art into an actor in the photograph. As a result of this hailing, the mythic president becomes rhetorically available as an authorizing figure.

George Washington is hailed in images made all over the White House. Indeed, perhaps no other figure signals so explicitly the continuity of the American presidency while inviting viewers to consider the capacity for dramatic change. Consider a photograph made one year into Obama's presidency (Figure 11.1). President Obama stands alone in the outer Oval Office; he is photographed from inside the Cabinet Room, where Charles Willson Peale's masterful 1776 portrait of George Washington dominates, hung high on a wall.[40] The two presidents have been put in visual association, but Obama is unaware of it; only the viewer sees the two in the same frame. Washington the mythic president is pictured here,

Figure 11.1 *President Barack Obama stands in the Outer Oval Office, viewed from the Cabinet Room of the White House, January 7, 2010. (Official White House Photo by Pete Souza)*

Figure 11.2 *President Barack Obama meets with advisors in the Roosevelt Room of the White House, May 4, 2009. (Official White House Photo by Pete Souza)*

but not at the expense of Obama; despite their differences in height, both are given equal compositional weight. Deep inside the presidency (note the nested series of doors), Obama is a visual echo of Peale's Washington, gazing off in the same direction, holding roughly the same facial expression and body position, his hands in his pockets a twenty-first century echo of Washington's hand in vest. Washington's hailing thus invites attention both to continuity and change. Obama represents the continuity of the American republic, while his role as the first African American president signals something new; as *The New Yorker*'s inauguration week cover of Obama dressed as Washington declared, both men may be understood to be "the first."[41]

The Roosevelt Room, a meeting room in the West Wing, enables White House photographers to advance a variety of associations with its eponymous mythic presidents. One Roosevelt Room shot features President Obama meeting with his advisors in May 2009 (Figure 11.2). While everyone else in the room sits, Obama stands. Gesturing as he makes a point, his assertive stance and body positioning (note especially his left arm) echoes the 1909 Tade Styka oil of Theodore Roosevelt above the mantel.[42] Obama may not have the masculine trappings of horse and Rough Rider uniform, but he does have a rather phallically placed football. The football functions here as something of a visual joke, resonating not only as a prop of traditional American masculinity, but also as a commentary on Obama's own habits. As the White House Flickr photostream illustrates, Obama frequently is photographed tossing a football around the office as a way to relax or wind down.[43] Here the football frames President Obama as relaxed but active and engaged, a quarterback on offense. Such images are structured to offer a contemporary parallel to Roosevelt's famed early twentieth-century public construction of masculinity.[44] Styka's Roosevelt authorizes Obama's performance of masculinity, one key requirement of the mythic presidency.[45]

In some cases, authorizing figures were compositionally presented as direct participants in the proceedings rather than simply as spectators. Note, for example, how Obama and his economic advisors were photographed in the Roosevelt Room just days after the inauguration in 2009[46] (Figure 11.3). Obama's pointing gesture hails a confident-looking FDR, inviting him into the scene. Smiling and seeming to look directly at the

Figure 11.3 *President Barack Obama meets with economic advisors in the Roosevelt Room of the White House, January 2009. (Official White House Photo by Pete Souza)*

Figure 11.4 *President Barack Obama, Vice President Joe Biden, and senior staff, react in the Roosevelt Room of the White House, as the House passes the health care reform bill, March 21, 2010. (Official White House Photo by Pete Souza)*

president, pen and paper in hand, the thirty-second president appears to be taking notes. In a room full of glum faces, FDR stands out for his easy affability and calm. Jonathan Alter writes of the first few weeks of Obama's presidency that the White House's goal was to show through its "ceaseless activity" that the public could have confidence in the new president in the face of major economic crisis: "While markets and polls would respond in large part to what happened in the economy, the tone at the top was critical. As Roosevelt had shown, public confidence was connected to the president's personal confidence."[47] In a time of economic crisis in which the Great Depression frequently was invoked as a point of comparison, FDR's portrait reminds the viewer of the mythic president's leadership in that earlier crisis. The photograph thus hails FDR both ideologically and affectively, encouraging viewers to recognize in the new president's inclusive gesture both the immense challenges of the day and the need to maintain optimism for the future.[48]

Both Roosevelt portraits are activated as authorizing figures in a widely-circulated photograph dated March 21, 2010, the night the House of Representatives passed the Obama health care plan[49] (Figure 11.4). A group of advisors is gathered with the president and the vice president in the Roosevelt Room to watch the televised vote on Capitol Hill. By nearly every compositional measure of line, spatial organization, light, and color, Obama visually dominates the scene. Dressed in a white shirt and red tie but wearing no jacket, Obama contrasts sharply with others in the room who wear jackets and darker clothes. The skylight over the President's head illuminates his crisp, white shirt and further emphasizes the visual contrast. Obama also occupies the precise center of the frame; the left third of the photograph is occupied by the portrait of Franklin Roosevelt and the right third is taken up by the portrait of Theodore Roosevelt. Taken as a unit, Obama and the two Roosevelts each make up one point of an equilateral triangle, the former presidents structurally linked with the current one through lines created by Press Secretary Robert Gibbs's gaze on the left and the echoing body positions of Obama, Vice President Joe Biden, and Theodore Roosevelt on the right. Obama's visual dominance is thus authorized by his visual association with the portraits of the two Roosevelts. As in Figure 11.3, Franklin D. Roosevelt's leadership is acknowledged in the photo, but here it is Theodore Roosevelt who shares the spotlight with Obama. Throughout the health care debate, President Obama emphasized the first Roosevelt's role. In his September 9, 2009, address to a joint session of Congress, Obama stated, "I am not the first President to take up this cause, but I am determined to be the last. It has now been nearly a century since Theodore Roosevelt first called for health care reform."[50] The warm glow of the light hung above Styka's painting visually emphasizes Roosevelt's role as an early national health care advocate; Styka's Roosevelt perhaps also serves to acknowledge Obama's own "rough ride" through the formidable process.

Hailing photographs visually associated the president with mythic presidents, linking Obama with masculine, larger-than-life leaders and ideological forebears. Recall what I noted above about the use of presidents as exemplars: they provide models for leadership, suggest behavior to imitate, and offer avenues for interpretation of American political culture. Photographs of President Obama with portraits of Washington emphasized both men's unique institutional roles as "the first" and at the same time performed the continuity of the American presidency. Affectively, images of Obama with portraits of the two Roosevelts pointed to

FDR's ability to create public confidence during crisis and to TR's iconic masculinity. Ideologically, in the context of the economic crisis and the health care debate, both Roosevelts were hailed in ways that authorize Obama's leadership on these issues. Far from merely sharing the frame with these presidents, Obama was authorized by these White House portraits in ways that sanctioned his leadership in the messy immediacy of the policy-making present while implicating him in the long history of the American presidency itself.

Dissociation: Inviting Reflection upon the Mythic Presidency

Up to this point I have highlighted how photographs of Obama with White House art sought positively to relate Obama to the mythic presidency. But a smaller group of photographs worked differently: in these photographs, the viewer is invited to see Obama as a figure of dissociation. Chaim Perelman tells us that dissociation "aims at separating elements which language or a recognized tradition have previously tied together," observing that "reasoning by dissociation is characterized from the start by the opposition of appearance and reality."[51] Dissociative photographs compositionally separated Obama from past presidents, dissociating the appearances of the mythic presidency from the realities of twenty-first century governance. In doing so, they elevated Obama by inviting reconsideration of the mythic presidency and by encouraging the viewer to scrutinize the presidency as an object of study. Ultimately, then, both the associative and the dissociative photographs worked to authorize Obama's leadership.

In one of these dissociative images, white porcelain busts of Abraham Lincoln and Thomas Jefferson anchor the left and right sides of a doorway leading from a white marble hallway into the Diplomatic Reception Room[52] (Figure 11.5). Each bust occupies its own pedestal and looks off in a different direction, away from the doorway; a large, gold presidential seal dominates the space above the door. The wallpaper in the Diplomatic Reception Room, installed by Jackie Kennedy in 1961, after a nineteenth-century pattern, depicts "Views of North America" in vibrant blues, greens, and yellow.[53] As President Obama leaves the room and moves into the hallway, he departs a space full of color and enters one that is pristine, marble, and white. Poised to walk through the doorway and literally introduce color to the space, Obama the flesh-and-blood African American president

Figure 11.5 *President Barack Obama leaves the Diplomatic Reception Room after a statement on the confirmation of Judge Sonia Sotomayor to the Supreme Court, on Aug. 6, 2009. (Official White House Photo by Pete Souza)*

is caught unawares in the middle of a triangle created by the presidential seal and the disembodied busts of Lincoln and Jefferson on the left and right. Whereas in Figure 11.1 a similarly unaware Obama was authorized by Washington's giant presence, here Obama is a material disruption to the white marble continuity of the mythic presidency. Obama's ambiguous racial visibility, assiduously marked by his campaign as both black and white, visually contrasts with the other presidents in the frame.[54] Note that the photograph not only calls our attention to Obama's color but to the materiality of the room he is leaving too; the abandoned lectern and microphone over his left shoulder are testament to his executive duties in the here and now. As Jefferson and Lincoln anchor that white, pristine, idealized space of appearances, Obama materially complicates whatever seamless narrative the busts, the seal, and the marble might profess. By highlighting Obama's difference from the men enshrined in the porcelain busts, the photo invites recognition of the difference between the presidency as myth/appearance and the presidency as job/reality.

Certainly Obama's racial difference or, as he is fond of putting it, the fact that he does not "look like the guys on our money," is part of what creates dissociation. But he is not only a black man visually disrupting a long history of white men with his difference. Some of the photographs I term dissociative sacrificed Obama's association with the mythic presidency for identification with the viewer. Such photographs echoed what Obama declared throughout his presidential campaign, that he is more "like us" than "like them." This was made visible especially in a group of photographs in which Obama is pictured looking at presidential portraits. In these photos Obama functioned as the viewer's surrogate, inviting us to contemplate these figures enshrined in public memory along with him. In doing so, he seemed to encourage the viewer to reflect upon the presidency itself.

In one of these photographs, Obama studies John Vanderlyn's portrait of James Madison in the Blue Room[55] (Figure 11.6). As he waits for his first press conference to begin, "forty-four" is caught in a moment of engage-

Figure 11.6 *President Barack Obama looks at a portrait of President James Madison while waiting in the Blue Room of the White House before his press conference in the East Room, February 9, 2009. (Official White House Photo by Pete Souza)*

ment with "four." Standing with his back to the camera and looking up at the Madison portrait, Obama serves as a kind of visual intermediary: we look at him looking at Madison's portrait, and as a result we study Madison's portrait ourselves. Because the photograph essentially puts us in the same place as Obama the viewer, it invites us to consider Obama's own viewing experience: What is he thinking about as he contemplates the canvas? The constitutional law professor contemplates the drafter of the Constitution? The president studies the author of the Bill of Rights just before he jumps into a live, televised arena with a free press? The first African American president studies a slaveholding one? The commander in chief overseeing two wars thinks about the first president to sign a declaration of war? Perhaps. But this photograph is different from the images of authorizing figures discussed earlier. It is the aura with which portraits of presidents are supposedly infused that activates the mythic presidency. Yet here the enthymeme implicit in the hailing photographs, the one that collapses the gap between "presidential portrait" and "president," is missing. The photograph instead calls explicit attention to the portrait *as a portrait*. Madison's face is obscured by the harsh light bouncing off it, revealing the rough texture of the canvas. The viewer is thus invited to see the Madison portrait more as an art object than as an iconic founding father. As much about the paintings as they were about the president, photos of Obama looking at presidential portraits complicated an easy association of Obama with mythic presidents: he is not like them.[56]

Not surprisingly, Lincoln frequently is hailed in photographs of Obama with White House art. He appears especially often in Oval Office photographs, where George Henry Story's 1915 painted portrait and a bronze bust by Augustus Saint-Gaudens occupy prominent places.[57] These photographs activate ubiquitous comparisons of Obama to Lincoln, comparisons Obama himself actively cultivated throughout the 2008 campaign.[58] But a few photographs that associate President Obama with Lincoln are more dissociative. Early in 2010, the president chose to display a copy of the Emancipation Proclamation in the Oval Office and to unveil it on the Dr. Martin Luther King Jr. holiday.[59] In this photograph President Obama is not so much a viewer as he is a museum docent, interpreting the Emancipation Proclamation for a multigenerational group of mostly African Americans. Gesturing toward the document in a professorial way, Obama hails the *text* of Lincoln rather than the image. Indeed, Lincoln in the form of the George Henry Story portrait is present but left out of the

Figure 11.7 *President Barack Obama views the Emancipation Proclamation with a small group of African American seniors, their grandchildren, and some children from the Washington, D.C., area, in the Oval Office, January 18, 2010. This copy of the Emancipation Proclamation, which is on loan from the Smithsonian Museum of American History, was hung on the wall of the Oval Office today and will be exhibited for six months before being moved to the Lincoln Bedroom where the original Proclamation was signed by Abraham Lincoln on January 1, 1863. (Official White House photo by Pete Souza)*

action entirely; the eyes of everyone in the room (even the professional historian Taylor Branch) are on Obama and the text he interprets. As he encourages his audience to reflect upon the text, the President is literally reflected in it, his likeness mingling in ghostly fashion with Lincoln's signature on the document.

It may be tempting to view this photograph as a tidy, condensed narrative of racial progress: Emancipation leads to King, leads to Obama. But the Emancipation Proclamation is far from an unproblematic document. As Kirt Wilson has argued persuasively, the Emancipation Proclamation was a paradoxical performance of presidential leadership. Rather than decisively freeing the slaves, the ambivalent president worked within the institutionalized, bureaucratic structures available to him to accomplish the task; only through its later reworking in the culture has it attained the moral status it has today.[60] Obama himself is most certainly familiar with the text's ambivalence as a document of racial progress. Biographer David Remnick states that as a law professor Obama taught a course on racism and the law in which he assigned "the essential legislation and court cases," including the Emancipation Proclamation.[61] By displacing the mythic Lincoln of the portrait and making Obama's hermeneutic performance central, the photograph presents the iconic document in a way that recognizes this ambivalence. First, Obama is figured as the interpreter of the document; it is not something, apparently, to be engaged on one's own. Note also the presence below it of a bronze bust of Dr. Martin Luther King Jr.[62] Whereas Lincoln's image is shunted to the side, it is King who is brought into the picture, the bust triangulating with the Emancipation Proclamation above and the president on the left. The very composition of Souza's photograph implies the Emancipation Proclamation cannot hang on its own; it needs the King bust to warrant its iconicity and, most importantly, a hermeneutic president to interpret it.

Made on the Martin Luther King Jr. holiday at the end of a year in which Obama attempted to translate the "hope" rhetoric of the campaign into public policy, the Emancipation Proclamation photograph not only invited reflection upon the torturous path African Americans have taken to full citizenship in the United States, it illustrated that the presidency is the product of the hard choices of governance. In the here and now, Obama seemed to be saying, presidents often need to compromise; leadership is messy and often morally ambivalent. By encouraging us to recognize the ways in which the nation's story—its presidential myths—are more complicated than they may initially appear, the Obama of these photographs not only negotiated but appeared to welcome that uneasy space between the cool, white, pristine appearances of presidential myth and the messy, colorful reality of actual governance.

Although they were only a small portion of the total number of photographs depicting President Obama with White House art, the dissociative photographs do compelling rhetorical work. Whereas the photographs I discussed in the first section of this essay visually cited past presidents in ways that authorized Obama's leadership, in the dissociative images President Obama himself functioned as an authorizing figure. Through their compositional emphasis on Obama's own bodily performances, the photographs invited the viewer to identify with Obama. As a result, he became an authorizing figure himself—like the presidents hanging on the White House walls—one who enabled the viewer to reflect upon the complex narrative of the American presidency.

Conclusion: The Visual Politics of Presidential Invention

Philip Abbott writes, "Any president carries with him the successes and failures of past presidents as burdens to be borne, or as opportunities to be explored, or, as often, both."[63] In this regard, during his first eighteen months in office President Obama was in many ways unexceptional. Like all presidents, he engaged in "forms of rhetorical action" that allowed him to play a "role as the symbolic, as well as the real, head of state."[64] Using social media to circulate a visual chronicle of life in the White House, the early Obama administration employed White House art as one mechanism by which to authorize Obama's leadership and invite reflection upon the presidency itself. Yet citation of presidential exemplars is an inexact science; as Abbott observes, "popular attachment to these figures is often extremely general and unfocused."[65] For viewers of the White House Flickr photostream, visual invocations of Washington and Madison may have conjured up little association beyond that of "founder." Even the seemingly more specific visual associations of Obama with the Roosevelts, economic crisis, and health care reform would necessarily diminish over time as the images lost their immediate link to the policy debates of 2009–10. Yet presidents do not mobilize exemplars for purely instrumental means; no one supported President Obama on the economy simply because he was pictured with a painting of Franklin Roosevelt. For these reasons, we would do better to evaluate the images for the constitutive work they did and continued to do, to examine the photographs as products of hermeneutic acts of presidential "inventiveness" and imagination.[66] When we view the photographs this way, then we see that the visual citation of presidential exemplars broadly affirmed the continuity of the American presidency and authorized Obama's rightful place in that long history. Given that Obama consistently faced challenges not only to the legitimacy of his presidency but even to his American citizenship, such visual invention was wise. Yet the use of the presidents of White House art to visually authorize Obama's leadership meant also picturing a history as white and male as the first forty-three presidents themselves. (One is tempted to imagine how a President Hillary Clinton might have mobilized the visual politics of White House art differently.) Ultimately, the photographs aligned President Obama with a vaguely positive, yet deeply conventional image of the presidency. Although such alignment may have had instrumental and constitutive value, during his first eighteen months in office White House art arguably constrained him as much as it enabled him.

Despite their dependence upon the conventionality of presidential portraiture, however, the Flickr photographs do convey rhetorical prowess. Much has been made of candidate and President Obama's prodigious oratorical skills, and for good reason. Yet apart from praise for the campaign's general skill in mobilizing social media, much less has been said of Obama's visual eloquence. Above all, the White House Flickr photostream reveals that the president was from the beginning the author of his own image. The White House mobilized images produced for epideictic purposes—portraits of presidents—and made them doubly epideictic by placing Obama in the frame. Over time, systematic study of these photographs will enable critics to access not only the ways that Obama wished to be pictured in the present but also the ways he sought to be preserved for history. Despite the constraints mentioned above, the dissociative photographs suggest that, even in his early months in office, Obama thought carefully about visibility. Using a visual logic of dissociation, some photographs subtly picked away at the idea that the presidency exists above or apart from the materiality of history.[67] In these photographs from Obama's first eighteen months in office, we are invited to consider the rhetoric of presidential expectations through Obama's eyes. Obama invites the viewer to join him in scraping away at the mythic canvas of White House art—and at the presidency itself—to reveal the materiality of its facture.

Notes

The author wishes to thank Michael Shaw, Justin Vaughn, Jennifer Mercieca, and Jason Edwards for feedback and suggestions on earlier versions of this essay, and George Boone for his research assistance.

1. *The Rachel Maddow Show,* "Message in White House Paintings?" MSNBC.com, November 16, 2009, http://www.msnbc.msn.com/id/26315908/ns/msnbc_tv-rachel_maddow_show/#33980329.

2. Laura Rozen, "In W.H., Are Pictures Telling a Story?" Politico.com, November 16, 2009, http://www.msnbc.msn.com/id/26315908/ns/msnbc_tv-rachel_maddow_show/#33980329.

3. James A. Abbott and Elaine M. Rice, *Designing Camelot: The Kennedy White House Restoration* (New York: Van Nostrand Reinhold, 1998).

4. Hugh Sidey, "Editing the First Lady: Life Magazine Goes to the White House," *White House History* 13 (Collection Set 3): 13–14.

5. Elaine Rice Bachmann, "Circa 1961: The Kennedy White House Interiors," *White House History* 13 (Collection Set 3): 81.

6. William Kloss, *Art in the White House: A Nation's Pride* (Washington, DC: White House Historical Association, 2008), 23.

7. Forrest McDonald, *The American Presidency: An Intellectual History* (Lawrence: University Press of Kansas, 1995), 466.

8. Jeffrey Walker, *Rhetoric and Poetics in Antiquity* (New York: Oxford University Press, 2000), 9.

9. The term *rhetoric of display* comes from Lawrence J. Prelli, *Rhetorics of Display* (Columbia, SC: University of South Carolina Press, 2006). Prelli defines *display* as that which evokes "commonplace associations about 'how things look or appear'" (1–2).

10. Mary Lynn Kotz, "Art in the White House: The Clintons' Choice," ARTnews, September 1994, 138.

11. On the history of this painting see Kloss, *Art in the White House*, 146–49.

12. Kotz, "Art in the White House," 138.

13. There is much to be said about the works of art the Obamas borrowed, though that is beyond the scope of this study. See Carol Vogel, "A Bold and Modern White House," *New York Times*, October 7, 2009, http://www.nytimes.com/2009/10/07/arts/design/07borrow.html.

14. Amy Chozick and Kelly Crow, "Changing the Art on the White House Walls," *Wall Street Journal* May 22, 2009, http://online.wsj.com/article/SB10001424052970203771904574175453455287432.html.

15. See Scott Horner, "The Illustrated President," *Harper's* January 24, 2008, http://www.harpers.org/archive/2008/01/hbc-90002237; and Sidney Blumenthal, "From Norman Rockwell to Abu Ghraib," *Salon*, April 26, 2007, http://www.salon.com/opinion/blumenthal/2007/04/26/torture_policy/index.html. Horner's claims about the origins of the painting are incorrect; see Cara Finnegan, "A Funny Thing Happened at the Archive," *first efforts*, January 20, 2010, http://caraf.blogs.com/caraf/2010/01/funny-thing-happened-at-the-archive-or-how-i-busted-a-lefty-internet-meme-about-george-w-bushs-taste.html.

16. On the official portrait, see Mark Landler, "Wisecracks in White House As Bush Portrait Is Unveiled," *New York Times*, June 1, 2012, A16.

17. The photograph is available at http://www.flickr.com/photos/whitehouse/3484818188/.

18. The book is most visible in the highest-resolution version of the photograph, available at http://www.flickr.com/photos/whitehouse/3484818188/sizes/o/.

19. See Rodger Streitmatter, "The Rise and Triumph of the White House Photo Opportunity," *Journalism Quarterly* (1988): 981–85; Lawrence J. Mullen, "The President's Visual Image From 1945 to 1974: An Analysis of Spatial Configuration in News Magazine Photographs," *Presidential Studies Quarterly* 27 (1997): 819–34; Kiku Adatto, *Picture Perfect:*

Life in the Age of the Photo Op (Princeton: Princeton University Press, 2008); and Keith Erickson, "Presidential Rhetoric's Visual Turn: Performance Fragments and the Politics of Illusionism," *Communication Monographs* 67 (2000): 138–57.

20. Scholarship on the visual politics of presidential communication has tended to focus on three areas: how news and entertainment media represent presidents and the presidency; the mediated features of elections, campaigns, and debates; and the relationship between presidents and the press. See, among many others, the work of Trevor Parry-Giles and Shawn Parry-Giles, including *The Prime-Time Presidency: The West Wing and U.S. Nationalism* (Urbana, IL: University of Illinois Press, 2006) and *Constructing Clinton: Hyperreality and Presidential Image-Making in Postmodern Politics* (New York: Peter Lang, 2002); Kathleen Hall Jamieson, *Packaging the Presidency,* 3rd ed. (New York: Oxford University Press, 1996) and *Eloquence in an Electronic Age: The Transformation of Political Speechmaking* (New York: Oxford University Press, 1990); and Roderick Hart, *Seducing America: How Television Charms the Modern Voter* (New York: Oxford University Press, 1994), *Campaign Talk: Why Elections Are Good for Us* (Princeton, NJ: Princeton University Press, 2000), and *The Sound of Leadership: Presidential Communication in the Modern Age* (Chicago: University of Chicago Press, 1989). See also Janis L. Edwards, *Political Cartoons in the 1988 Presidential Campaign* (New York: Routledge, 1997); Doris A. Graber, *Mass Media and American Politics,* 8th ed. (Washington, DC: CQ Press, 2009); W. Lance Bennett, Regina G. Lawrence, and Steven Livingston, *When the Press Fails: Political Power and the News Media from Iraq to Katrina* (Chicago: University of Chicago Press, 2008); and Samuel Kernell, *Going Public: New Strategies of Presidential Leadership,* 4th ed. (Washington, DC: CQ Press, 2006). Art historical writing on images of presidents includes Joseph B. Hudson, "Banks, Politics, Hard Cider, and Paint: The Political Origins of William Sidney Mount's 'Cider Making,'" *Metropolitan Museum Journal* 10 (1975): 107–18; Georgia Brady Bumgardner, "Political Portraiture: Two Prints of Andrew Jackson," *The American Art Journal* 18 (1986): 84–95; David Ward, *Charles Willson Peale: Art and Selfhood in the Early Republic* (Berkeley: University of California Press, 2004); and Adam Greenhalgh, "'Not a Man but a God': The Apotheosis of Gilbert Stuart's Athenaeum Portrait of George Washington," *Winterthur Portfolio* 41 (2007): 269–303.

21. Philip Abbott, *The Exemplary Presidency: Franklin D. Roosevelt and the American Political Tradition* (Amherst: University of Massachusetts Press, 1990), 8.

22. Ibid., 10–11.

23. Ibid., 11–12.

24. Jason Edwards, "Sanctioning Foreign Policy: The Rhetorical Use of President Harry Truman," *Presidential Studies Quarterly* 39 (September 2009): 455.

25. Ralina L. Joseph, "Imagining Obama: Reading Overtly and Inferentially Racist Images of Our 44th President, 2007–2008," *Communication Studies* 62 (2011): 390.

26. For an example of Michael Shaw's work along these lines, see BagNewsNotes Blog, "Right-Wing Focus," http://www.bagnewsnotes.com/category/right-wing-focus.

27. Dora Apel, "Just Joking? Chimps, Obama, and Racial Stereotype," *Journal of Vi-*

sual Culture 8 (2009): 134–42; Pearl K. Ford, Angie Maxwell, and Todd Shields, "What's the Matter with Arkansas? Symbolic Racism and 2008 Presidential Candidate Support," *Presidential Studies Quarterly* 40 (2010): 286–302; Spencer Piston, "How Explicit Racial Prejudice Hurt Obama in the 2008 Election," *Political Behavior* 32 (2010): 431–51; and Catherine Squires, "Reframing the National Family: Race Mixing and Re-telling American History," *The Black Scholar* 39 (2009): 41–50.

28. Flickr began in 2004 as a small feature of an online game created by software engineers in Vancouver; see Daniel Terdiman, "Photo Site a Hit with Bloggers," *Wired,* December 9, 2004, http://www.wired.com/culture/lifestyle/news/2004/12/65958. Julian Stallabrass's short essay on photos of Obama on Flickr mentions the White House Flickr photostream but suggests that vernacular images of Obama on Flickr are "more interesting" (197); see Stallabrass, "Obama on Flickr," *Journal of Visual Culture* 8 (August 2009): 196–201.

29. In 2009, the Obama administration established an Office of New Media as part of its communications operation. On the Obama White House's media strategy, see Jennifer Senior, "The Message is the Message," *New York,* August 2, 2009, http://nymag.com/news/politics/58199/; and Ken Auletta, "Non-Stop News," *The New Yorker,* January 25, 2010: 38–47. For a substantive history of the White House communications office, see Martha Joynt Kumar, *Managing the President's Message: The White House Communications Operation* (Baltimore: Johns Hopkins University Press, 2007).

30. Geoffrey Batchen defines vernacular photography as "ordinary photographs, the ones made or bought (or sometimes bought and then made over) by everyday folk from 1839 until now." See Geoffrey Batchen, "Vernacular Photographies," *History of Photography* 24 (Autumn 2000): 262.

31. See National Public Radio, "A Front-Row View Of Obama's White House," January 15, 2009, http://www.npr.org/templates/story/story.php?storyId=99353598; and Rino Pucci, "Photographing Power," *News Photographer* August 2009: 39–43.

32. "Inside View of the White House is Not What It Seems, Says Professor," interview with Cara Finnegan, *States News Service,* March 4, 2010, Academic OneFile.

33. Donald E. Rice, *The Rhetorical Uses of the Authorizing Figure: Fidel Castro and José Martí* (New York: Praeger, 1992), xiv. See also Edwards, "Sanctioning Foreign Policy." On the broader question of how presidents appropriate the rhetoric of iconic figures, see Denise M. Bostdorff and Steven R. Goldzweig, "History, Collective Memory, and the Appropriation of Martin Luther King, Jr.: Reagan's Rhetorical Legacy," *Presidential Studies Quarterly* 35 (2005): 661–90; Lara M. Brown, "The Greats and the Great Debate: President William J. Clinton's Use of Presidential Exemplars," *Presidential Studies Quarterly* 37 (2007): 124–38; and John M. Murphy, "Bill Clinton, Martin Luther King, Jr., and the Orchestration of Rhetorical Traditions," *Quarterly Journal of Speech* 83 (1997): 71–89.

34. Edwards, "Sanctioning Foreign Policy," 454.

35. Rice, *The Rhetorical Uses of the Authorizing Figure,* 13.

36. Patricia S. Misciagno, "Rethinking the Mythic Presidency," *Political Communication* 13 (1996): 329. See also Janis L. Edwards and Stacey M. Smith, "Myth and Anti-Myth in

Presidential Campaign Films, 2000," in *The Millennium Edition: Communication in the 2000 Campaign,* ed. Linda Lee Kaid (Lanham, MD: Rowman and Littlefield, 2003), 17–25.

37. Edwards and Smith, "Myth and Anti-Myth," 20.

38. Warren G. Rochelle, "The Literary Presidency," *Presidential Studies Quarterly* 29 (1999): 409.

39. Chaim Perelman and Lucie Olbrechts-Tyteca, *The New Rhetoric: A Treatise on Argumentation,* trans. John Wilkinson and Purcell Weaver (Notre Dame, IN: University of Notre Dame Press, 1969), 190.

40. A color version of the image is available at http://www.flickr.com/photos/white-house/4330708633/. The portrait at the White House is Peale's late 1776 copy of a portrait made on commission for John Hancock; see Kloss, *Art in the White House,* 58–59.

41. The image, by Drew Friedman, appeared on the January 26, 2009, cover, http://archives.newyorker.com/?i=2009-01-26.

42. A color version of this photograph is available at http://www.flickr.com/photos/whitehouse/3531554769/. On Styka's painting, see Kloss, *Art in the White House,* 379.

43. As of June 17, 2010, there were more than a dozen photographs on the White House Flickr photostream featuring Obama with a football.

44. On Theodore Roosevelt's construction of masculinity, see Arnaldo Testi, "The Gender of Reform Politics: Theodore Roosevelt and the Culture of Masculinity," *Journal of American History* 81 (1995): 1509–33; Gail Bederman, *Manliness and Civilization: A Cultural History of Gender and Race in the United States, 1880–1917* (Chicago: University of Chicago Press, 1995); and Leroy G. Dorsey, *We Are All Americans, Pure and Simple: Theodore Roosevelt and the Myth of Americanism* (Tuscaloosa: University of Alabama Press, 2007), 19–23.

45. On the necessity for the president to be masculine, see Edwards and Smith, "Myth and Anti-Myth," 20.

46. A color version of this photograph is available at http://www.flickr.com/photos/whitehouse/3483999361/.

47. Jonathan Alter, *The Promise: President Obama, Year One* (New York: Simon and Schuster, 2010), 110–11.

48. This specific visual analogy was not new; *Time* magazine's postelection cover of Obama as FDR, complete with cigarette in holder, similarly but clumsily trumpeted that the election portended "A New New Deal." The photo illustration, by Arthur Hochstein and Lon Tweeten, appeared on the November 24, 2008, cover, (http://www.time.com/time/covers/0,16641,20081124,00.html). In 2010, it was featured in a National Portrait Gallery exhibition on the history of *Time*'s covers of presidents. See "Comings and Goings," *Washington Post,* February 5, 2010: WE39.

49. A color version of this photograph is available at http://www.flickr.com/photos/whitehouse/4455976349/.

50. Barack Obama, "Remarks by the President to a Joint Session of Congress on Health Care," whitehouse.gov, September 9, 2009, http://www.whitehouse.gov/the-press-office/remarks-president-a-joint-session-congress-health-care.

51. Chaim Perelman, *The Realm of Rhetoric* (Notre Dame, IN: University of Notre Dame Press, 1982), 49, 134.

52. A color version of this photograph is available at http://www.flickr.com/photos/whitehouse/3860760104/. The Lincoln bust is by Sèvres after Leonard Volk. The Jefferson bust, also by Sèvres, is after Jean-Antoine Houdon. See Kloss, *Art in the White House*, 374.

53. On the wallpaper, see Abbott and Rice, *Designing Camelot*, 120–122.

54. On Obama's racialization as white during the 2008 campaign, see Shawn Michelle Smith, "Obama's Whiteness," *Journal of Visual Culture* 8 (2009): 129–33.

55. A color version of this photograph is available at http://www.flickr.com/photos/whitehouse/3484009761/. On the 1816 portrait, see Kloss, *Art in the White House*, 82–83.

56. For further examples supporting this claim, I would turn the reader's attention to photos of Obama viewing portraits of John Kennedy (http://www.flickr.com/photos/whitehouse/3483999881/) and Abraham Lincoln (http://www.flickr.com/photos/whitehouse/3684030052/), both of which are composed to emphasize the portraits as portraits, not presidents.

57. On these art objects, see Kloss, *Art in the White House*, 373, 378.

58. David Remnick tracks Obama's interest in and invocations of Lincoln in *The Bridge: The Life and Rise of Barack Obama* (New York: Knopf, 2010), 23, 473, 475–76. See also David Zarefsky, "Obama's Lincoln: Uses of the Argument from Historical Analogy," *Proceedings of the Alta Conference on Argumentation* (Washington, DC: NCA/AFA, 2010), 572–78.

59. A color version of this photo is available at http://www.flickr.com/photos/whitehouse/4285414839/. On the choice to display the Emancipation Proclamation, see Sheryl Gay Stolberg, "Marking the Day, From Oval Office to Soup Kitchen," *New York Times*, January 19, 2010, A19; and Stolberg, "Frustration at Obama's Nuanced Style on Race," *New York Times*, February 9, 2010, A14.

60. Kirt Wilson, "The Paradox of Lincoln's Leadership," *Rhetoric and Public Affairs* 3 (2000): 15–32.

61. Remnick, *The Bridge*, 263.

62. The King bust belongs to the National Portrait Gallery. When it was lent to the Clinton White House in 2000 for display in the White House library, it was the first image of an African American to be displayed in a public room of the White House. See Jake Tapper, Political Punch Blog, "Bust of MLK Joins President Obama in Oval Office," March 18, 2009, http://blogs.abcnews.com/politicalpunch/2009/03/bust-of-mlk-joi.html.

63. Abbott, *The Exemplary Presidency*, 14.

64. Karlyn Kohrs Campbell and Kathleen Hall Jamieson, *Presidents Creating the Presidency: Deeds Done in Words* (Chicago: University of Chicago Press, 2008), 7.

65. Abbott, *The Exemplary Presidency*, 13.

66. Ibid., 184. On constitutive rhetorics, see James Jasinski and Jennifer R. Mercieca, "Analyzing Constitutive Rhetorics: The Virginia and Kentucky Resolutions and the 'Principles of '98," in Shawn J. Parry-Giles and J. Michael Hogan, eds., *The Handbook of Rhetoric and Public Address* (London: Wiley-Blackwell, 2010), 313–41.

67. The Obama White House continued to use visual culture dissociatively in order to make issues of race and America's racial history more visible in the spaces of the White House. In the summer of 2011, Norman Rockwell's 1964 painting of a Black schoolgirl, Ruby Bridges, being pelted with rotten tomatoes while being escorted to her newly integrated school was hung just outside of the Oval Office. Bridges herself was invited to the White House to see the painting and meet with the President, and the White House posted photographs to Flickr as well as a video of the visit to its Web site. Media commentators seemed most interested in the fact that the "N-word" appeared in the painting; see, for example, Adam Martin, "White House Painting Puts N-Word Just Outside of Oval Office," *Atlantic Wire,* August 24, 2011, http://www.theatlanticwire.com/national/2011/08/white-house-painting-puts-n-word-just-outside-oval-office/41665/.

CHAPTER 12

Michelle Obama, "Mom-in-Chief"

Gender, Race, and Familialism in Media Representations of the First Lady

BONNIE J. DOW

On February 24, 2009, when President Barack Obama made his first address to a joint session of Congress, First Lady Michelle Obama watched from the gallery, wearing a sleeveless purple dress. Mrs. Obama's apparel became the subject of media discussion in the days that followed, primarily for its featuring of her bare arms in the dead of winter. In a March 7 column titled "Should Michelle Cover Up?" Maureen Dowd reported a conversation with her *New York Times* colleague David Brooks about the first lady's "amazing arms." Brooks complained that the first lady's overt display of her "physical presence" was inappropriate for "sensually avoidant" Washington, DC, and remarked, "She's made her point. ... Now she should put away Thunder and Lightning."[1] As ABC News reported on its Web site that same week, in the course of a month Mrs. Obama's bare arms had appeared not only at the president's speech but in her official White House portrait and on the cover of *Vogue,* provoking considerable public discourse. That discourse ranged from admiring comments about her well-toned biceps and her much-publicized workout regimen to critiques that her fashion choices were too informal and ill-suited to the season.[2] Yet, as Joan Faber McAlister has observed, the issue was not as much about the sleeveless style as it was about the arms themselves and how they signified. Critics were "animated by the anxiety over the sight of muscular arms (fit for manual labor but unfit for display in polite company) on the figure of the first lady."[3]

This is not an essay about the first lady's body, but the eruption of "Sleevegate," as one reporter termed it,[4] brings into focus one of the specific personal burdens faced by Mrs. Obama as mass media attempted to make sense of her meaning as the nation's first African American first lady:

the long history of dominant white culture's obsession with black female bodies as icons of otherness, difference, primitivism, and aberrant sexuality. This "ageless drama of defining the black female form" can easily be traced through the fame of the exotic physique of the "Hottentot Venus" in early nineteenth-century Europe, to cultural constructions of American slave women as commodities, breeders, and sexual lures, to public commentary on the physiques of tennis stars Venus and Serena Williams over the last decade or so.[5] Cultural anxiety regarding the "difference" (from white norms) attached to their bodies by majority white publics is merely one aspect of the burden that black women historically have carried. For Mrs. Obama, it is but one constituent of the array of burdens borne by a black first lady forced to reconcile her all-too-visible difference—and its links to racial stereotypes—with the normative expectations attached to an institution previously occupied exclusively by white women.[6]

Much of what follows relies on a comparison of representations of the first lady in mainstream media directed at white audiences and in mainstream media directed at black audiences. My experience with this discourse indicates that white-targeted media have talked about the first lady's body in a way that black-targeted media have not. The "body problem" offers a useful entry point into a broader discussion of a central dimension of Mrs. Obama's personal burden (as well as a central dimension of her rhetorical/cultural significance) as our first African American first lady: her function as a signifier for the dialectic between sameness and difference that swirls around her and the first family in the public imaginary. For example, in stories from the early days of the Obama presidency, magazines targeting white women tended to talk about Mrs. Obama's muscular arms as impressive and enviable—as somehow otherworldly and unbelievable on someone who does not train her body for a living.[7] They fetishized her difference from ordinary (white) women, seemingly doing so to praise her, while also domesticating her somewhat transgressive physique by framing it within the postfeminist and maternalist politics of self-care, that is, "Mommy works out so that she can be a happier and better Mommy."[8] Importantly, profiles of Mrs. Obama in white health and lifestyle magazines did not mention the health problems that disproportionately affect African American women—obesity, diabetes, heart disease, tuberculosis—focusing instead on the First Lady's fitness regimen and reinforcing a "postfeminist discourse wherein individual action is decontextualized from social health realities."[9]

Michelle Obama's inescapable blackness, her unusually tall and fit body, and her well-publicized fashion sense (which can be understood as exemplifying the ways that class can function to make racial difference more palatable) are all constituent parts of how she signifies the tensions between sameness and difference in the most basic, visual, and visceral senses.[10] Attention to her body may be the most visible (literally and figuratively) aspect of this dynamic, but it plays itself out in multiple ways. What philosophers and political theorists have termed the "politics of recognition," the enduring conflict between universalism and specificity in our understandings of citizenship, serves as a loose backdrop for understanding this issue. Cultural movements of the late twentieth century geared toward developing awareness of diversity and multiculturalism have highlighted the conflict between understandings of citizenship founded on sameness—the abstract equality of rights and privileges all are presumed to possess—and those based in difference—the specific identities of individuals and groups linked to, for instance, some combination of gender, race, ethnicity, and sexuality. The latter recognize the "distinctness … that has been ignored, glossed over, assimilated to a dominant or majority identity."[11] Importantly, that distinctness often is produced by and productive of histories of discrimination and oppression. More recently, political theorist Danielle Allen has explored a similar dynamic operating through what she calls the metaphors of "oneness" and "wholeness" that figure in struggles to understand citizenship in ways that "bring trustful coherence out of division without erasing or suppressing difference."[12]

The Obamas bring this issue into sharp relief. As a candidate, President Obama faced personal burdens predicated on public uneasiness, emanating from multiple directions, with his "uniqueness" as an African American contender for the White House. Was he really born in the United States? Was he "black enough?" Or was he "too black" and the captive of black radicals (e.g., Jeremiah Wright)? Mrs. Obama also was subject to some controversial and racially charged characterizations during the last year of the 2008 presidential contest, as she became increasingly visible on the campaign trail. Michelle Obama biographer Liza Mundy has argued that many of these problems derived from Mrs. Obama's role as a campaign surrogate deployed to appeal to black voters and their concerns, "freeing her husband to seem more postracial, or even nonracial, in his self-presentation." Moreover, journalists focused on a "running theme of her narrative, the idea that there is something vaguely wrong with contemporary America," casting Mrs. Obama as "the darker, contentious, and hidden side of her husband."[13] As Kimberly Moffitt has observed in a useful summary of Mrs. Obama's personal burden as aspiring first lady, there was "no established lexicon for a woman like Michelle Obama who was a presidential candidate's wife but also an African-American," thus "news coverage relied upon recycled stereotypes of African-American women to discuss her."[14] The image problems that arose during the campaign prompted a media makeover to produce "a new Michelle, carefully edited for public consumption" and, as one Obama adviser remarked, designed to avoid controversy by emphasizing "'a much more traditional woman's role.'"[15]

Such observations foreground the first lady's function as an integral component of the presidential ethos; as Karlyn Kohrs Campbell has argued, the presidency is a "two-person career" that "requires their cooperative efforts if it is to be pursued successfully."[16] Like the president, the first lady functions as a representative of the nation, but she is peculiarly burdened by the role's lack of official definition and its indistinct combination of state and domestic duties. The role has evolved over time, and first ladies have emphasized different aspects of it. Shawn Parry-Giles and Diane Blair have argued that the contemporary first lady role can be understood as an enactment of the ideology of twentieth-century republican motherhood (sometimes expressed through a "first mother" persona), which stresses women's concern with social welfare generally and with the health and morality of the nation's women and children in particular. Both as private partners and as public advocates, first ladies are circumscribed by traditional gender expectations. Even so, Parry Giles and Blair conclude that the role of first lady can serve as a "site for the performance of archetypal femininity" and also as "a location for feminist advancement that challenges gender stereotypes."[17] As Lisa Burns has argued in *First Ladies and the Fourth Estate,* mass media provide the primary arena in which the first lady's image is managed and discussed, always with an eye to her function as a "model for American womanhood." With this context in mind, I am specifically interested in the mediated construction of Mrs. Obama's identity *after* the campaign and during her initial year in the White House, a period when, Burns concludes, first ladies' identities are traditionally cemented in public consciousness.[18]

Mrs. Obama's journey from the campaign's "Angry Black Woman," who held a less sanguine view of America than her husband, to her status as a popular first lady whose approval ratings began to outstrip her husband's shortly after they entered the White House, has led to much speculation about the engineering behind this image transformation.[19] I am less concerned with Mrs. Obama's (or her handlers') intentions than I am with the rhetorical and ideological dynamics resulting from whatever combinations of motives might be in play on behalf of the White House, the varying producers and audiences for the discourse I examine here, and Mrs. Obama herself. As Dana Cloud explained in her 1996 analysis of what she termed Oprah Winfrey's "tokenist biography," my goal is to understand the implications of Michelle Obama's persona "as it is constructed and performed both with and without her direct participation."[20]

In short, I focus on the ways that mass-mediated representations of Michelle Obama have negotiated the cultural stresses produced by two sets of expectations: that she embody universalized (and idealized) conceptions of womanhood, motherhood, and citizenship expected of all first ladies and that her unique relationship to those categories as an African American be recognized as well. I explore that dynamic as it manifested in verbal discourses by and about the first lady in mass-market magazine cover stories about her that began to appear after the 2008 election. I trace the tensions between sameness and difference around the first lady as they were negotiated in two distinct media arenas: print magazine discourse produced for a predominantly white audience and print magazine discourse produced for a predominantly black audience. I argue that these tensions are rhetorically managed through their containment within a variety of historical and contemporary discourses that are invoked by and alluded to in media coverage of her and the first family. In the first section, I discuss the ways that black and white media make sense of Mrs. Obama in seemingly disparate ways. Next, I argue that those differences are usefully understood as contemporary instantiations of historical frames that have been deployed at various times in American history to make black women intelligible to white majority publics. I conclude by discussing the commonalities in the contemporary iterations of these frames in black and white media, including their reliance on a nostalgic and universalizing rhetoric of familialism that negotiates the tensions between sameness and difference in some familiar yet problematic ways. Such a discourse serves some obvious strategic functions for the packaging of Mrs. Obama as our first African American first lady, but I am ultimately most concerned with the ideological and exclusionary effects of articulating exemplary citizenship to familialism.

Michelle Obama in Black and White

Although one might come at a discussion of the sameness/difference dialectic in representations of Michelle Obama from several directions, I focus here on the discourses surrounding Mrs. Obama's role within her family: as a daughter, as a wife, and, most importantly, as self-labeled "Mom-in-Chief." I suggest that the possibilities offered by familial roles provided the first lady, and her interpreters, with the richest possibilities for constituting her meaning as, simultaneously, a first lady unlike any other as well as one who, like previous occupants of her position, is expected to somehow represent the American familial imaginary that all citizens are presumed to share.

Two contrasting cover stories, both featuring a head shot of the first lady accompanied by a cover line announcing "The Meaning of Michelle," provide an initial illustration. These appeared in two national news magazines, *Time* and *Newsweek*, publications that generally offer similar takes on similar subjects. Yet one of the Michelle Obama stories was written by two white journalists—a man and a woman—whereas the other was written by an African American woman. The *Time* journalists' race is unmarked in the article itself, but *Newsweek* correspondent Alison Samuels announces her race in the first line of her essay when she begins with an anecdote about discussing Michelle Obama with her "'sista friends'" at a "recent Sunday brunch after church."[21] This anecdote is below a story title that reads "What Michelle Means to *Us*" (my emphasis). The *Time* and *Newsweek* articles are both celebratory; both note Mrs. Obama's "uniqueness," and both are speculative about what impact that uniqueness might have. A central difference between them, however, is the context in which that uniqueness and its impact are discussed.

The *Time* writers, Nancy Gibbs and Michael Scherer, are seemingly cognizant of the function of the first lady and first family as "ideals or culture types" when they mention the "sheer symbolic power of the role."[22] They also appear to recognize the way that "the first lady institution has served as a site of contestation regarding women's 'proper' place."[23] For example, after quoting former First Lady Hillary Clinton's memoir, in which she laments that the first lady represents an "'ideal—and largely mythical—concept of American womanhood,'" Gibbs and Scherer claim that "Michelle's true advantage" over Clinton is that "she appears at peace, even relieved, that her power is symbolic rather than institutional. It makes her less threatening, and more potent at the same time—especially since her presence at the White House has such unique significance." Noting that Mrs. Clinton sent staffers to policy meetings, *Time* quotes Mrs. Obama as follows: "I don't want to have a say ... Don't tell me what happened today at work ... I want the home space to be really free of that."[24]

This *Time* essay exemplifies the dominant approach to Mrs. Obama in journalism targeted at white women: she is a postfeminist and postracial success story. *Time* describes her "unique significance" this way: "The great-great-granddaughter of slaves now occupies a house built by them, one of the most professionally accomplished First Ladies ever cheerfully chooses to call herself Mom in Chief, and the South Side girl whose motivation often came from defying people who tried to stop her now gets to write her own set of rules." Generally, the article only mentions blackness in terms of something Mrs. Obama has triumphed *over,* as when it notes her successful image rehabilitation after a campaign in which she was depicted as an "Angry Black Woman" or as a "black radical in a designer dress." Now that she is "a New American Icon," the article implies, race need not be mentioned.[25]

The dominant postfeminist theme of "choice" suffuses this description of the first lady. Put simply, postfeminist ideology, as widely disseminated in popular media, asserts that feminism has done its work, has created gender equality, and any problems that remain are the result of women's "choices."[26] For example, women make less money because they "choose" lower-paying jobs that are more adaptable to childrearing, or as Lisa Belkin put it in her famous "Opting Out" essay in the *New York Times Magazine,* "Why don't women run the world? Maybe it's because they don't want to."[27] Postfeminism has some profound race and class blinders, and it posits a false universalism that is often predicated on the assumed intractability of women's maternal aspirations. Thus, Michelle Obama "cheerfully chooses" to be Mom-in-Chief, and liberated from working for wages, "gets to write her own set of rules," which include "suspending her career in favor of helping her husband get elected, then getting her daughters settled and her garden planted."[28] In the Q and A section of the *Time* article, under the heading "Women's Choices" Mrs. Obama is quoted as follows: "Find your space. Find your spot. Wear what you love. Choose the careers that may have meaning for you. ... I think that's one thing that we as women sometimes do—we don't make choices that have meaning to us."[29] Here and elsewhere, the article, like most postfeminist discourse, does not address how women's raced and classed positions affect their access to postfeminist "choices," and it elides a "structural analysis that might suggest that unequal pay at work, the intersection of racism and sexism, and cultural assumptions about femininity make the concept of 'free choice' an oxymoron."[30]

The *Newsweek* essay by Alison Samuels offers a strong contrast to the *Time* story, initially visible in Samuels's succinct rejection of a postracial universalism. She notes, for instance, that Mrs. Obama has "two very different constituencies—African Americans and everyone else."[31] Moreover, Samuels is not as interested in seeing Mrs. Obama through the prism of previous first ladies as she is in answering the question asked by Hortense Spillers: "How might a First Lady who is black insinuate a revision of the idea of the 'black woman' in the national imaginary?"[32] Samuels makes her focus clear in the first paragraph of the *Newsweek* story, in which she transforms Mrs. Obama's burden into an opportunity: "The new First Lady will have the chance to knock down ugly stereotypes about black women and educate the world about American black culture more generally. But perhaps more important—even apart from what her husband can do—Michelle has the power to change the way African Americans see ourselves, our lives and our possibilities."[33]

Samuels and the black women with whom she speaks about Mrs. Obama are deeply committed to the first lady's particularity as an African American woman and to her very specific meaning for an imagined black community. They embed her meaning in the context of discourses of black womanhood—particularly those around marriage and family life—and in opposition to black stereotypes. They celebrate her difference from former first ladies and from dominant black stereotypes while insisting, at the same time, that she and her family represent an unrecognized (silent?) black majority. For example, Samuels's first interviewee pointedly rejects the individualism that permeates the *Time* article when she says, "'I think she's always going to be classy, because she knows she's not just representing herself. ... She knows she's fighting stereotypes of black people that have been around for decades and that her every move will be watched.'" Pointing out that 50 percent of African American women are single, Samuels asks what the Obamas' relationship might mean for black marriage and reports this reply: "'I want my son to see first-hand what two people can do when they work together and respect each other. ... His father and I divorced when he was 2—so he never had the chance to see the way a relationship works. Many of his friends have single moms too, so the Obamas are going to teach us that love and happiness is not just for others but us too."[34]

Like Gibbs and Scherer in *Time*, Samuels refers to what she calls the "flare-up" in the "white mommy wars" over Mrs. Obama's "Mom-in-Chief" persona. Her response is double-sided: she applauds the Mom-in-Chief choice while recognizing how rare it is for black women in particular: "[M]ost African American women I know are thrilled she's in a position to make that choice. The average African-American family can't survive without two incomes—the poverty level among black families hovers above 30 percent, according to 2006 U.S. Census figures. And for single moms, that can mean working two jobs, leaving precious little time with the children."[35] Here, Samuels points out that the postfeminist frame deployed by white media has little resonance for many black women for whom working for wages is hardly a "choice." Even so, in her account, black women celebrate rather than resent Mrs. Obama's fortune in being able to focus on motherhood. These two different accounts of "the meaning of Michelle" suggest obvious conclusions. For example, the *Time* writers generally elide the first lady's difference through an assimilationist mode of representation in which "whiteness is the privileged yet unnamed place from which to see and make sense of the world."[36] Conversely, Samuels insists on the visibility and centrality of race, and her story emphasizes the importance of role modeling and positive representation for a black community that recognizes the "difference" produced by racism and racial stereotypes.

Samuel's story is unusual in that it appears in a mainstream, national newsmagazine with a predominantly white readership; nevertheless, it has much less in common with the *Time* story than it does with the dominant approach to Michelle Obama in mainstream black print media outlets. By black print media, I mean mass-market publications directed at an African American audience, editorially controlled by African Americans, and in which shared racial identity is an overt editorial theme. Some black media (e.g., *Ebony*) are wholly owned by African Americans; some others (e.g., *Essence* is owned by Time, Inc.) are not.[37] For purposes of easy contrast, in what follows I use the term *white media* to refer to what media critics usually term *mainstream media*, that is, mass-market publications generally editorially controlled by whites and directed at a predominantly white readership.

The contrasts between representations of Mrs. Obama and her family in black and white media are evident in two exclusive interviews granted by the first lady shortly after moving into the White House. The first of these appeared in the April 2009 issue of *O, The Oprah Magazine,* which is sometimes assumed to have a majority African American audience because of the race of its founder, Oprah Winfrey. In fact, the readership for *O* is only 25 percent black (although its ratio of black and white readers is less imbalanced than that of any other mass-market women's magazine), and all three of its editors-in-chief have been white women. Mrs. Obama's other early interview was published in the May 2009 issue of *Essence.* The readership for *Essence* is about 85 percent African American women.[38] The dominant topic in these interviews is adjustment to life in the White House, with an emphasis on the Obamas' family life. In both interviews, Mrs. Obama notes that the first family enjoys a kind of "normalcy" that they have lacked for several years, symbolized by the Obama daughters' access to their father and by the family's ability to eat dinner together most nights. Mrs. Obama stresses the importance of parenting in her own life, remarking to Oprah, for instance, that she was "able to breathe" once she saw that her children were thriving in the White House.[39]

Family life—Mrs. Obama's childhood, the quality of the Obamas' life in the White House, and the importance of family in American life generally—dominates these interviews. Although *O,* the publication with a majority white audience, does not mention race explicitly, the *Essence* story, which also interviews Mrs. Obama's mother, Marian Robinson, raises race immediately in its teaser paragraph, previewing the story as a chat with the two women about "retaining their family values, what it takes to raise good kids, and being role models for the Black community."[40]

All roads lead back to family in these interviews. In the interview with Winfrey, asked about how the campaign changed her, Mrs. Obama responds: "I saw our shared values. We fundamentally want the same things for ourselves and for each other. We want our kids to be safe and to grow up with some resources and aspire to a slightly better life than ours." Asked about work–life balance, the first lady begins with a nostalgic vision of her upbringing: "And we once lived in small enough communities where people could help each other. Families were together. That's how I grew up. My grandmother lived around the corner, my grandfather lived two blocks away, they each lived with aunts and uncles."[41] That Mrs. Obama grew up in an intact African American family with a stay-at-home mother, as well as hails from a solid working-class background, are key components of her life story that are repeatedly offered as proof of her embodiment of an American ideal in which "family values" and individual responsibility make the difference between success and failure.

That the first lady's background receives so much attention in profiles of the first family is partially related to her mother's continuing presence in the first family's life. In addition, Mrs. Obama's family of origin, in contrast to the president's, fits the idealized template of American family life that she advocates in these interviews. Thus, in addition to fulfilling the general expectation that the first lady enact a normative gender role that includes attention to the quality of family life, Mrs. Obama's discourse about her idyllic upbringing functions as a counterweight to President Obama's much less traditional background as the product of a mixed race marriage, a broken home and absent father, and a childhood partially spent being raised by his white grandparents.

Mrs. Obama's reminiscing about her childhood and its impact on her development is equally present in the *Essence* interview, and it is used in service of the role-modeling and representation themes evident in the earlier *Newsweek* article. For example, when asked what she can do as first lady to "advance the interests of girls and women around the world," Mrs. Obama responds, "the thing I have the most control over is serving as an example of what's possible when women from the very beginning of their lives are loved by the people around them." The somewhat therapeutic tone of this reply arises again when she is asked about the rise of HIV among African American women and how she might address it. Though the first lady begins with a recommendation for "testing and education and information," she then says, "Truthfully, I think the answers to a lot of the issues come from self-esteem. Young girls and women have to believe that they are worth something more, they have to see opportunities for themselves beyond a relationship or beyond what's right there in front of them." Finally, when asked about how to get more African Americans involved in improving their communities, Mrs. Obama replies: "Individual responsibility is the first step. We all have complete control over the decisions and choices we make in our lives with our own families, whether it's turning off the TV and making sure that your kids have some structure and do their homework. Whether it's making sure that you cut your lawn and pick up the garbage in front of your house. If we are all tending to our gardens, that will strengthen the Black community, first and foremost."[42]

A difference between the *O* and *Essence* interviews is that the latter includes questions that allow Mrs. Obama the opportunity to comment on issues (e.g., AIDS) with potential connections to public policy affecting African Americans. Yet in her replies, Mrs. Obama invariably returns to family life as the locus of control, shifting the focus to seemingly universal themes that protect her from potential accusations of favoritism toward the black community. As I discuss next, this kind of family-centered discourse—the central similarity in white and black media coverage of Mrs. Obama—has important historical antecedents.

The Uses of History: The Obamas, White True Womanhood, and African American Racial Uplift

The white-targeted media I examined make Mrs. Obama and her life culturally intelligible within the ostensibly universal and racially unmarked discourses familiar to its presumed white, middle-class, and largely female audiences. While celebrating America's progress in putting a "different" kind of American family in the White House, this discourse takes pains to represent Mrs. Obama and her family in ways that assimilate them to a discourse of presumed "shared and universal similarity."[43] The complex dance of recognizing difference while stressing similarity has abundant antecedents in historical relationships between black and white women in the United States, particularly when supposedly universal links to motherhood are available to be invoked. Susan Zaeske, for example, has persuasively detailed the ways that early antislavery petitions penned by white women dramatized the vulnerability of slave women through identification strategies that relied on discourses of white true womanhood and motherhood.[44] Antislavery reformers told the story of slave women's suffering in ways that feminized it and "endowed [it] with all the moral value generally attributed to nineteenth-century [white] American womanhood."[45] Scholars such as Zaeske and Jean Fagan Yellin have made clear that this strategy benefited white women far more than black slave women—it rationalized the political agency of the former while consigning the latter to "the role of the passive victim."[46]

I use a historical example because I am interested in the perseveration of a discursive strategy in which cultural norms derived from white womanhood are rhetorically deployed to make sense of black women's lives for dominant cultural audiences. Just as female abolitionists used ideals of white womanhood to humanize female slaves and to make their suffering intelligible to white northern women, mainstream white media have made Mrs. Obama intelligible by nesting her within familiar discourses of white postfeminist womanhood while presenting those discourses as race and class transcendent. Additional examples of interpretations of black women's lives through frames derived from white womanhood are not difficult to name. They include, for instance, the "black matriarchy" thesis (predicated on the idealization of the white, patriarchal family) promulgated by interpretations of the 1965 Moynihan report, or the ways that white feminists' claiming of Anita Hill as a representative victim of sexual harassment in 1991 forced her into the frame of a universalist white female narrative.[47]

In contrast, the centrality of race to the emphasis on role modeling and positive representation in black media treatment of Mrs. Obama reflects the kind of "double consciousness" that W. E. B. DuBois identified more than a century ago when he wrote of "this sense of always looking at one's self through the eyes of others."[48] Consider this opening paragraph from a fall 2009 cover story in *Today's Black Woman*: "As I've watched Michelle Obama on television news programs and talk shows and have seen her face on the internet and gracing the covers of numerous publications, there is an aspect of her presence that has given me an immense amount of joy. She actually *looks* like a Black woman. You don't have to wonder if this woman, who is revered as beautiful and intelligent, is of African descent. And she is the *First Lady*" (emphasis in original).[49] The historical antecedent for such discourse is racial uplift rhetoric, long a presence in black middle-class women's mass media as well as in middle-class black advocacy.[50] In the post-Reconstruction period, the founders of the National Association of Colored Women took as their motto "Lifting As We Climb," a phrase that succinctly expressed the ideology of racial uplift. For many black middle and upper-class club women, advocacy of the "politics of respectability" was an important step toward proving free blacks were "worthy of equal civil and political rights."[51]

As Evelyn Brooks Higgenbotham has explained it, the discourse of many black club women "equated normality with conformity to white middle-class models of gender roles and sexuality," linking "mainstream domestic duties, codes of dress, sexual conduct, and public etiquette with both individual success and group progress."[52] The contemporary iteration of the politics of respectability around Mrs. Obama is well summarized by a line from the *Today's Black Woman* feature on the first lady: "To have a Black woman in that position [of first lady] brings Black women into the forefront as full-fledged American women, and, more importantly, ladies. … It affirms Black women's womanhood, their humanity, their femininity."[53] Like white postfeminist discourse, contemporary iterations of the rhetoric of respectability and racial uplift superimpose a "'natural' unity over a plethora of historical, socioeconomic, and ideological differences among blacks themselves."[54] Such discourse, in the past and in the present, presents a paradox: "While invoking a discursive ground on which to explode negative stereotypes of black women," it stays "locked within hegemonic articulations of gender, class, and sexuality."[55]

Of course, in the nineteenth century, racial uplift was more than a rhetorical maneuver; it also was a community-organizing strategy with political goals, including forestalling white violence against blacks. Today, the continuing power of stereotypes of black Americans—and of black women, black mothers, and black families, in particular—helps explain contemporary iterations of uplift rhetoric. Yet as I conclude, in our present historical moment the uplift discourse that permeates black media representations of the first family is a constituent in a broader public discourse of hegemonic familialism that, in contradistinction to the historical goals of uplift activism, works to narrow rather than to expand our understandings of citizenship.

Citizenship and Hegemonic Familialism

Two different kinds of implications emerge from this analysis. The first can be termed *rhetorical implications* and are primarily about efficacy and expediency. That familialism offered the most efficient grounds on which to rehabilitate Michelle Obama's image—and concomitantly for mass media to negotiate the tensions between sameness and difference that she presents—is a marker of the continuing cultural power of ideologies attached to both gender and race. I suspect that the decisions to offer Mrs. Obama's initial interviews after entering the White House to *O* and *Essence,* and for those interviews to be dominated by talk about family, were deeply considered by White House strategists. Other first ladies with troubled images have gone the same route, as anyone who remembers Hillary Clinton's cookie baking and "It Takes a Village" phases might recall.

Such strategies foreground the importance of private, gendered behaviors—especially those linked to heterosexual and heteronormative family life—as transparent indicators of authenticity, stability, and normalcy. Discourses rooted in familialism not only partake of already normative rhetorics of family, they simultaneously function to give them additional public, political weight. Because the first lady is our access to the private side of the president, she functions as "a reliable sign of the values or underlying beliefs of her husband."[56] Mrs. Obama is not just any mother; she is the "Mom-in-Chief," an oft repeated title that functions to position the president even more firmly as the nation's patriarch, as well as to embed the first lady's public role in discourses of idealized familialism. Representations of Mrs. Obama frame her within dominant white middle-class understandings of "good parenting" (she is "just like us") and at the same time present her as a particular kind of exemplar (the first lady is an extraordinary parent in an extraordinary situation). In addition to the coverage of her personal parenting practices and philosophy, Mrs. Obama's public activities, largely centered on children and families, have worked to stabilize this persona. In *The Obamas*, Jodi Kantor observes that the Obama staff learned the formula early in the administration: "Put Michelle Obama in a roomful of kids—especially kids who were outsiders in one way or another—just let them interact, and they were likely to end with a Moment that generated warm, positive images and video."[57]

Just as framing the first lady within familialism is a reliable strategy for white media attempting to assimilate Mrs. Obama's difference, it is also an attractive strategy for a black community that labors under the burden of centuries of pathologizing racial stereotypes. The influence of long-standing and widely circulated negative depictions of black mothers and the black family (often referred to in public discourse in just such a way—"the black family"—as though it is monolithic) cannot be overstated.[58] Black media are acutely attentive to this context and, as the examples cited here indicate, they address it repeatedly in explicit ways. Although they do not explicitly note it in the same fashion, white media accounts of the Obama's family life are unavoidably operating against this backdrop as well, and it is an unspoken aspect of what makes Mrs. Obama so extraordinary.

The second facet of this evaluation is rooted in political concerns rather than strategic rhetorical ones. As the historical comparisons I have offered here suggest, these framing strategies function as rhetorics of citizenship. Antislavery reformers and racial uplift advocates argued for African Americans' humanity and eligibility for political agency and participation using deeply gendered discourses of domesticity and familialism; in our present moment, black and white media accounts of Michelle Obama and her family perform a variation on this theme. Mrs. Obama's speech at the 2008 Democratic National Convention signaled the outlines of her rehabilitation as an admirable citizen. She introduced herself as a sister, a wife, a mom, and a daughter, and she described the promise of America as a something enacted within and on behalf of families.[59] The many postelection stories about Mrs. Obama merely fleshed out the framework provided in that speech. As a feminist critic, I am deeply concerned about the retrograde gender politics of the first lady institution as well as about the ways the discourse by and about our current first lady has adapted to them. At the same time, I am sympathetic to black media desire to claim the Obamas as proof of the category of functional black middle-class families. But I also contend that deploying familial ideology for political purposes is generally problematic, no less in this moment than in the past.

The fetishizing of family in public discourse takes different meaning at different times, just as "family" itself means different things at different times. For example, dominant familial ideology in the mid-nineteenth century had a basis in white true womanhood; in our present moment, I would characterize the underpinnings of idealized white middle-class family life as neoliberal postfeminism.[60] But because the invocation of family always depends on a normative ideal, that invocation is always already exclusionary. The lessons of racial uplift are especially pertinent here. Racial uplift discourse depends on class differentiation as a signifier of racial progress, leaving in place "the racist logic of black pathology" and using a "preoccupation with … building black homes and promoting family stability" to displace "a broader vision of uplift as group struggle for citizenship and material advancement."[61] Or, as Melissa Harris-Perry has remarked in relation to the first lady, "Michelle Obama's traditionalist public persona could be used as a weapon against women who do not conform to this domestic ideal." More broadly, it "could easily be deployed to undercut support for public policies that focused on creation of a just and equal political and economic structure and to focus instead on 'marriage' and 'family values' as solutions to structural barriers facing black communities."[62]

More contemporary examples offer variations on the same lesson, particularly in terms of the intersections of familialism and citizenship in the political arena. In an analysis of the "rhetoric of family values" that emerged in the 1992 presidential campaign, Dana Cloud argued that "mythic familialism ... justified the exclusion of women from political arenas by constructing the domestic realm as a utopian space of freedom and authenticity" at the same time that discourse about the "poverty of values" worked to scapegoat the poor for their own problems and to promote the "privatization of social responsibility."[63] Similarly, Shawn Parry-Giles has argued that mass media constructions of the electorate as composed of "NASCAR Dads" or "security moms" during the 2004 presidential campaign legitimated those occupying these discursive categories as "ideal citizen participants," suggesting that the vote and voice of "others" were less valuable.[64] More recently, the many ongoing battles over gay marriage, gays and lesbians in the military, gay adoption, and the rights of gay workers make clear how exclusionary heteronormative familialism can be, and with profoundly material effects. Lauren Berlant has argued that our public discourse has been on a path since the 1980s of positing that "mass-mediated political identifications can only be rooted in traditional notions of home, family, and community."[65] From that perspective, media images and interpretations of Michelle Obama, who is widely celebrated as a "new" and "different" kind of first lady (a claim that is always about race, even when it is not explicitly mentioned), are simply offering an updated iteration of a familiar strategy.

Citizenship, these images tell us, is performed most appropriately from within families and on behalf of them; as Mrs. Obama put it to *Essence*, "Now is the time we need everybody rolling up their sleeves and finding a way to add value to their families and their communities."[66] In the *People* magazine interview with the First Couple at the conclusion of their first year in office, President Obama described his goals for the next year as "refocusing on how—whether we're Democrats or Republicans—we all have common values and care about our kids; we all want work that's satisfying, pays the bills, and gives children a better future and security."[67] Such discourses of familialism are troubling because they are presumed to be extra-political, apolitical, or transcendent of the political, suggested by the President's claim that "we" share them regardless of party affiliation. Family is presented as an authentic space of feeling "protected from the harsh realities of power."[68] Similarly, Parry-Giles argues that mass media labeling of voters through familial terminology depoliticizes them, "hailing their familial and nonpolitical commitments as badges of ideal citizenship" as they are reduced to the single act of voting for the best father-protector for the nation. Family affiliation replaces political affiliation and brings with it the hidden advantage of assumed neutrality; it functions as a kind of identity politics that goes unrecognized as such.[69]

Certainly, as feminist scholars have pointed out, one of the central problems with such discourse is that "Western families are not uniformly the havens of love, good will, and affection that prevailing public discourses construct them to be and that we ourselves would like to believe they are."[70] Such discourses of familialism not only present "family" as a utopian sphere of safety and love, but also function to fundamentally restrict the range of subject positions available for the performance of citizenship. We have a long history of such restrictions on women's civic identities, a history that includes varied manifestations—from republican motherhood to "soccer mom" voters—of the notion that "women's political space is somehow different from men's."[71]

My larger point, however, is that all citizens bear the consequences of a culture in which hegemonic familialism can be used to trump the political claims of difference—whether that difference is articulated to gender or race or sexuality or, more likely, some combination. The Obamas—and/or those who represent them in mass media—need not desire such an outcome in order to facilitate it. Much of the meaning of the first family is linked to what Berlant terms "the marketing of nostalgic images of a normal, familial, America" that defines the "utopian context for citizen aspiration."[72] Such images are political in the sense that they advantage some political agents and disadvantage others. Citizen subjects who must claim their political agency through what Elizabeth Cady Stanton, in "The Solitude of Self," called "the incidental relations of life," are disempowered as political actors.[73] The greater authenticity and moral superiority granted to claims on behalf of family undermine the rhetorical power of claims made on behalf of nonfamilial identities—for example, as workers, as victims of discrimination, as members of sexual minorities. Acceding to a public discourse in which the quality of family life is an implicit qualification for participating in political life, as well as the central motivation guiding that participation, is consent to a form of conditional citizenship. That the mediated constitution of our first African American first family works to enable rather than to challenge such a prospect seems especially ironic. Yet, considering the limited range of options available, I am not sure that the Obamas and their advisers had better rhetorical choices than to fall back on nostalgic familialism.

Notes

1. Maureen Dowd, "Should Michelle Cover Up?" *New York Times,* March 7, 2009, WK10.

2. Imaeyen Ibanga, "Obama's Choice to Bare Arms Causes Uproar," *ABC News,* March 2, 2009, http://abcnews.go.com/GMA/story?id=6986019&page=1.

3. Joan Faber McAlister, "_____Trash in the White House: Michelle Obama, Post-Racism and the Pre-Class Politics of Domestic Style," *Communication and Critical/Cultural Studies* 6 (2009): 311–15, 312.

4. Dayo Olopade, "Armed and Not Dangerous," *The Root,* March 11, 2009, http://www.theroot.com/views/armed-and-not-dangerous.

5. Ibid.

6. In *Sister Citizen: Shame, Stereotypes, and Black Women in America* (New Haven: Yale University Press, 2011), Melissa Harris-Perry provides a lengthy discussion of the stereotypes attached to black women's bodies and calls "the public dissection" of Michelle Obama's body "reminiscent" of the treatment of the Hottentot Venus (279).

7. The October 2009 issue of *Women's Health* magazine featured this cover teaser: "Michelle Obama talks to *WH* ... Plus How She Got Those Amazing Arms!"

8. Discussing her exercise routine in her *O* interview, Mrs. Obama remarked: "After I had Malia, I began to prioritize exercise because I realized that my happiness is tied to how I feel about myself. I want my girls to see a mother who takes care of herself, even if that means I have to get up at 4:30 so I can do a workout." See "The O Interview: Oprah Talks to Michelle Obama," *O Magazine,* April 2009, 146.

9. Amanda Hinnant, "The Cancer on Your Coffee Table: A Discourse Analysis of the Health Content in Mass-Circulated Women's Magazines," *Feminist Media Studies* 9 (2009): 317–333, 325. For examples of coverage of Mrs. Obama's fitness, see "The First Lady's Fitness Secrets," *Women's Health,* October 2009, 132; and Liz Vaccariello, "Michelle Obama: Happy, Healthy, and Strong," *Prevention,* November 2009, 136–41.

10. McAlister, "_____Trash in the White House," 312.

11. Charles Taylor, "The Politics of Recognition," in *Multiculturalism: Examining the Politics of Recognition,* ed. Amy Gutmann (Princeton, NJ: Princeton University Press, 1994), 38.

12. Danielle S. Allen, *Talking to Strangers: Anxieties of Citizenship Since* Brown v. Board of Education (Chicago: University of Chicago Press, 2004), 16. For a useful discussion of black women's experiences with the problem of recognition, see Harris-Perry, *Sister Citizen,* chapter 1.

13. Liza Mundy, *Michelle* (New York: Simon and Schuster, 2008), 282, 288; and D. Soyini Madison, "Crazy Patriotism and Angry (Post) Black Women," *Communication and Critical/Cultural Studies* 6 (2009): 321–26, 321.

14. Kimberly R. Moffitt, "Framing a First Lady: Media Coverage of Michelle Obama's Role in the 2008 Presidential Election," eds. Heather E. Harris, Kimberly R. Moffitt, and Catherine R. Squires, *The Obama Effect: Multidisciplinary Renderings of the 2008 Campaign* (Albany, NY: SUNY Press, 2010), 239. In chapter 7 of *Sister Citizen,* Harris-Perry also discusses the use of racial stereotypes in representations of Mrs. Obama.

15. Jodi Kantor, *The Obamas* (New York: Little, Brown, 2012), 31.

16. Karlyn Kohrs Campbell, "The Rhetorical Presidency: A Two-Person Career," in *Beyond the Rhetorical Presidency,* ed. Martin J. Medhurst (College Station: Texas A&M University Press, 1996), 180.

17. Shawn J. Parry-Giles and Diane Blair, "The Rise of the Rhetorical First Lady: Politics, Gender Ideology, and Women's Voice, 1789–2002," *Rhetoric & Public Affairs* 5 (2002): 567.

18. Lisa Burns, *First Ladies and the Fourth Estate: Press Framing of Presidential Wives* (DeKalb, IL: Northern Illinois University Press, 2008), 134.

19. Rachel L. Swarns, "First Lady in Control of Building Her Image," *New York Times,* April 25, 2009, A9. At the time of the inauguration, Michelle Obama's favorability ratings lagged ten points behind her husband's, but by April 2009 she had an 84 percent overall approval rating specifically linked to how she was handling her role as first lady. After a year in office, the President's approval rating was at 50 percent, but Mrs. Obama's was at 78 percent. See Charles M. Blow, "The Magic of Michelle," *New York Times,* October 24, 2009, A21, and "President Obama at One Year," *CBS News* Poll, January 18, 2010, http://www.cbsnews.com/htdocs/pdf/poll_obama_011810.pdf.

20. Dana Cloud, "Hegemony or Concordance? The Rhetoric of Tokenism in 'Oprah' Winfrey's Rags-to-Riches Biography," *Critical Studies in Mass Communication,* 13 (1996): 115–37, 116.

21. Alison Samuels, "What Michelle Means to Us," *Newsweek,* December 1, 2008, 28–32.

22. Campbell, "The Rhetorical Presidency," 181; and Nancy Gibbs and Michael Scherer, "Michelle Up Close," *Time,* June 1, 2009, 28.

23. Burns, *First Ladies and the Fourth Estate,* 145.

24. Gibbs and Scherer, "Michelle Up Close," 30, 33.

25. Ibid., 30, 28.

26. Bonnie J. Dow, *Prime-Time Feminism: Television, Media Culture, and the Women's Movement Since 1970* (Philadelphia: University of Pennsylvania Press, 1996); and Mary Douglas Vavrus, "Opting Out Moms in the News: Selling New Traditionalism in the New Millennium," *Feminist Media Studies,* 7 (2007): 47–63.

27. Lisa Belkin, "The Opt-Out Revolution," *New York Times Magazine,* October 26, 2003, 45.

28. Indeed, the *Time* writers attribute controversy over "the sacrifices she was having to make in terms of her own identity," symbolized by giving up her job and her independence, to feminists. Reporting Mrs. Obama's denial that "she has had to sacrifice at all," the article rejects the feminist analysis and posits that the first lady's "choices" are unconstrained by external factors (such as gender ideology). See Gibbs and Scherer, *First Ladies and the Fourth Estate,* 30.

29. Gibbs and Scherer, *First Ladies and the Fourth Estate*, 31.

30. Sarah Projansky, *Watching Rape: Film and Television in Postfeminist Culture* (New York: NYU Press, 2001), 73.

31. Samuels, "What Michelle Means to Us," 28.

32. Hortense Spillers, "Views of the East Wing: On Michelle Obama," *Communication and Critical/Cultural Studies* 6 (2009): 308.

33. Samuels, "What Michelle Means to Us," 28.

34. Ibid., 28, 30.

35. Ibid., 31.

36. Herman Gray, *Watching Race: Television and the Struggle for "Blackness"* (Minneapolis: University of Minnesota Press, 1995), 86.

37. For a discussion of the difficulties of defining "black media," see Catherine Squires, "Black Audiences, Past and Present: Commonsense Media Critics and Activists," in *Say It Loud! African American Audiences, Media, and Identity,* ed. Robin R. Means Coleman (New York: Routledge, 2002), 45–76.

38. On the readership for O and *Essence,* see *African American/Black Market Profile* (New York: Magazine Publishers of America, 2008).

39. "The O Interview," 143.

40. Angela Burt-Murray, "A Mother's Love," *Essence,* May 2009, 105.

41. "The O Interview," 146–47.

42. Burt-Murray, "A Mother's Love," 111, 113.

43. Gray, *Watching Race*, 85.

44. Susan Zaeske, *Signatures of Citizenship: Petitioning, Antislavery, and Women's Political Identity* (Chapel Hill: University of North Carolina Press, 2003).

45. Karen Sanchez-Eppler, "Bodily Bonds: The Intersecting Rhetorics of Feminism and Abolitionism," *Representations* 24 (Fall 1988): 32.

46. Jean Fagan Yellin, *Women and Sisters: The Anti-Slavery Feminists in American Culture* (New Haven: Yale University Press, 1989), 79.

47. On black matriarchy and the Moynihan report, see Patricia Hill Collins, *Black Feminist Thought: Knowledge, Consciousness, and the Politics of Empowerment* (New York: Routledge, 1990), 75–78. On Hill and Thomas, see Kimberlé Crenshaw, "Whose Story Is It Anyway? Feminist and Anti-Racist Appropriations of Anita Hill," in *Race-ing Justice, En-gendering Power: Essays on Anita Hill, Clarence Thomas, and the Construction of Social Reality,* ed. Toni Morrison (New York: Random House, 1992), 402–36.

48. W. E. B. DuBois, *The Souls of Black Folk: Essays and Sketches* (Chicago: A.C. McClurg & Co., 1903), 3.

49. Gerrie E. Summers, "Michelle Obama: A Relevant Role Model to the World's Women," *Today's Black Woman,* September 2009, 30–31, 31. See also "25 Most Influential African Americans: The First Family," *Essence,* December 2009, 130–31, which describes the Obamas as "a captivating portrait that's changing hearts, minds, and perceptions about Black men, Black women, Black children, and Black love."

50. Neliwe M. Rooks, *Ladies' Pages: African-American Women's Magazines and the Culture That Made Them* (New Brunswick, NJ: Rutgers University Press, 2004).

51. Evelyn Brooks Higginbotham, "African-American Women's History and the Metalanguage of Race," *Signs: Journal of Women in Culture and Society* 17 (Winter 1992): 251–274, 271.

52. Higginbotham, "African-American Women's History," 272, 271.

53. Summers, "Michelle Obama: A Relevant Role Model," 31.

54. Higginbotham, "African-American Women's History,"270.

55. Ibid., 271.

56. Campbell, "The Rhetorical Presidency," 181.

57. Kantor, *The Obamas,* 281.

58. See Harris-Perry, *Sister Citizen,* chapter 2.

59. "Michelle Obama's Remarks at the Democratic National Convention," *New York Times,* August 25, 2008, http://www.nytimes.com/2008/08/26/us/politics/26text-obama.html.

60. See Vavrus, "Opting Out Moms in the News," for a thorough discussion of neoliberal postfeminism.

61. Kevin K. Gaines, *Uplifting the Race: Black Leadership, Politics, and Culture in the Twentieth Century* (Chapel Hill: University of North Carolina Press, 1996), 259, 6.

62. Harris-Perry, *Sister Citizen,* 284, 285.

63. Dana Cloud, *Control and Consolation in American Politics: Rhetoric of Therapy* (Thousand Oaks, CA: Sage, 1998), 59, 62, 65–66.

64. Shawn Parry-Giles, "Constituting Presidentiality and U.S. Citizenship in Campaign 2004: NASCAR Dads, Security Moms, and Single Woman Voters," in *Rhetoric and Democracy: Pedagogical and Political Practices,* eds. Todd F. McDorman and David M. Timmerman (East Lansing: Michigan State University Press, 2008), 163–64.

65. Lauren Berlant, *The Queen of American Goes to Washington City: Essays on Sex and Citizenship* (Durham, NC: Duke University Press, 1997), 5.

66. Burt-Murray, "A Mother's Love," 113.

67. "An Exclusive Interview with the Obamas: Our First Year," *People,* January 25, 2010, 60–65, 64.

68. Berlant, *The Queen of American,* 11.

69. Parry-Giles, "Constituting Presidentiality and U.S. Citizenship," 148, 164–65.

70. Julia T. Wood, "Ethics, Justice, and the 'Private Sphere,'" *Women's Studies in Communication,* 21 (Fall 1998): 128.

71. Parry-Giles and Blair, "The Rise of the Rhetorical First Lady," 582.

72. Berlant, *The Queen of American,* 3.

73. Elizabeth Cady Stanton, "The Solitude of Self," In *Man Cannot Speak for Her, Volume II: Key Texts of the Early Feminists,* ed. Karlyn Kohrs Campbell (Westport, CT: Greenwood Press, 1989), 372.

Carrying the Burden

How Barack Obama Both Embraced and Diminished Heroic Expectations

JENNIFER R. MERCIECA

JUSTIN S. VAUGHN

On February 24, 2009, then newly inaugurated President Barack Obama believed that he had been called "to govern in extraordinary times," which was both "a tremendous burden" and "a great privilege." As the essays in this volume reflect, Obama's first term in office was defined, in large part, by the tremendous burden of those extraordinary times as well as by the rhetoric of heroic expectations. At times President Obama embraced and encouraged the nation's heroic expectations; at other times he dismissed and discouraged them. What is clear is that as a central feature of the nation's political discourse about the presidency, Obama could not ignore the nation's heroic expectations. For example, in the spring of 2010, after more than a month of oil spilling uncontrollably into the Gulf of Mexico, President Obama reported that his youngest daughter Malia had expressed her frustration with the delay in stopping the spill, asking him "Did you plug the hole yet, Daddy?" as he attempted his morning shave. Certainly Obama's daughter could be forgiven for the high expectations that she had that her dad could somehow personally stop millions of gallons of oil from contaminating the Gulf, but what about the 48 percent of Americans who Gallup reported also disapproved of the way Obama handled the oil spill?[1] Certainly their expectations were not less than those of Obama's young daughter. Obama held himself accountable for stopping the oil spill as well, telling reporters on May 27, 2010, "In case you're wondering who's responsible, I take responsibility. It is my job to make sure that everything is done to shut this down. That doesn't mean it's going to be easy. It doesn't mean it's going to happen right away or the way I'd like it to happen. It doesn't mean that we're not going to make mistakes. But there shouldn't be any confusion here: The Federal Government is fully engaged, and I'm fully engaged."[2] Although President Obama could not literally swim down to the bottom of the Gulf and plug the oil spill, he still assumed the role of presidential hero, determined to make the world right again. Yet while taking responsibility, Obama also sought to reduce heroic expectations—it was not going to be easy to stop the oil spill; it would take time; and mistakes would likely be made in the process. As with other issues during his first term in office, President Obama both embraced the nation's heroic expectations and attempted to diminish those expectations by forecasting the difficulties involved in resolving the nation's crisis.

From the outset, Barack Obama's leadership task was destined to be extraordinarily difficult, if not impossible. In addition to the burden of being the first African American president in a nation still grappling with a past scarred by slavery and subsequent (and ongoing) problems with racial discrimination and inequality, Obama inherited tremendous policy burdens, including two wars that were proving to be increasingly expensive and decreasingly popular and an economic collapse threatening to erode middle-class life as Americans knew it. Perhaps inspired by what he called the opportunity to "shape our world for good," Obama pushed ahead, pursuing a powerful legislative agenda that championed long-sought items from the liberal Democratic wish list such as health, energy, and immigration reform. The president's success was mixed, though, as his agenda triggered active opposition from emboldened Tea Party activists and a strategically recalcitrant Republican caucus on Capitol Hill. Obama's opposition pursued a strategy of protest, confrontation, and obfuscation, which led to declining presidential approval numbers and heavy losses for Democrats in the 2010 mid-term elections. By the 2012 election, the electorate would reverse themselves again, however, voting Obama a second term and generally re-endorsing his agenda.

His presidential approval ratings, which according to Gallup were at 69 percent when he assumed office in 2009, hovered below 50 percent for much of his presidency; yet after a tireless campaign against Republican Mitt Romney, Obama won reelection by 126 Electoral College votes and almost 3.5 million popular votes.[3] After Obama's reelection, Gallup polled Americans about their expectations for Obama's second term: compared to similar questions asked in 2008, 21 percent fewer Americans (33 percent) believed that Obama could "heal political divisions in this country"; 13 percent fewer (57 percent) believed that Obama could "improve the quality of the environment"; 11 percent fewer (56 percent) believe that Obama could "reduce unemployment"; 10 percent fewer (54 percent) believed that Obama could "create a strong economic recovery," and so forth.[4] Clearly, Americans in 2012 were much less optimistic that Obama could successfully meet their heroic expectations than they had been in 2008. Nevertheless, a majority of voters chose to return him to office, with only marginal drop-off from his 2008 vote total (i.e., less than 1 million fewer, in an election with more than 126 million votes cast). The dynamics and eventual outcome of the 2012 election yield countless intriguing research questions, but to us one of the most important is why the electorate voted the way that it did in a context typically unfavorable to incumbents: Why did the electorate choose to return this heroically burdened president to the Oval Office? Had Obama's rhetorical performance somehow prepared the electorate to contextualize his leadership efforts, to avoid what Stephen Medvic refers to as "the expectations trap"?[5] We believe the essays in this volume might help us to answer this question.

The essays in this volume identify not only the sources of Obama's burdens but also the extraordinary difficulties involved in meeting the heroic expectations of the modern presidency. From these essays we can learn a great deal about how Obama dealt with the nation's heroic expectations and how at times he embraced them, whereas at other times he diminished them. The path of this volume winds through institutional, contextual, and personal burdens by focusing on consubstantiality, public leadership, the economy, American exceptionalism, America's self-image, religion, and race. The common link between these dimensions has been the particularly dialogical way in which Obama practiced rhetorical leadership.[6]

Four scholars examined how Obama responded to his institutional burdens. Jay Childers and Eric Dieter each demonstrate different dimensions of Obama's vision of leadership as a form of engagement, one that is geared toward achieving understanding, demonstrating reciprocity, and reaching mutually acceptable, legitimate agreements. The chapters authored by Brandon Rottinghaus and Matthew Eshbaugh-Soha are explicitly interested in the response Obama's leadership efforts have engendered, looking to the causal consequences of the "acting-together" that Dieter discussed between Obama and his audience. In so doing, Rottinghaus's conclusion that Obama's ability to lead the public has been primarily present when key contextual factors are aligned in the president's favor is consistent with a growing body of empirical literature. Eshbaugh-Soha presciently critiques this leadership model, demonstrating the pervasive filtering power possessed by the media, an institution that negotiates the transmission of information and thus manipulates the prospect for unidirectional presidential leadership. Obama has endeavored to break free of this media-imposed communication burden, one that has also constrained his predecessors, but has been largely unsuccessful, as Eshbaugh-Soha indicates with particular respect to the president's success on health care reform–related communication.

Three scholars examined how Obama responded to his contextual burdens. David Zarefsky and Jason Edwards examined the content of several of Obama's most important speeches delivered abroad to inquire whether and how Obama reset "America's role in the world." Zarefsky showed that Obama's understanding of the relationship between the United States and the rest of the world is characterized by much more egalitarian and cooperative impulses than proponents of American exceptionalism traditionally convey. Similarly, Edwards introduced the notion of democratic exceptionalism, demonstrating its importance in Obama's preference for messages of international partnership and interdependence. Both Zarefsky and Edwards take away from Obama's foreign policy rhetoric a message of measured humility and desire for communication and reciprocity between states that is quite consistent with what earlier essays in this volume find in how Obama approached politics on an individual level as well as a racial level. James Arnt Aune argued that Obama did not take advantage of the rhetorical opportunities presented to him with the collapse of previous economic narratives inherent in the financial crisis, and thus that Obama's failure to construct a new economic narrative has left the nation floating in the discursive abyss, without a rhetorical anchor with which we can tether our economic arguments.

Finally, four scholars examined how Obama responded to his personal burdens. Catherine Langford and Dave Tell focus on Obama's position relative to key currents in modern American religious history, with Langford detailing the religious roots of Obama's secular political discourse and Tell relating Obama's rise to Exodus narratives in both the general biblical and American historical senses. In both cases, each author details Obama's external foci, with Langford commenting upon Obama's rhetorical inclusiveness and Tell noting the agency Obama's auditors receive. Essays by Cara Finnegan and Bonnie Jean Dow have in many ways contributed to an evolving discussion on how the conversations about Obama—and the Obamas—reflect the state of American politics and political identity today. Finnegan's analysis of photographs of Obama and fine art show a variety of ways in which the president has to engage with the expectations of the nation about what it is to be president, a commentary that builds upon the discussion of heroic leadership discussed in the introduction to this volume. Similarly, Dow's analysis of First Lady Michelle Obama argued that Americans had difficulty translating their expectations for the First Family into the reality of the Obama family in the White House. Like each of the essays in the volume that precede them, the chapters authored by Finnegan and Dow hang on concepts of leadership, identity, communication, and power; most importantly, these essays consider the ways these weighty concepts intersect at the level of the body in the case of America's forty-fourth president.

Taken together, these scholars have demonstrated throughout the preceding chapters that Obama both embraced and diminished heroic expectations in his first term in office. Jay Childers explained that while Obama can be thought of as a deliberative democrat, his agonistic approach to public debate seeks to integrate multiple perspectives rather than to pursue his own agenda. We would expect a heroic leader to pursue his or her own agenda to the exclusion of all others, so although Obama's agonistic approach is laudable from a deliberative democracy standpoint, it may have prohibited him from fulfilling heroic expectations. Likewise, Eric Dieter's analysis of how Obama's 2008 campaign attempted to build consubstantiality between the candidate and his audience demonstrates that although Obama sought the heroic status of the presidency, he did so in a way that promised to elevate his audience as well as himself. Despite Obama's apparent reticence, essays by Brandon Rottinghaus and Matthew Eshbaugh-Soha demonstrated that Obama did attempt heroic leadership of public opinion, even if he was not always successful. According to essays by David Zarefsky and Jason Edwards, Obama's stress on the interconnectedness of the United States and the world, which paralleled his stress on community domestically, enabled him to play the role of heroic leader abroad while potentially threatening his ability to lead on American exceptionalism at home. James Arnt Aune invoked the nation's heroic expectations of Obama's economic rhetoric when he judged it lacking for failing to define a new economic narrative that would move the nation forward—certainly the task of a heroic leader. Catherine Langford explained how Obama's use of the secular messianic style allowed him to focus both his and his audience's efforts on the rewards of good works in the present, not in the afterlife, thereby rejecting the promise of eternal heroism. Dave Tell argued that Obama's use of the Exodus narrative both propelled him to attempt heroic status as well as restrained him from acting as the sole heroic leader. Cara Finnegan placed Obama within the mythic presidency, but also demonstrated the disjunctive elements of that placement so that Obama appeared to be both mythic and an outsider, commenting on the possibilities of the heroic presidency. And finally, Bonnie Dow demonstrated that Michelle Obama is only acceptable as the First Lady because she represents the heroic good mother, not because she inherently satisfies the nation's heroic expectations for the First Lady.

Reading these analyses together enables us to learn precisely how complicated it has been for President Obama to satisfy the nation's heroic expectations: his natural demeanor, political investments, rhetorical style, personal history, motivating narratives, and his race combined to make Obama an ambiguously heroic leader. On the one hand, the Exodus narrative, as well as our expectations for the office and his deep sense of obligation and responsibility, propels Obama to seek heroic status. On the other hand, his commitment to deliberative democracy, consubstantiality, cooperation, and the interconnectedness of community restrain Obama's heroic impulses, preventing the would-be hero from achieving mythic status. Therefore, we find Obama consistently embracing heroic expectations while also seeking to diminish those same expectations. Because Obama's embracing and diminishing strategies have evolved from his political and personal commitments, it is unlikely that he will resolve these contradictions in his second term; it is likely that we will continue to see him embracing, while diminishing, heroic expectations. How these strategies will affect opinion polls or presidential rankings is unclear. Perhaps Obama's approach is best suited for a nation weary of the consolidation of power in the executive branch, or perhaps the nation will judge Obama weak for not living up to heroic expectations.

Likewise, Obama's performance of the rhetorical markers of the heroic presidency—rhetoric that seeks "to unify the nation, to demonstrate a high degree of agency (the ability to control world history), and seeks to consolidate power in the executive branch"[7]—was also complicated. The preceding essays certainly provide us with many examples of Obama seeking to unify the nation—indeed, Obama's stress on community and interconnectedness not only required him to seek unification but also perhaps even hindered his ability to act as the heroic leader. Yet Obama's mere election triggered vitriol the likes of which the United States had not seen for several decades. Obama's rhetoric may have always aimed at the unification of the nation through transcending difference, but his policies led to division. The preceding essays likewise provide us with ample opportunity to judge whether Obama's rhetoric demonstrated a high degree of agency. Clearly, Obama attempted to give his audience agency, while stressing the interconnectedness of the United States with the rest of the world—a decidedly non-heroic, if egalitarian, approach to international relations. Yet, much of the nation seemed to approve of how Obama "reset" America's role in the world—campaign season allegations of an apology tour by members of the right wing notwithstanding—so perhaps Obama's non-heroic approach to international leadership was precisely what was needed after the dismal failure of George W. Bush's confrontational foreign policy. Finally, based on the preceding essays it is difficult to determine whether Obama's rhetoric sought to consolidate power in the executive branch—certainly his many attempts to reinforce interconnectedness and community and his repeated attempts to diminish heroic expectations could be read as an attempt to reduce the power of the executive branch. Yet, as his Tea Party and Republican Party critics have constantly protested, Obama and his policies have reduced individual liberty. Because none of the essays in this volume addressed this particular question, it is not possible to make determinations about the veracity of Obama's critics' accusations.

What the future holds for Barack Obama and his disparate burdens is, as always, uncertain and immediately unknowable. What we can know, however, is that we will continue to ask questions about the rhetoric of heroic expectations and the institutional, contextual, and personal burdens faced by anyone who occupies the Oval Office. It is likely that new burdens will confront President Obama in his second term as the crises of 2008–12 fade into the nation's political memory and are replaced by other more immediate challenges. Based upon what we have observed about President Obama thus far, regardless of the precise nature of the challenges he and his administration face, it is clear that he will use his presidency to focus on problem solving, transcending difference, and involving as many perspectives as possible into the decision-making process. Will the nation remember him as a heroic leader? Only history can judge.

Notes

1. Barack Obama, "Address Before a Joint Session of Congress," February 24, 2009, in *The American Presidency Project* [online], eds. John Woolley and Gerhard Peters, http://www.presidency.ucsb.edu/ws/?pid=85753; and "Obama Receives 44% Approval on Oil Spill While BP Gets 16%," *Gallup Politics*, June 21, 2010, http://www.gallup.com/poll/140957/obama-receives-approval-oil-spill-gets.aspx.

2. Barack Obama, "The President's News Conference," May 27, 2010, in *The American Presidency Project* [online], eds. John Woolley and Gerhard Peters, http://www.presidency. ucsb.edu/ws/?pid=87963.

3. "Presidential Job Approval Center," *Gallup Politics*, December 15, 2012, http://www. gallup.com/poll/124922/Presidential-Approval-Center.aspx.

4. "Americans Assess What Obama Can Accomplish in Next Term: Americans Generally Less Positive than in 2008," *Gallup Politics*, November 15, 2012, http://www.gallup.com/poll/158843/americans-assess-obama-accomplish-next-term.aspx.

5. Stephen K. Medvic, *In Defense of Politicians: The Expectations Trap and Its Threat to Democracy* (New York, Routledge, 2013).

6. M. M. Bakhtin, *Dialogic Imagination: Four Essays* (Austin: University of Texas Press, 1982), 282. "In point of fact, word is a two-sided act. It is determined equally by whose word it is and for whom it is meant. As word, it is precisely the product of the reciprocal relationship between speaker and listener, addresser and addressee. Each and every word expresses the 'one' in relation to the 'other.' I give myself verbal shape from another's point of view, ultimately, from the point of view of the community to which I belong. A word is a bridge thrown between myself and another. If one end of the bridge depends on me, then the other depends on my addressee. A word is territory shared by both addresser and addressee, by the speaker and his interlocutor" (V. N. Volosinov, *Marxism and the Philosophy of Language* [Cambridge: Harvard University Press, 1986], 86).

7. From Chapter 1, page 22, of this volume.

Contributor Biographies

JAMES ARNT AUNE served as Professor and Head of the Department of Communication at Texas A&M University. He is the author of *Rhetoric and Marxism* (Westview Press) and *Selling the Free Market: The Rhetoric of Economic Correctness* (Guilford Press) and coeditor of *Civil Rights Rhetoric and the American Presidency* and *The Prospect of Presidential Rhetoric* (Texas A&M University Press), as well as numerous articles and book chapters. His research, which focused on rhetorical theory and the philosophy of communication, has received several awards, including the National Communication Association's Diamond Anniversary Book Award. Aune died in January 2013.

JAY P. CHILDERS is Assistant Professor of Communication Studies at the University of Kansas. His research is focused on questions of democratic citizenship in rhetoric and political communication. He is the author of *The Evolving Citizen: American Youth and the Changing Norms of Democratic Engagement* (Pennsylvania State University Press), and the coauthor of *Political Tone: How Leaders Talk and Why* (University of Chicago Press). He has also authored a number of essays, including pieces that have appeared in *Presidential Studies Quarterly*, *Quarterly Journal of Speech*, and *Western Journal of Communication*.

ERIC DIETER is a doctoral candidate in the Department of English and coordinator of the dual credit rhetoric and writing program at The University of Texas at Austin, which serves students from Texas high schools underrepresented in postsecondary education. His research focuses on ethos and authenticity in American politics and on the pragmatic overlap between democracy and pedagogy, especially ways of teaching civic literacy in rhetoric and composition courses.

BONNIE J. Dow is Associate Professor and Chair of Communication Studies and Associate Professor of Women's and Gender Studies at Vanderbilt University. Her scholarship focuses on representations of women and feminism in mass media and the discourses of first- and second-wave feminism in the United States. She is the author of *Prime-Time Feminism: Television, Media Culture, and the Women's Movement Since 1970* (University of Pennsylvania Press), and the coeditor (with Julia T. Wood) of *The Sage Handbook of Gender and Communication* (Sage). She is also a coeditor of *The Aunt Lute Anthology of U.S. Women Writers, Volume One: 17th–19th Centuries* (Aunt Lute Books). Her current book project is tentatively titled *Framing Feminism: Television News, Women's Liberation, and 1970.*

Jason A. Edwards is Associate Professor of Communication Studies at Bridgewater State University. He is the author of *Navigating the Post-Cold War World: President Clinton's Foreign Policy Rhetoric* (Lexington) and coeditor of *The Rhetoric of American Exceptionalism: Critical Essays* (McFarland). Additionally, he has authored over thirty articles and book chapters appearing in venues such as *Rhetoric and Public Affairs, Communication Quarterly, Southern Journal of Communication, Presidential Studies Quarterly,* and *The Howard Journal of Communications.* He is currently at work on a book that traces the rhetorical contours of American foreign policy rhetoric.

Matthew Eshbaugh-Soha is Associate Professor of Political Science at the University of North Texas. He studies the presidency, media, and public policy and is coauthor of *Breaking through the Noise: Presidential Leadership, Public Opinion, and News Media* (Stanford University Press).

Cara A. Finnegan is Associate Professor of Communication at the University of Illinois at Urbana-Champaign. She is the author of *Picturing Poverty: Print Culture and FSA Photographs* (Smithsonian) and coeditor of *Visual Rhetoric: A Reader in Communication and American Culture* (Sage). Her research has been honored with the National Communication Association's Diamond Anniversary Book Award and its Golden Monograph Award.

Catherine L. Langford is Associate Professor of Communication Studies at Texas Tech University. Primarily interested in legal and political discourses, her research for the most part focuses on the nexus between constitutional interpretation and federalism. She is the author of numerous articles and book chapters, including pieces published in *Communication Law Review* and *Argumentation & Advocacy.*

JENNIFER R. MERCIECA is Associate Professor and Associate Department Head in the Department of Communication at Texas A&M University. She is the author of *Founding Fictions* (University of Alabama Press) as well as numerous essays published in *The Quarterly Journal of Speech, Rhetoric & Public Affairs,* and *Presidential Studies Quarterly.*

BRANDON ROTTINGHAUS is Associate Professor and the Senator Don Henderson Scholar at the University of Houston. His research interests include the presidency, executive-legislative relations, and public opinion. He is author of *The Provisional Pulpit: Modern Presidential Leadership of Public Opinion* (Texas A&M University Press). His work has been funded by the Dirksen Center for Congressional Research, the Eagleton Center for the American Governor, and the National Science Foundation.

DAVE TELL is Associate Professor of Communication Studies at the University of Kansas. He is the author of *Confessional Crises and Cultural Politics in Twentieth-Century America* (Pennsylvania State University Press). He has previously won the National Communication Association's Gerald R. Miller Outstanding Dissertation Award and the Karl R. Wallace Memorial Award for excellence in communication research, teaching, and service.

JUSTIN S. VAUGHN is Assistant Professor of Political Science at Boise State University. He has published several studies of presidential politics, including *Gendering the Presidency: Gender, Presidential Politics, and Popular Culture* (University Press of Kentucky) and articles in journals including *Presidential Studies Quarterly, Political Research Quarterly,* and *White House Studies.* He also currently serves as coeditor of the *Presidents & Executive Politics Report.* His current research projects include examinations of the rhetorical and administrative dimensions of the presidential policy czar phenomenon and the rise of the post-rhetorical presidency.

DAVID ZAREFSKY is Owen L. Coon Professor Emeritus of Argumentation and Debate, and Professor Emeritus of Communication Studies, Northwestern University. He studies presidential rhetoric and argumentation in public discourse. He is the author of *President Johnson's War on Poverty: Rhetoric and History* (University of Alabama Press) and *Lincoln, Douglas, and Slavery: In the Crucible of Public Debate* (University of Chicago Press), among other books and articles. He is a past president of both the National Communication Association and the Rhetoric Society of America.

Index